6-14-65

THIS new book by a leading authority traces the history of the ballet from its earliest classical forms in Ancient Greece and Rome and its appearance in France during the Renaissance, up to the present-day developments of modern ballet in Western Europe, Russia and America.

The author describes in detail the growth of ballet through the work of the great choregraphers and their colleagues and at the same time gives an account of those artists in this field whose influence has helped create and change various forms and styles of expressive dance.

Joan Lawson, who is the author of the leading works on mime and on European folk dance, and teaches at the Royal Ballet School, has travelled and studied widely in the Soviet Union and has lectured in Moscow and Leningrad, where she has had access to many sources previously unknown in the West.

The whole work is enriched with a wealth of fascinating illustrations. For serious students of the ballet and for ballet-lovers this book will remain a continued source of information and pleasure.

$ 8.75

1964-65

A HISTORY OF BALLET AND ITS MAKERS

To

TAMARA KARSAVINA

PEOPLE'S ARTIST GALINA ULANOVA *and* DAME MARGOT FONTEYN,

My Goddesses of the Dance

and to

DAME NINETTE DE VALOIS

and my Friends of The Royal Ballet

They pursued the Rules of the Drama in their mute Performances, by confining each Representation to a certain Action with a great Observation of the Manners and Passions, which the Action naturally produced.

JOHN WEAVER

A HISTORY OF BALLET AND ITS MAKERS

BY

JOAN LAWSON
Author of "European Folk Dance" and "Mime"

LONDON
SIR ISAAC PITMAN & SONS LTD.

First published 1964

SIR ISAAC PITMAN & SONS LTD.
PITMAN HOUSE, PARKER STREET, KINGSWAY, LONDON, W.C.2
THE PITMAN PRESS, BATH
PITMAN HOUSE, BOUVERIE STREET, CARLTON, MELBOURNE
22–25 BECKETT'S BUILDINGS, PRESIDENT STREET, JOHANNESBURG
ASSOCIATED COMPANIES
PITMAN MEDICAL PUBLISHING COMPANY LTD.
46 CHARLOTTE STREET, LONDON, W.1
PITMAN PUBLISHING CORPORATION
20 EAST 46TH STREET, NEW YORK 17, NEW YORK
SIR ISAAC PITMAN & SONS (CANADA) LTD.
(INCORPORATING THE COMMERCIAL TEXT BOOK COMPANY)
PITMAN HOUSE, 381–383 CHURCH STREET, TORONTO

Printed in Great Britain by Butler & Tanner Ltd, Frome and London

F4 —(G. 489)

Preface

BALLET today is an art without words. The dancer expresses everything through the movements of his body, which he uses as a sensitive instrument. The great Russian ballet-master, Mikhail Fokine, said that if it were necessary to read a libretto before the ballet was understood, the choregrapher had failed.

The search for expression through dance as a theatrical enterprise has been a long one and is not yet over. Both before and long after the famous *Balet comique de la Royne* poets, singers and actors played their part in explaining the action. It was not until 1717 that the first full ballet without words appeared in England. Since then European ballet-masters have been seeking to explain themselves solely through the movements of the dancers. On their way they have accepted ideas and methods from many countries and spheres of art, transforming and adapting these to their own special need. In the course of a long history the construction, content and style of ballet have been continually changing and each important choregrapher has made some contribution. In this book an attempt is made to define the development of ballet through the work of the choregraphers and their colleagues and to give an account as well of those artists in this field whose influence has helped to create and change the various forms and styles of expressive dance. It cannot be a full account because the subject is too vast to be contained in one book, particularly now that ballet is to be found in many different countries. Each of these has some kind of dance or theatre tradition which may have contributed to the development of ballet as a whole, even though that country at one time may have had no ballet of its own.

England has developed its own ballet only within the last thirty years or so, but its influence in that field prior to this period has always been underrated, although the dramatic qualities of its mimes were once highly valued on the continent. They, with other elements, certainly influenced continental methods of performance. France, as the founder of that specific form of entertainment known as ballet, determined its form and established the classical technique of dance. Russia has contributed much towards the musicality and expressiveness of dance movement in all spheres. Italy has added to the spectacle by way of both décor and technique. If other countries have had their share in the production, then I hope I have not neglected to state their case. If I have omitted the names of many famous dancers it is not because they are forgotten but because, for all their efforts as individuals, their dancing could not have made its effect without the work of those choregraphers, who have formed the traditions, principles and styles upon which present-day ballet is based.

I have neglected the work of some choregraphers because there has been no satisfactory and generally accepted method of notating their choregraphic design, with all the necessary indications for the quality of movement needed to express the dramatic content of both dance and role, and no method of indicating the vitally important phrasing and accenting of the steps. Today ballets can be filmed, a process that will give valuable information about dancers in a particular performance. There are also the notation systems of Srbouyi Lissitssian (U.S.S.R.), Rudolph von Laban (Germany and U.S.A.) and Benesh (England), which are all proving valuable but which are somewhat unwieldy for writing down a whole ballet. My choice of choregraphers to discuss has been decided by reading accounts of their work by their contemporaries and their own personal letters, plans and other data, and by the fact that they are choregraphers whose work is of special interest to performers. I have confined my choice mainly to those working within the classical medium, although I have cited those few modern dancers who have influenced and helped to free classically based ballet from the many conventions which continually grow round the basic principles of any art and often impede its progress.

I have not discussed the interesting developments that have recently been taking place in such countries as Belgium under Maurice Béjart, in England in the Western Theatre Ballets, or in the U.S.S.R.; the activities of both folk dance and classical choregraphers are in a state of flux, led by such interesting creative artists as Igor Belsky and S. Grigorovich, and attempts are being made to train choregraphers. The question is: will the State Institute of Theatrical Art (GITIS) succeed? I believe a true choregrapher, like every other creative artist, is born and not made. He can only express himself fully through movement, which is his instinctive solution to the problem of communicating ideas.

JOAN LAWSON

Acknowledgements

THIS book has been in the making for over twenty years, during which many people have helped my researches into the past. I must now offer them my most grateful thanks. I am particularly indebted to: the late P. J. S. Richardson, O.B.E. and to Peter Revitt for giving me the freedom of their libraries and collections of prints, etc., and sparing me so much of their time in discussion; Doctor Frances A. Yates of the Warburg Institute, London University for her generous permission to quote widely from her important book *French Academies of the Sixteenth Century* and for discussing several difficult questions of interpretation; my Soviet friends Yuri Ossipovitch Slonimsky for his inspiring letters and permission to quote from his books, Yuri Aleexevitch Bakroushine for sending me much valuable material and photos from Moscow, Natalie René for her help in discussing Russian and Soviet choregraphy with artists in the U.S.S.R., Sergei Alexandrovitch Morshchikhin of the Lunacharsky State Theatre Museum and Library for sending me valuable material from Leningrad, the Director of the Bakroushine State Theatre Museum for sending me valuable material from Moscow; Alan and Katharine Lawson for translations from the French and German; Elizabeth Bell, M.A. for translations from the Italian; the Director of the Bodleian Library, Oxford, the Librarian of the Brighton Public Library; and the Director of the Reading Room, the British Museum for giving me so many facilities and help with documents and papers; the late Edwin Evans and Frank Howes, C.B.E. for their endless patience with my musical problems; the late Seraphina Astafieva who started me on my search; Dame Ninette de Valois, Sir Frederick Ashton, Leonide Lavrovsky, the late Mikhail Fokine, and other choregraphers mentioned herein for talking about their work with me; and Madame Tamara Karsavina, Vittorina Ottolonghi, C. W. Swinson (of Messrs. A. and C. Black) and Anthony Crickmay for the loan of many photographs to illustrate my history.

JOAN LAWSON

Contents

List of Plates

CHAPTER 1

The Beginnings of Classical Ballet

Ballet must have a beginning, climax and end.
(NOVERRE, *Letters* 1760)

THE quotation above is capable of many interpretations. The *Balet comique de la Royne* (1581) has been a convenient point at which to commence a history of ballet. This spectacle, which bore little resemblance to present-day ballet, was the climax of seventeen fêtes given by Catherine de Medici to celebrate the betrothal of the Duc de Joyeuse to Marguerite de Lorraine-Vaudémont. It can also be interpreted as a climax of the Renaissance in France, when authors, having studied the theories, principles, technique and effects used in the plays of Greek dramatists, believed they were producing something similar.

The end (or object) of the production might be regarded as an expression of Catherine de Medici's hopes that by understanding the truths hidden in its symbolism and allegory: "Hearts would be softened and opposite opinions be brought together" (Champion) and the Protestant members of her court would see the errors of their ways and return to the Catholic church.

To find the seeds from which *Balet comique* and later ballets stem a search must be made amongst the dance rituals of primitive Greek tribes where originally the dancing of the group was everything, but where finally the priests and acolytes eliminated all others from the ceremony and continued their dance before a wondering audience. At this point in religious ritual the story of dance as entertainment might be said to begin because the performers had consciously to discipline themselves and their movements to communicate the meaning of the ritual and fill the now limited dance space. Thus a definite technique of dance started to develop. Although this bore little or no relationship to classical dance technique it had this in common with it: in both the movements had to be so displayed that the audience saw them to the best advantage.

THE BIRTH OF GREEK TRAGEDY

The dramatis personae and themes of classical ballet began to emerge as the *tragodia*—or goat-song—took shape under a priest who was also a poet. As he sang the tale of his god, so his acolytes danced and mimed that god's deeds, whilst the audience at the climax or end of the recital, would join in the ritual by performing the appropriately expressive dance of rejoicing, sorrow, Bacchic frenzy and the like.

This form of ritual changed character when, inspired by the poems of Homer, a secular form of dramatic entertainment appeared in which bard and dancer-mime expressed through chant and gesture the deeds of some great hero, his relationship to the gods and the fates determining his life and death; Thespis, the father of Greek tragedy, introduced actors, thereby allowing dialogue in which the players could respond and exchange comment, and thus enlarged the scope of the drama.

The public love of this form of entertainment grew as the second actor became as important as the first and led a chorus, who not only interpreted the words directly into action, as the first dancer-mimes had done, but also reacted expressively to the speech of both actors. This task ultimately led the chorus also to create the background and atmosphere against which the hero's deeds could be depicted. At a later stage poets began to compete for the honour of presenting such plays at the Olympic Games and other events linking the citizens of the Greek towns together.

The tragedy chosen was played as an act of homage to a city's god. Its purpose was to fire the imagination and spirit of the townsfolk. It had to appeal to everyone, therefore its plot was limited to certain traditional themes in which the heroes, who were likened to gods, performed or were expected to perform deeds and acts that were known. There had to be generalization because both the characters and their actions had to be recognized as belonging to that theme upon which a particular plot was based. It is from the generalizations of action and character that the libretti of many later dramatic plays and ballets have developed, and the techniques of classical choregraphic design.

THE GENERALIZATION OF ACTION AND CHARACTER

The tragedy frequently took the form of a trilogy with each play forming, as it were, an act of the whole in which the events presaging and influencing a hero's deeds and his life in the hands of the gods and the fates were so discussed that they would convey some political or moral lesson.

The same characters appear in play after play and their actions, emotions and moods are discussed by the various authors in much the same terms. The heroes Theseus, Jason, Hercules and Ulysses not only have similar types of adventure, but are likened to each other in gesture, action and looks. The sad heroines Andromache, Hecuba, the faithful sisters or daughters Antigone, Elektra, Iphigenia and the tragic Cassandra are given similar dramatic manifestations of emotion, mood and action. Those beauties Helen and Phaedra battle against similar destinies, as do Orestes and Oedipus before their fate is fully realized. Even strange Tiresias, the soothsayer, demonstrates in some plays the magical qualities of the tragic sorceress Medea.

The gods and goddesses make infrequent appearances, but, like their servants Mercury and Iris, when they do it is always with those qualities and attributes with which they have been associated. Moreover from the time of Euripides, their main task was frequently to descend as the *deus ex machina* and deliver some comment or explanation of the drama, or even make some prophecy as an epilogue to the play.

TECHNIQUES

If such generalizations were found in the plots, characters and actions of these plays, then generalizations were also made to govern the techniques of production, particularly the work of the chorus, because these represented the background of ordinary people above whom the heroes and heroines had been raised to play a leading part in the drama. If the chosen tragedy were to convey its message correctly, then the chorus would have to use only certain recognized types, tones and qualities of speech, song and movement in order to transfer their own emotions and reactions to the situation to the onlookers, and inspire them to respond.

By the time that the tragedies began to be played in the enormous theatres, Greece possessed innumerable dance rituals each of which served a different purpose, and each of which had its specific physical, musical and emotional qualities of movement. Elements from such dances would be borrowed by the leader of the chorus and author of the play to create the necessary background and atmosphere for the tale unfolded by the actors on the stage, whose size prevented much dramatic movement. The chorus, in fact, supplied far more than background and atmosphere to the plot. They were the visual embodiment of the action.

The Part of the Chorus

In Greek drama the chorus had three functions: they interpreted or they reacted to the actors' words. (Their third function will be discussed later.) In certain ballets, particularly those which can be called national or character in the modern sense, the *corps de ballet* still perform these two functions, with this difference, the term *word* must now be interpreted as *action*. Therefore, in modern usage the *corps de ballet* can directly assist the hero or heroine in the development of the plot (as do the Wilis in dancing Hilarion to his death in *Giselle*), or play the main parts in the drama (as in parts of *The Rake's Progress* and *The Green Table*); or else they can react positively to the actions of the principal players and thus heighten the effect of the drama (as in Helpmann's *Miracle in the Gorbals*).

The third function of the Greek chorus was to create atmosphere and form the background to the drama, a task also performed by the modern *corps de ballet*.

Certain technical developments, which came to govern the content and choregraphic design of all later ballet arose from these three functions of the chorus.

Interpretation of Words or Actions

This led, firstly, to the development of strongly active movements and gestures descriptive of the deeds and tasks performed by the leading players. Such gestures could be borrowed from the movements of everyday life, from man's varied occupations and particularly in the actions of the heroes, from the Pyrrhic dance and athletic rituals. Secondly there arose those movements describing the way in which such direct actions should be performed; thus the chorus helped to build up a full portrait of the characters portrayed on the stage.

Reaction to Words or Actions

If the portraits thus built by directly active gestures were to be fully valid then their effect upon others had immediately to be perceived. From this premise developed those emotionally expressive gestures descriptive of the reactions of the chorus to the words spoken or to the deed performed.

An important point to remember about this category of chorus work is that in Greek drama all violent deeds of murder, suicide, fratricide and the like were banished from the stage for fear of the effect that the actual sight of such an act might have on the audience. It was all the more important, therefore, that the chorus should show their immediate reaction to such horrors as were being described by the actors.

Creation of Atmosphere and Background

Similarly if the reaction of the chorus to events taking place offstage were to be obvious then they had firstly to create a background and atmosphere of normality. Any deviation from this normality would immediately throw the cause of the change into high relief. That is, the results of the leading character's actions would be made much clearer because of the immediate effect they had on those who were the representatives of the audience.

Perhaps however the most important task for the chorus in most Greek plays was to link the various episodes together by their constant presence and movement; thus the chorus gave to drama, as it gives now to ballet, continuity and flow of line.

Music

The development of any theatrical technique arises from the need of making the most effective use of the materials at hand. The essential need of any Greek play, classical drama or ballet produced today is for the action and line of movement of the dance to flow onwards, achieving continuity at the same time as the plot develops and reaches its climax.

The work of the Greek chorus in linking the episodes of the play was very dependent upon the tones and qualities of the music and chant accompanying the dance and movement. This acted as a unifying element in the same way as the specially written scores of modern ballets like *Petrushka* and *The Firebird.*

The Stage and Chorus Movements

The numbers of a Greek chorus ranged from twelve to fifty and could be of either sex, according to the needs of the drama. With rare exceptions, they were present throughout the play and this meant that their activities had to be carefully regulated, whether they were moving or static. It is not possible to discover how they were deployed in the orchestra (or dancing space) which lay in front of and below the level of the stage upon which the actors played. Nevertheless, although modern Greek producers do not pretend to stage replicas of the ancient dramas in their great open-air theatres their practices can be some guide to what happened. Believing that these tragedies are in direct contact with the flow of life from past to present they make use of material from their oldest dance rituals.

The stage, like an altar, is the focal point of all chorus activities because it is here that the principal players act out the drama. All chorus groupings made in static moments are directed towards a single area and this, being in line with the audience's own viewpoint, directs attention where and when it is most needed.

So that these groupings may be pictorially effective great variety is allowed in the static pictures formed during the most dramatic moments; each dancer perhaps strikes an individual pose in keeping with the situation. But each member of the group is seen to be part of the whole, although they may be widely disposed about the orchestra. For this reason much use is made of movements and steps from the traditional *chains* and *kolos,* which can carry the dancers from place to place whilst linked together by hands, elbows, shoulders, or by hands in each other's belts.

These traditional *kolo* forms are also a valuable way of moving the chorus throughout the breadth and depth of the orchestra, particularly during those moments of the play when the creation of proper atmosphere and background is needed.

Scenery, Costumes and Props

The fact that the chorus were usually present and there were few facilities for change of scene or costume no doubt helped Aristotle (384–322 B.C.) to suggest certain rules for drama which were seized upon by Renaissance academicians and moulded into a rigid discipline of the unities of time, place and action, that exercised a stranglehold on ballet for nearly one hundred and fifty years. But in fact few Greek authors conformed absolutely to these rules and the lack of facilities for changing did not prevent the actors heightening the effects of their playing by using mask-like head-dresses, built-up soles to the footwear and other additions which would help paint a fuller picture of the character played. *Periaktoi*, or triangular prisms were also used, each side of these was painted with a scene and could be revolved as the play progressed. The Greek chorus had no special dress, but the lack of appropriate costume has never prevented dancers anywhere from expressing themselves through movement, even when conforming to the stern technique of classical dance, provided they approach their task in the right frame of mind. The example of certain modern ballets proves that the very lack of costume and props can make dancers more expressive because they have to rely entirely on their own ability to convey meaning through movement. This was the main task of the Greek chorus, as it was of later performers, the *pantomimi* of the Roman Empire, who not only became entertainers in the great theatres and circuses but also interpreters of commands given by the conquering legions. They could communicate meaning through movement and gesture to the enormous crowds, few of whom could understand the language of the conqueror.

GREEK COMEDY AND PARTICULARIZATION

Ballet has a purpose, if only to entertain.
(Fokine)

Although Fokine's major works are in a serious vein, his lighter ones play an equally important role in the development of ballet. Similarly, although Greek tragedy showed the way for the many generalizations made by choregraphers and teachers using classical techniques, the various types of Greek comedy have equally important elements to offer to the designers of *demi-caractère* and character works.

Tragedy and comedy develop from ritual, but comedy has an entirely different effect on the audience. It is meant for laughter and requires a particular technique. It is based on the actions and reactions of more ordinary people to everyday happenings, both congruous and incongruous. It can laugh with or at the man who slips on a banana-skin and it is his attitude to his misfortune which determines the way the laugh should go. The fact that the laugh can be for or against the player or situation makes comedy a powerful weapon in times of stress. But, if the player wishes to make his point, instead of generalizing, as in classical tragedy, he must particularize. He must clearly define what type of man he is playing, underlining the foibles, idiosyncrasies and other personal attributes which lead to his discomfiture or triumph. The audience should be left in no doubt about the manner and behaviour of a particular man in a particular situation. This was essential in those Greek comedies which pilloried the petty officials, local tradespeople and other characters, whose actions and personalities amused, upset or irritated the life of the community. Moreover when reverence for the gods and their servants began to abate and they too took their part in comedy, becoming figures of fun, the need to particularize was essential.

The chorus played little or no part in these comedies because the audience needed no intermediaries to help them understand the predicaments of gods, or others like themselves and their neighbours, coping with some domestic, civic or political problem, and suffering the same trials and tribulations because of clumsiness, misplaced zeal, surprising interference, or some other cause familiar to themselves.

If laughter is to rise spontaneously from the audience, then an element of surprise from one source or another is vital. This means that the players' technique must be flexible and ready to deal with any situation as it arises, even if only negatively. Nevertheless the ancient comedians, like their counterparts today, kept an appropriate stock of tricks, jokes, gags and similar material in hand to deal with each situation as it arose. Each player was also engaged to play if not the same, then at least a similar role throughout the repertoire, and from these dramatis personae there have descended some of the figures of the Commedia dell'Arte companies and thence, the Harlequins and Columbines and their counterparts as well as stylized ways of playing certain roles in modern character ballets.

ROME AND THE PANTOMIMI

Although the seeds of choregraphic design sown by Greek tragedy did not develop during the long period between the fall of the Greek Empire and the Renaissance, the technique of expressive gesture, which later dancers in the classical *ballet d'action* would use to tell their story, made great progress. The need for communication with the conquered as the Romans spread through Greece and other Mediterranean areas found the legions calling on the *pantomimi* amongst their captives to interpret their commands. This meant that the interpreters, who had sometimes been players in the Greek theatres, would strive to make authoritative all those gestures which they used when directly interpreting the words and expressing the action to be done.

But at the same time, the *pantomimi* were developing a more subtle, flexible form of play. As Greek tragedy lost its popularity there developed from the literary drama a form of pantomimic dance in which the actor (*histrio*) used danced-mime to act the tale of some traditional hero and was accompanied by a singer and flute-player, to give his movements continuity and emphasis. This type of interlude became more important than the drama when the *pantomimi* had so perfected their technique of representation that they required no singer to explain the action and he quitted the scene.

DEVELOPMENT OF TECHNIQUE

This perfection of technique grew out of their various tasks. The *pantomimi* not only acted as interpreters and entertainers for the crowds in the vast arenas built to celebrate victories, they also provided entertainment at the courts of the new rulers. This led to two forms of play, and ultimately to two types of player. The more serious type of tragedian and the subtle comedian would be more effective in intimate surroundings, whilst an altogether broader kind of performer would find success in the great open-air theatres and circuses. Nevertheless the magnificent dancer-mimes, Bathylus and Pylades and other players were successful in both places and their methods of play seem to have developed in three ways.

Firstly, because the *pantomimi's* argument was stated without words and without the help of an intermediary to direct the audience's attention to the events taking place on the stage, as the Greek chorus had done, a much clearer definition of the characters and their deeds, actions, emotions, and moods was needed. It was this that led to greater stylization of gesture and movement.

The fact that the most expressive part of the action was no longer taking place in the orchestra, but on the stage would lead to a broadening and flattening out of the movement because the players needed to direct their faces and gestures outwards to the audience, now usually seated in a semicircle in front, instead of round three parts of an oval, as in the Greek theatre.

Secondly, the lack of a chorus to create atmosphere and background led the *pantomimi* to be more emotionally expressive and move more freely than the earlier actors had done. They also emphasized the meaning of their play by the use of sounding boards on the stage to strengthen the effect of the significant gestures in a phrase with deliberate movements of the feet.

John Weaver sums up the wonderful play of the famous Roman *pantomimi* thus—

> In a word, a Pantomime, to deserve that name, must be everything exactly and do all things with Order, Decency and Measure like himself, without any Imperfection have his Thoughts properly composed, yet excel in a Vivacity of Mind, a quick Apprehension and deep Judgment, and his Applause must be the necessary Consequence of his Performance in which every Spectator must behold himself acted, as in a Glass, all that he himself is us'd to do and suffer.

Thirdly, although these great mimes seem to have relied entirely on their own efforts to convey meaning, it is certain that others, particularly the comedians, were not so adept and made further extravagant additions to their costumes and props. They also padded out their performance in the circuses with spectacular acts of rope-walking, juggling and acrobatics that were sandwiched in between the chariot races, athletic contests and wild-animal processions. Such elements do not at first sight seem to lend themselves to balletic treatment, but they did ultimately develop into the magnificent technical effects of many later ballet spectacles.

THE DEVELOPMENT OF DANCE BETWEEN THE FALL OF ROME AND THE RENAISSANCE

It was not until the establishment of the first Provençal courts that a distinction seems to have been made between the dances performed by everybody and those of high society. The first differentiation was probably made unconsciously when steps were performed inside a building on smoother floors, instead of on rough ground, and the footgear and clothes of the courtiers ceased to be like those of the peasant.

A further development of dance took place with the Revival of Learning when philosophers began to study the classical writers on education. The value of dance in society is frequently discussed by these early scholars, and the troubadours who were amongst the learned men of their time, gave advice on deportment and dance amongst their other activities. In his *Advice to a Young Lady*, Amanieu de Sescas suggests how she should comport herself in the dance as well as behave before people. Similar advice can be found in other works by troubadours and *jongleurs*, who are also supposed to have been among the first teachers of courtly dance.

But, and this is perhaps more important in the development of that specific form of dance which ultimately became the basis for classical ballet, the troubadours laid down strict rules for the composition of their poems and musical accompaniments. They clearly understood differences in musical style and their *chansons à danser* are the forerunners of the dance tunes and forms used in later *ballets du cour*. An old Provençal writes thus about composing a *dansa*—

> It must have a slightly joyous tune not quite so long as those for the Vers or Canso, but a little more lively as is suitable for dancing. But nowadays people use this tune badly for singers hardly know how to get into a good dance rhythm.
>
> (From *Leys d'Amor*)

The argument that the tunes for the dance had changed is made more impressive when it is realized that church musicians and choirboys frequently accompanied the balls and other entertainments given in noblemen's houses.

THE DEVELOPMENT OF THE SPECTACLE

Throughout the long period between the decline of the Roman Empire and the Renaissance, the traditions of danced-mime established by the Greek chorus and Roman *pantomimi* were continued in one way or another by groups of travelling players, who were usually responsible for the people's entertainments as well as that of the slowly developing courts. In addition, as the Greeks and Romans had developed their own forms of theatre, so the barbarian tribes elsewhere in Europe had developed their own dramatic forms of ritual.

Relics of these are still found in many folk plays, mummings, sword and morris dances and the like, in all of which are strong elements of dance and/or mime.

As soon as the Christian Church came into power, it quickly found that, despite the edicts passed by first one prelate then another, it was powerless entirely to suppress the people's own dances and rituals. It, therefore, began to turn some of this rich dramatic material to its own use for the early liturgical and later mystery, miracle and morality plays. Certain curious legends arose from this amalgam of pagan and Christian elements, which later proved to be valuable sources for the themes of such ballets as *Balet comique de la Royne* and *The Sleeping Beauty*, where some pagan rite is either explained or transformed into a fairy-tale by Christian philosophers. But what is more important was the effect that working for the Church had upon the technique of the *pantomimi*.

Realizing that the *pantomimi* had developed a definite technique of movement for interpreting words through expressive gesture, the Church began to employ them to dramatize parts of the new rituals and make their significance clear to a congregation not all of whom understood Latin. The *pantomimi* entrusted with so meaningful a task as interpreting passages from the life of Jesus and his Mother would need to discipline their gestures severely, particularly as not all prelates seem to have approved this means of communication. That some form of discipline was enacted is clear from de Martène's *De Antiquis Monarchum* where he quotes a tenth-century document analysing over three hundred gestures used by Benedictine, Cistercian and other religious orders during the hours of silence and in Divine Service. It cannot be said that these gestures were the exclusive property of the Christian Church. Nothing could be further from the truth as many of them are used and understood by people of all creeds and nations today. It would seem, therefore, that the *pantomimi* themselves gave regular form to the most common of their gestures, and the monks and nuns in their desire for regulation, directed these into rigid formulas of movement. Amongst these formulas are many which are the conventional gestures of the classical *ballets d'action*.

THE FIRST BALLET SPECTACLES

It is impossible to date with any accuracy the first spectacle to be associated with the term ballet. Father Ménestrier mentions the thirteenth-century horse ballets. Others find the elaborate masking, mummings, masquerades and balls of a slightly later period, a more feasible beginning as then a definite style of court dance with a proper technique of movement began to be used. Some of these were organized round a theme which demanded little more than the wearing of appropriate costumes. A more useful pointer to the future shape of ballet as a spectacle might be an entertainment quoted by Prunières in *Le Ballet du Cour en France avant Benserade et Lully*.

When Philip the Good of Burgundy married Isabel of Portugal (1430) he founded the knightly Order of the Golden Fleece to the Glory of God and the Propagation of the Holy Faith. Following the example of the Church's religious processions, he introduced into the solemn proceedings a cart containing mummers who enacted the story of Jason and the Golden Fleece, whilst a bishop preached a sermon likening the story of Jason to the Crusading Knights battling to rescue the Holy land from the Infidel.

The fact that this story lent itself so easily to symbolism and allegory made it a popular theme for other festive occasions, notably that staged by Bergonza di Botta for his famous dinner-ballet in honour of the marriage of Isabella of Aragon to the Duke of Milan (1489). But this was only one of many magnificent entertainments given throughout Savoy and Northern Italy during the late fifteenth and early sixteenth centuries. Each was given to celebrate some notable event, staged throughout the town by the various authorities and contained wonderful scenic devices designed by such artists as Leonardo da Vinci.

FURTHER READING

CHAMBERS, SIR E. K., *Medieval Stage*, 2 vols. (1902).
CHAMBERS, SIR E. K., *Elizabethan Stage*, 4 vols. (1922).
CHAMBERS, SIR E. K., *Shakespeare*, 2 vols. (Clarendon Press, 1930).
DUCHÂRTRES, PAUL, *The Italian Comedy* (trans. by Randolph T. Weaver) (London, Harrap, 1929).
HARRISON, JANE, *Ancient Rite and Ritual* (London, 1931).
LAWSON, JOAN, *European Folk Dance* (London, Pitman, 1953).
LAWSON, JOAN, *Mime* (London, Pitman, 1957).
LAWSON, JOAN, *Classical Ballet, its Style and Technique* (London, A. and C. Black, 1960).
MÉNÉSTRIER, FATHER CLAUDE FRANÇOIS, *Des Ballets anciens et modernes* (Paris, 1682).
NICHOLL, ALLARDYCE, *The Development of the Theatre* (London, Harrap, 1949).
NICHOLL, ALLARDYCE, *Masks, Mimes and Miracles* (London, Harrap, 1931).
NICHOLL, ALLARDYCE, *British Drama* (London, Harrap, 1927).
PRUNIÈRES, HENRI, *Le Ballet du Cour en France avant Benserade et Lully* (Paris, 1914).
PRUNIÈRES, HENRI, *L'Opéra italien en France avant Lully* (Paris, 1913).
SACHS, CURT, *Rise of Music in the Ancient World* (London, Dent, 1944).
SACHS, CURT, *World History of Dance* (London, Allen & Unwin, 1937).
WEAVER, JOHN, *Essay towards a History of Dancing* (London, 1712).
WEAVER, JOHN, *A History of Mimes and Pantomimes* (London, 1728).
YATES, FRANCES, A., *The French Academies of the Sixteenth Century* (London, Jarrolds for the Warburg Institute, London University, 1948).

CHAPTER 2

The Mould of Classical Ballet: I The Academic Background

Ballet can be linked to contemporary events.
(KHUDEKOV, a nineteenth-century Russian journalist)

WHILST the fantastic *spectacula* were staged outside in the streets and squares of the North Italian towns, they contained something for everyone. Scenes from plays by Terence and other classical authors were jostled by highly symbolical processions and groupings, fire-works, water-shows, juggling, acrobatics, circuses and the rest. There was a place for the many different kinds of player. Those performers descended from the *pantomimi* and *jongleurs* were perhaps the most valued because they fitted into any form of entertainment. They were both vocal artists and dancer-mimes, and on being thrown out of some noble household for a ribald joke, or offending by clever innuendo, could go out into the streets and poke fun at those who irritated or oppressed the townsfolk, or indulge in some other popular "ploy." But once dinner-ballets and similar entertainments began to be staged in-side the palaces of prince or prelate, only the more serious player could be used, because the scope of such spectacles was more limited. They were staged for some specific purpose, therefore only those who would conform to the discipline of words fraught with meaning and dance-steps moulded to spell out some complicated symbol would be employed.

THE PART OF THE PHILOSOPHERS

The production of the dinner-ballets and similar entertainments given in honour of a marriage or of the signing of a treaty, the welcoming of a hero or other like occasion was the responsibility of learned philosophers. On all such occasions the leading figures brought important spiritual advisers in their train, thus the various alliances united families, states and also learned men.

The task of these last was to advise on political and other eventualities and to help produce the spectacles which, it was hoped, would strengthen the significance of the union and be a compliment to those participating.

These meetings of philosophers sometimes led to the forming of academies where discussions took place to elucidate the writings of the great classical authors and bring about the reconciliation of pagan and Christian dogmas by the use of symbolism and allegory. The academicians seized upon this material when they were producing their magnificent entertainments. Their main concern was to ensure these would have the right effect, therefore—

> The fables of the poets were to be interpreted as veiled statements of truth . . . The poet must hide his meaning in myth and image.
>
> (JEAN DORAT, a noted French scholar)

The Revival of Learning in France gained impetus when Francis I invited leading philosophers and artists such as Leonardo da Vinci to his court. But it was not until his son, Henri II, married Catherine de Medici that lavish entertainments began to be staged. Catherine was an astute woman and realized that the struggle for power between the various religious factions had to be resolved. She was quick to invite the help of learned Frenchmen of all parties to take part in the religious and political debates, and also to help stage the numerous festivities which she felt were needed to enhance the prestige of the court.

Coming from Florence, the home of the first academy and the earliest type of *spectacula*, she believed in the "effect" such activities could have on the morals of those participating. It is not surprising that her son Charles IX decided, after listening to the debates and concerts given at the home of a wealthy and learned Frenchman, Jean-Antoine de Baïf, to grant him letters patent to found an academy because—

> It is the opinion of many great personages, both ancient legislators and philosophers that it is of great importance for the morals of the citizens of a town, that the music current and used in the country should be retained under certain laws, for the minds of most men are formed and their behaviour influenced by its character, so that where music is disordered, there morals are also depraved, and where it is well ordered, there men are well disciplined morally.
>
> (*Préambule* dated 1570)

Jean-Antoine de Baïf was a member of the group known as the *Pléiade* amongst whose interesting activities was their attempt to revive the theatre of the Greeks. De Baïf invented a system of *vers mesurés* in order "To unite music with dance, song and measure as in the ancient days of Greece," so that the moral effects of the music would bring about the desired result. In practice this system was a method of making the metrical rhythm of the words form the basis of the musical rhythm. Thus the verbal declamation determined the timing and phrasing of the notes and these in their turn, determined the timing of the steps and gestures.

Theoretically the work of De Baïf and the *Pléiade* was far more than drawing up rules for the composing of *vers mesurés*. Like academicians elsewhere they interpreted the term *music* in the widest possible sense—*everything to do with the Muses*—and believing that no art, particularly that of living, could be practised without strict ethical and intellectual discipline, they drew up and discussed the educational syllabus required by those who wished to join in their activities. It suggested that the education of the French academicians, who were also courtiers, was to be complete in every detail as was that of the earlier Italians, whose education has been so brilliantly analysed by Castiglione in *The Courtier* (1528).

Henri III (Catherine de Medici's third son) became interested in the work of De Baïf's academy on hearing of the "effects" it supposedly had on its audience. Being a highly religious man and inheriting the throne of a country still torn between rival factions, despite his mother's efforts to unite the parties, he felt the need of staging religious processions to the great cathedrals and monasteries as well as more lighthearted entertainments in an attempted reconciliation.

After he had visited a concert given by De Baïf and taken part in some of the debates of the *Pléiade*, a contemporary, Sauval, wrote "All Ballets and masquerades were conducted by De Baïf and Maudit." The king was so impressed by the "effects of the music," that De Baïf and his colleagues were invited to compose the anthems and music and to help design the symbolical attributes and banners to be carried by Henri and his courtiers in penitential processions, as well as to take part in the debates, which Henri arranged at his own palace, and in the entertainments arising therefrom.

BALET COMIQUE DE LA ROYNE 1581

It was at a palace debate that the French philosopher, Jamyn, first expounded his theory of Circe, upon which *Balet comique de la Royne* was to be based. His argument throws light upon the way in which the allegory and symbolism used by the authors of this work came to be put into effect—

> I will touch upon the opinions of the Stoics, who held that virtues and vices were animals, and not only virtues and vices, but our passions also such as rage, anger, grief, malignity and others . . . The magic potion by which Circe transformed men into animals is to be interpreted as the power of bad habits, which if not resisted in the outset, degrade men into beasts.

The author of *The French Academies of the Sixteenth Century*, Frances A. Yates, not only gives the history but also a brilliant analysis and interpretation of the many spectacular entertainments given throughout the life of Catherine de Medici and notes that a Huguenot,

Agrippa d'Aubigné, who attended the palace debates when a member of the captive Henri of Navarre's suite, claims to have invented *Balet comique de la Royne.*

The ballet is always attributed to Balthazar de Beaujoyeulx (or Baltazarino Belgiojoso), who came to Paris as *valet de chambre* with Catherine de Medici. This Italian musician and dancing-master seems to have acted as producer for a work prepared by many hands chosen for the task by Catherine herself. There is no evidence that the *Pléiade* was collectively involved in the production, but individually they and their followers were extremely active in staging the seventeen fêtes given in honour of the Joyeuse marriage. Moreover as the De Baïf academicians had had much experience in staging similar entertainments, it is not surprising that certain items found in their earlier works were repeated and enlarged upon, because their influence undoubtedly penetrated all spheres of art, and *Balet comique de la Royne* must be quoted as one of the first ballets in which a proper synthesis of the arts was made in the sense that Diaghilev was to make it more fully understood some four hundred years later. It is perhaps useful to take note of some of these earlier items in order to emphasize the importance of the *Pléiade* in establishing the recognized style of the *ballets du cour.*

At the Fontainebleau fêtes (1564) when he received the Papal Ambassadors after the Council of Trent, Charles IX was wakened one morning by Three Sirens on the canal outside his window singing verses by Ronsard describing how Charles would restore peace. They were followed by Neptune (who symbolized the king) and immediately a nymph appeared on the rocks to signify "That the woodland deities would return with the return of peace," an item to be repeated with little alteration in the first part of *Balet comique.*

The Bayonne fêtes (1565) were given in honour of Catherine's daughter, Isabel, wife of Philip of Spain and for these De Baïf wrote a masquerade where the King of France vanquished the Fairy of the Pyrénées, who had enchanted some knights and maidens; an action to be repeated in *Balet comique* where Circe twice casts a spell over some nymphs. But it is more important to note that this masquerade introduced groups of peasants, each group performing a folk dance as an allegorical figure representing their province was brought into the hall. This idea was copied in later French ballets and it undoubtedly helped to introduce new steps into classical dance.

After the *Pléiade* became a recognized academy they included a ballet, *Paradis d'Amour*, in the fêtes they organized for the wedding of Henry of Navarre and Marguerite de Valois (1572). Parts of the action of this work closely resembled that of *Balet comique* and it contained an elaborate sequence of geometrical figures danced to *musique mesurée* by Twelve Nymphs representing the Virtues, whilst the diagrams themselves were supposed to represent Eternal Truths; a subject to be repeated and enlarged upon in the grand finale of *Balet comique.*

SYMBOLISM AND ALLEGORY

Another important link between the De Baïf academicians and *Balet comique* is the use of identical items of allegory and symbolism, which influenced the whole proceeding. The work was intended as a compliment to the parties involved in this alliance between two ruling houses. But it was also a comment on contemporary events. Baltazarino states—

> It is intimately connected with the times . . . After long wars peace has come at last and these magnificences of the Joyeuse wedding will show that the country has not been weakened or impoverished by them.

In their desire to ensure that the audience fully understood the implications of the tale of Circe, the authors appended four explanations of the fable to their libretto, the first pointing to the physical allegory; the second to the moral allegory; the third relating the story to Time and the Four Seasons; and the last (written by le Sieur Gordon, gentleman of the King's bedchamber who came to France with Mary Queen of Scots and was later Dean of Salisbury) was an enlargement of the moral and physical allegories. All these explanations are highly complex and are derived from a famous sixteenth-century book on mythology by Natale Conti. It becomes clear when reading the text of the words spoken during the action and the meaning hidden in the four explanations, that only those fully acquainted with subjects discussed by philosophers and academicians could appreciate the full significance of the spectacle as a short analysis of some of the difficulties facing a member of the audience can show.

The ballet took place in the Salle de Bourbon which was divided into four parts. The King, Queen Mother, Bride and Groom with their attendants sat facing Circe's garden, which represented the world of evil from whence emerged a stag, a dog, an elephant, a lion, a tiger and a pig, each representing some vice. Above the garden hung a golden sun and at its side a fountain. These signified not only that Circe was a daughter of the Sun and of Perseis a daughter of the Ocean, but also emphasized the belief that the enchantress was a mixture of heat and water, sun and ocean, matter and form from which arise those instincts leading men into all kinds of vice unless restrained by reason.

On the bridal group's right hand was the world of Nature represented by Pan seated in an oak wood from which came satyrs and wood nymphs to implore the god to rescue Circe's victims. On the bridal group's left hand was a vault covered with billowing clouds and representing the Vault of Heaven wherein sat singers and musicians. When their music was heard those onlookers who were "better instructed in the Platonic disciplines esteemed it to be the true harmony of heaven."

A great star-spangled cloud was suspended in the centre of the hall through which would descend such gods as Mercury, Minerva and Jupiter to pay their tribute to Catherine de

Medici who, the audience were assured by one actor after another, sat supreme in the world of reason and wisdom.

In addition to the significance of the words and the set, there was the significance of some of the characters and the properties they carried. For example: The Three Sirens with two tails, who sang the King's praises in *musique mesurée*, and were answered by the singers in the Vault of Heaven, were to be interpreted as "daughters of the Muses whose song guided the celestial spheres" (CATARI, a fifteenth-century author on mythology). The Four Ladies who opened the third part carried their conventional attributes: Fortitude, a pillar to denote strength and a musical instrument resting on her side to denote that it had been subjected to will; Justice, a pair of scales; Temperance, a pitcher of water; and Prudence, who also represented Virginity, carried a snake, a symbol of fertility.

With so much symbolism and allegory to be presented by words, scenery, costumes and props it is not surprising that the dancers seemed to play only a very decorative part and formed the links between the episodes. But even some part of their solemn processions and movements had the greatest significance. When the Twelve Naiads danced, their first figure was a triangle, representing Justice or the theological and intellectual disciplines, and this was followed by other significant geometrical figures, which were supposed to represent the alphabet of the Druids. According to Paul Lacroix, who gives some diagrams and their meanings found in a ballet of 1610, these signified the following: three circles conjoined represented Truth Known; a square within a square represented Virtuous Design; three circles within each other—Perfect Truth; and two equilateral triangles within a circle—Supreme Power. The need for this geometrical configuration arose from the Renaissance philosophers' belief that "All things were related to number, both in the outer world of nature and the inner world of man's soul." Following the example of Pythagoras, the Greek mathematicians too, tended to work everything out through geometrical and numerical associations.

The working out of the floor patterns of these figures led to many intricate windings. The author of the published description of the ballet writes how each time the Twelve Naiads crystallized into a group, the Four Dryads broke it with another, once the audience had appreciated its design. He also notes that half-way through there was a grand chain formed by four different kinds of interlacings and "So dexterously did each dancer keep her place and mark the cadence, that the beholders thought Archimedes himself had not a better understanding of geometrical proportions than these princesses and ladies in the dance."

It is not possible to say what was the form or quality of the steps used during the *entrées*. In De Baïf's academy, dance obeyed the same principles as words and music. That is the steps were measured in time in the same way that appropriately phrased steps can express the metres of Greek verse, each series falling into its proper cadence. Caroso describes this in *Il Ballarino* (1581).

THE FOUNDING OF THE ACADEMIES

Unfortunately the splendours of the Joyeuse wedding did not bring about the desired results. It was not until the conclusion of the Civil Wars and the coming into power of Cardinal Richelieu that any development took place in the arts. Although spectacles continued to be staged, they were still performed by amateurs and directed by literary men. These were mostly, if not entirely, educated by the church and had no knowledge of dance in its primitive expressive form. Both academicians and Jesuit Fathers, who staged equally impressive ballets, were only concerned with the "effects" these would have on their audiences. They concentrated on the outward form of the poetry, music, décor, costume and props, and not on the expressive movements of the dancers. Dancing was a social accomplishment and not a means of communication. The designing of significant geometrical shapes was the only way learned academicians were able to bring their passion for allegory and symbolism to bear on the dances in their ballets. And as the dancers were amateurs, the dancing-masters had only to see that their steps conformed to the design, music and above all, the niceties of social behaviour.

Cardinal Richelieu however paved the way for the development of all official forms of French art when he became political as well as spiritual adviser to Louis XIII and later to Louis XIV. His aim, which was furthered by Cardinal Mazarin and Chief Minister Colbert, was to establish the French kings firmly on their throne and make their courts the first in Europe. To achieve this it seems as if these astute men said "If the arts are to enhance the reputation and prestige of King and State, then they must be linked to contemporary events and ideas. And if they are to bring about the desired results, then there must be official bodies to ensure the proper planning of the effects." They then set to work to found the various Academies which were to organize the artists in every field and direct their energies into the proper channels. By the last years of the reign of Louis XIV, their aim had been achieved. The French court set the fashion and example for all other European monarchs.

Although not all these academies had a direct influence on ballet, their work must be considered because the result of dividing the arts into separate categories was to hinder the development of dance as an expressive medium.

THE FUNCTION OF THE ACADEMIES

L' Académie française was the first to be granted letters patent (1635). Its work was to study the French language, compile a dictionary and establish the grammar. It wished also to ensure that the rules of the classical theatre as laid down by Plato and Aristotle were maintained as they, the Academicians, understood them. Amongst these principles were the all-important ones frequently to crop up in ballet: the unities of time, place and action.

But the academicians were not content to deal with mere literary problems. Saint-Simon in his *Memoirs* gives an account of their debates on etiquette, behaviour and the rules of precedence. This last was a sore point in Saint-Simon's day and one which strongly influenced the staging of *Le Ballet royal* (1662) in which the Court Gazette solemnly states: "The origin and grandeur of the Royal House of France was represented by Fifteen Families with which they had alliance, all appearing in strict order of precedence." These rules of precedence guided later French dancing-masters when professionals took the place of the amateur courtiers and then demanded their right to a certain place in the order of appearance.

The Academy of Painting and Sculpture was founded in 1648 and some points of its manifesto give a clear indication of what was expected from any artist aspiring to become a member of so official a body and of the type of work produced—

1. Art should deal with grand and important subjects and never with the familiar things of life.
2. All such subjects are to be found in the ancients.
3. Art must serve the state and not the individual.
4. Nature is low, common and vulgar.
5. The ancient poets and sculptors have selected from nature all that is dignified and inspiring; rely, therefore, upon them, because observation is degrading.
6. Drawing is all-important not colour.
7. Painting should imitate the grandeur and severity of sculpture.
8. The judge of painting is not the artist, nor the public, but the infallible king.

Colbert, whose first academy this was, also expected the academicians to lay down a golden rule for French architecture, and although they did not succeed, there is little doubt that their calculations on the relative proportions allotted to the breadth, height and depth of the stage, when allied to the Italian views on perspective, led French ballet to those valuable types of set where the eye, undistracted by detail, is always drawn towards the spaciously centred dancing area. This became one of the most valuable elements in period décor designed by Bakst and Benois for Diaghilev.

In 1661 Colbert decided to found *L'Académie royale de Danse*: "To reform dancing of the abuses introduced into it during the disorders of the civil war and to debate upon ways of raising the standard of this art." But his efforts were ineffectual and the workings of his academy are not known. According to Frances A. Yates (*see* page 14) it seems that these new academicians ran foul of the powerful *Confréries de St. Julien* (whose first "charge," made by Royal Letter in 1334, was confirmed by Charles VI in 1406). Its leader, *roi des violons*, possessed the right to grant licences for the teaching of dance and expected his members to understand choregraphy or the methods of writing down a dance. Louis XIV

granted the *confrérie* letters patent in 1658, but Colbert does not seem to have consulted or invited its members to join him when he founded the new academy.

In a most interesting pamphlet, *Le Mariage de la Musique avec la Danse* (1664), the then *roi des violons*, Guillaume du Manoir, accuses these new academicians of not knowing their job and argues this from several important angles. Firstly he questions their right to issue licences to dancing-masters. This is an important point because at this time the *confrérie* was run on very strict lines. As with other guilds, an apprentice had to study four years under a master before he could submit a master-work or *chef-d'œuvre* (some music and a dance with its music and choregraphy) before twenty-four masters. And only when they approved his work was he entitled to call himself master and take apprentices.

This does not mean there were no other dancing-masters and fiddlers. During this period there were three kinds of artists and craftsmen in France and other European countries. Firstly those who worked for the royal households, they were known as *valets de chambre* and paid an annual salary. Secondly came those who belonged to the guilds and whose work or personal performances were bought by wealthy clients. Lastly there were those who hawked their wares and themselves round the people's fairs and theatres. Some dancers and comedians belonging to this group played a very great and important part in the development of ballet because, as will be found later, both the ballets and the classical technique practised in state theatres were frequently enriched when some outsider from the *théâtres du foire* came to play on the stage or take over the teaching at the school.

Du Manoir next brings up the question of the purely technical abilities of the new academicians and questions their right to call themselves masters. He asks whether they can grant licences since their system of apprenticeship has yet to be tried. He also accuses them of being a merely money-making concern and even trying to create a monopoly.

But Du Manoir's most important argument against them is lack of musical knowledge. After quoting how they have phrased a minuet to a sarabande merely because it has the same time signature, and the *pas de bourrée* to the movement of a gavotte, he accuses them of "Breaking this art from the true framework of music as understood by the ancients. Dancing is but an imitation of music, whereas music includes all the sciences and a greater part of art."

There is little doubt that as the various academies were founded, the literary men, composers, artists and dancing-masters who jointly had made the earlier ballets, lost contact with each other; the dancing-masters in particular, having been deprived of advice from other experts, began to concentrate purely on technical problems.

As if to counter the accusation that the division of the arts was failing to raise the prestige of the French courts, Colbert next founded *l'Académie des Inscriptions et des belles Lettres* (1663). Its original purpose was to provide expert mythological advice on the designs used for medals, tapestries and what could be called slogans. It also directed all courtly performances and, like a Ministry of Propaganda it ensured that all art was to the glorification of its king—*le roi soleil*. It was to this body that Quinault, the poet, had to submit the libretti of Lully's opera-ballets when he was appointed Director of Ballet. He obediently accepted their directions about the subject and details of each production, which were almost entirely based on classical themes and thus easily acquired the necessary allegory and symbolism.

Colbert next persuaded the king to grant letters patent to Abbé Perrin and Robert Combert to found *l'Académie royale de Musique* (1669), whose function was "To establish throughout the Realm academies of opera, representations in music and in the French language after the manner of Italy." It was in 1672 that Louis XIV authorized "His faithful and well-beloved Jean-Baptiste Lully to add to this academy a school to educate pupils as much for dancing as for singing and also train bands of violins and other instruments."

These new French opera-ballets set out to rival the Italian operas introduced earlier by Cardinal Mazarin and were an amalgam of ballet and opera. They derived from the interest taken not only in the Italian *opera seria*, but also in the playing of the Commedia dell'Arte companies, who had been introduced to Paris by Catherine de Medici. The wholly professional acting of these companies and their mime, dancing, methods of play and the introduction of gay interludes between the acts of their comedies had already influenced Molière to produce similar episodes between the acts of his plays, and to borrow some of their characters and methods of acting. Lully, in staging his opera-ballets, attempted something similar and required players more adaptable and accomplished than the amateur courtiers hitherto adequate for the simpler *ballets du cour*. Even though the dancers were still subservient to the vocal text, a far more accomplished style was beginning to evolve, which demanded longer rehearsal and more technical ability than that required for fashionable court dances.

The first professional dancers to appear in *ballets du cour* were the dancing-masters themselves, notably Pierre Beauchamps, the King's dancing-master, whose nephew Charles Louis became choregrapher in chief to *l'Académie royale de Musique* (later *l'Opéra*). The first professional ladies did not appear until 1691, when the academy produced a group of four dancers led by Mlle. Lafontaine at a public performance of *Le Triomphe d'Amour* at the *palais royal*. These ladies were not trained by the academy, whose school for dancers was only started in 1714 and whose school for children did not come into being until 1784. It would seem that the dancing-masters, who joined Lully at the Academy, furnished their own students for the production and that their work as academicians was confined to the discussions of technical problems, like that of the other academies.

THE WORK OF L'ACADÉMIE ROYALE DE MUSIQUE ET DE DANSE

There is no record of the deliberations of the first academicians of the dance. The manuscript said to have been prepared by Charles Louis Beauchamps has never been found. Yet studying the two books by Feuillet, his pupil, it is possible to surmise that their task was to define the steps and their exact performance, and the *ports de bras* and similar technical problems. Feuillet also makes an attempt to ally steps to music and gives the rules and time signature for the fashionable dances of the day.

The founding of an academy of dance within the academy of music marks the beginning of the everlasting struggle between those dancing-masters solely interested in technical problems and those ballet-masters who believe dance is a means of expression—a means of communicating through movement the moods, emotions and actions of the characters as they live them in the ballet. The French dancing-masters and their dancers working in the academy during the last years of the seventeenth and first half of the eighteenth centuries were the servants of literary men, who in their turn obeyed the dictates of experts in allegory and symbolism. It is not surprising, therefore, that they concentrated on perfecting the technique which produced the great dancers of the eighteenth century.

THE SUBJECT AND THE AUDIENCE

The rulings of the academic bodies might not have been so effective if there had not been a general desire for order and discipline amongst the circles for whom the official arts were intended. The desire was fostered by noble ladies of the time, who founded the *salons*. The first was created by a wealthy Italian, Mme. de Rambouillet, who found the rude manners of French soldiers newly returned from the civil wars impossible in an elegant drawing-room. She gradually drew round her a group of ladies and gentlemen with a knowledge of the behaviour of the Italian nobility brought up according to the courtly rules laid down by Castiglione in *The Courtier*. Gradually other wealthy ladies followed her example and vied with each other not only in employing important dancing-masters and tutors to ensure good manners and education, but also in attracting leading minds of the day. It thus became fashionable to discuss, superficially, the latest ideas and developments in the arts and sciences because learned men found it valuable to air their views in some *salon*. By so doing they could bring themselves to the notice of influential circles, particularly when both legitimate and illegitimate sons and daughters of the kings set up establishments as their fathers had done. In these *salons* ballets, masquerades and operas were staged and the themes chosen for production reflected the superficial interests of these people of fashion.

THE FÊTES AT SCEAUX

The sixteen fêtes given by the Duchesse du Maine at Sceaux in 1708 give some idea of the diversity of these spectacles. The Duchesse, an illegitimate daughter of Louis, had as her adviser the Abbé Malézieu, a member of the *Académie française*, who directed a sumptuous programme.

The first night was dedicated to the Goddess of Night and introduced the main theme of the fêtes. The Duchesse suffered from insomnia and much of the allegory and symbolism was devoted to the idea of banishing sleep and welcoming entertainment by the muses. The following nights were devoted to cards, music plays, to intriguing discussions on such subjects as Copernicus's theory of the sun, the virtues of the sabbath and a debate between Archimedes and Descartes, the philosophers, and Euripides, Terence and Corneille, the playwrights as they sat in the Inferno, to ballets, and on the fourteenth night there appeared as the fourth episode among scenes of the Greek gods, the famous mimed scene from an episode in Corneille's *Horace* given by two professional dancers, M. Balon and Mlle. Prévost This has been called the first *ballet d'action*. That is a scene without words in which the dancers expressed their meaning solely through movement.

But were M. Balon and Mlle. Prévost really incorporating emotionally expressive movements into the dance steps as happened in later *pas d'action*? Were they not rather using well-phrased conventional gestures such as were used in later *scènes d'action*? John Weaver casts doubts on Balon's ability to convey meaning through movement after seeing him dance in London—

> He pretended nothing more than a graceful Motion with strong and nimble Risings and the casting of the Body into several agreeable Postures. But for expressing anything in Nature, it was never in his Head. The Imitation of the Manners and Passions of Mankind he knew nothing of, nor ever therefore pretended to show us.

These sentiments were echoed in *The Spectator* when Addison and Steele launched their attack on the artificiality and meaningless virtuosity of the French dancers appearing and teaching in London in 1712 (*see* page 27).

It is not possible to be so certain about Mlle. Prévost's lack of expression. When she danced *Les Caractères de la Danse*, a solo specially written for her in which she characterized the eleven dances then in vogue (such as the *gavotte*, *gigue*, *passe-pied*, etc.), she is said to have turned it into a charming pantomime by changing her facial expression and poses so that they were appropriate to each dance and the dancers likely to perform them. Moreover, one of her pupils, Marie Sallé, was to become the most expressive dancer of the next generation (*see* page 3).

The Sceaux performance was perhaps unique in that it was performed by dancers trained in academic methods and not by actors. Similar scenes to this dramatic episode from *Horace*, where a brother kills a sister before recognizing her and killing himself, had been enacted in the earliest religious plays, in the first English drama *Gorboduc* (1561), in Shakespeare, in the Commedia dell'Arte and other popular theatres. Neither M. Balon, nor Abbé Malézieu, who designed these fêtes, could have been unaware of such practices for both had visited England, where more natural methods of dancing expressively had already reached the stage.

Perhaps this fourteenth scene has been so widely noted because it was the first time a death scene was shown before an audience in an official French theatre; such scenes were hitherto banned by the *Académie française* in their effort to maintain the principles of the Greek classical theatre (*see* pages 4 and 8). In addition it was the first scene of its kind to be presented at a court theatre which was without symbolical or allegorical meaning.

FURTHER READING

BISSON, L., *A Short History of French Literature* (Penguin, 1943).
BLAZE, CASTILE, *La Danse et les Ballets* (Paris, 1832).
MÉNESTRIER, FATHER CLAUDE FRANÇOIS, *Des Ballets anciens et modernes* (Paris, 1682).
PRUNIÈRES, HENRI, *Le Ballet du Cour en France avant Benserade et Lully* (Paris, 1914).
PRUNIÈRES, HENRI, *L'Opéra italien en France avant Lully* (Paris, 1914).
ROEDERER, P. L., *Mémoire pour servir á la Histoire de la Société polie en France* (Paris, 1892).
WEAVER, JOHN, *Essay towards a History of Dancing* (London, 1712).
WEAVER, JOHN, *A History of the Mimes and Pantomimes* (London, 1728).
WEAVER, JOHN, *Orchésographie* (translation of Feuillet's book) (1706).
YATES, FRANCES, A., *The French Academies of the Sixteenth Century* (London, Jarrolds for Warburg Institute, London University, 1948).

CHAPTER 3

The Mould of Classical Ballet: II The Staging of the Classical Ballet d'Action

Dancing must interpret meaning, it must not be mere gymnastics, an end in itself.
(FOKINE)

BY the beginning of the eighteenth century the formulas for creating classical ballets were set. The various French academicians laid down that the Greek or Roman themes be given proper allegory and symbolism to suit the purpose of the entertainment. The action was set in words and music, and divided into three or four parts linked and enlivened by *entrées* of dancers. The formulas for classical technique were being developed by French academicians from the work of earlier dancing-masters, and the amateur courtiers were rapidly giving place to professionals in the opera-ballets where solo virtuosity instead of the configuration of group dance commanded attention.

The development of virtuosity was largely due to the Commedia dell'Arte companies. These groups of players, originally servants of noble Italian households, were expected to behave like courtiers. This was particularly true of the *innamorati* (serious lovers) who received similar education. Because they were actors playing the roles of courtiers, they understood the need of perfecting the requisite techniques of dancing, music and the like in order to create the right impression by properly phrasing and accenting each step, gesture and pose. Similarly the comic characters, particularly the Harlequins and Columbines, who were the dancers of the companies, not only studied fashionable court dance so as to poke fun at grand manners, but enlivened their technique with newly invented steps or borrowed from some folk dance, acrobatics or tumbling. Something of the virtuosity of the Commedia dell'Arte dancers is described by De Brosses, who speaks of one young woman who executed twenty *entrechats* without pausing and "clicked her heel eight times at each leap. And she did this for all the *entrepas* for which our masters are so admired. Indeed compared with her supple grace, La Camargo seems like a block of stone."

These remarks were written about a beautiful pupil of Fassano, leader of a group of travelling players, when he introduced her to Paris. Fassano himself introduced complex steps of elevation and *batterie* to the Russian dancers of St. Petersburg, when he took over their training from Landé (*see* page 47). He was perhaps the most prominent of the Italian dancers to enrich the technique of the classical dancers when the state and court theatres began to be established. Having a technique of their own, the Italian Commedia dell'Arte players were probably the only type of professional able to teach young artists the various kinds of ballet, whether tragic or comic. The ordinary dancing-master had still to make his dancing theatrically effective, instead of making it conform to the etiquette of the ballroom.

But the Italian comedians did not rely on virtuosity only. Like other travelling players they performed in the popular theatres as well as at court, and in the former a freer type of play, not dependent on words, was more acceptable, especially during the interludes where miming, dancing and the like were welcomed "Because the eye is quicker to seize upon the meaning of a gesture than the ear to seize upon the meaning of a word—unless one has been specially educated to rely on hearing instead of seeing." (George Robey)

THE ENGLISH SCENE

For all the influence of the Commedia dell'Arte and other travelling players on both official and unofficial French theatres, the next step forwards in the development of ballet was taken by John Weaver in England when he presented *The Loves of Mars and Venus* at the Theatre Royal, Drury Lane (2nd March, 1717). This was the first classical *ballet d'action* in which the dancers conveyed meaning through movement without the aid of actors or singers to explain the action.

Although *The Loves of Mars and Venus* can be considered as a development of the French *ballet du cour* and the opera-ballets, and is closely linked to their traditions, it is also a development of certain English theatrical traditions. England had an extremely vigorous theatrical life of her own whilst these French and Italian entertainments were developing and it differed slightly from that on the continent.

Firstly there were no official bodies to direct all art towards one purpose. Even the elaborate court mummings, maskings and masques had something for everyone as had the earlier mystery, miracle and morality plays, and the drama which developed from these sources; Shakespeare's plays are superb examples of the rich variety of the English theatre. There are symbolism and allegory in them as in the work of other playwrights, but these are only secondary considerations, the action is the essential ingredient.

Secondly "the dancing English," whose love of dance was first noted by Saint Augustine, were making greater use of dance and mime in all their entertainments by the reign of Elizabeth I than were other peoples. This was particularly important in the masques and anti-masques which frequently included specially arranged dances, perhaps to create the necessary atmosphere for a more important piece of poetry, or to depict some comic characters playing a major part in creating satirical or witty diversion during a serious production.

Thirdly professional dancers appeared in English masques earlier than in ballets elsewhere. The masque sometimes required as long as fifty days' rehearsal. The producer, therefore, seems often to have used the highly accomplished morris dance teams, whose virile stepping had played an important part in earlier folk and religious dramas. Indeed the morris dance had served as a basic technique for such players as Will Kempe and George Jolley, whose lively performances in England and on the continent have been well recorded.

JOHN WEAVER (1673–1760)

A glance at the advertisements of *The Daily Courant* from 1702 to 1730 will give any reader an excellent idea of the various items presented on one evening at the London theatres of that time. Plays of Shakespeare and other dramatists appear and as well Italian singers, acrobats, jugglers and novelty acts. Messieurs Balon and Dupré are advertised to dance on the same bill as Mrs. Santlow (later Mrs. Booth), Misters Weaver and Thurmond, to name only a few of the stars. Amongst their items are a *New Morris*, *The Highland Lilt*, *The Whip of Dunboyne*, *The Dutch Skipper* (who later becomes drunken!), Spanish and Italian *entrées* and dances for Harlequins, Scaramouche and other Commedia dell'Arte characters.

John Weaver worked in London from 1702 to 1733 as a dancer (sometimes playing Harlequin, which suggests a more than average technique), as teacher, and ballet-master. He brought an analytical as well as a practical mind to the problems of dance on the stage, which, he asserted, differs from that performed in society and made out his case in his reply to Addison and Steele in *The Spectator* (*see* page 23) when he also mentions the publication of his *Essay Towards a History of Dancing*.

Weaver clearly states therein the need for style in dance when he describes how it always has been and always should be an expressive medium—

> By Serious Dancing I would be understood to mean not only that genteel Dancing in which the French have excelled, whether Brisk or Grave; and where Air, Firmness and a graceful and regular Motion of all Parts are required; but also where such Dancing shall represent any Character that is either Natural or belonging to ancient Fable or otherwise, where a nice Address and Management of the Passions and Gestures take up the Thought of the Performer and in which he is to show his skill.

> By Grotesque Dancing I mean only such Characters as are quite out of Nature, as Harlequin, Scaramouche, Pierrot and c. tho' in the Natural Sense of the Word, Grotesque amongst Masters of our Profession, takes in all comic Dancing whatsoever.

Weaver had a third and vitally important style of dance which he calls *scenical*. This requires a plot through which the action is expressed by "Dance and Dumb show." It was his practical application of the principles of these three forms of dance that became his greatest contribution to the development of the *ballet d'action*. Moreover, it was his practical viewpoint that made him present *The Loves of Mars and Venus* purely as a story shown by dance and mime without any hint of symbolism or allegorical significance, a course to be taken by all later choregraphers until the twentieth century.

THE LOVES OF MARS AND VENUS

The Parts of the Classical Ballet d'action

Although Weaver does not use the terms *pas d'action* and *scènes d'action*, he does make a distinction between those sections of his libretto where his dancers express their emotions whilst dancing and those where they are moving more or less as actors. For example in scene IV where Venus and Mars meet he writes—

> This Performance is alternate as representing Love and War. It is somewhat in Imitation of a Dancing among the Ancients . . . one singular Beauty in this sort of Dance is; that Strength and Softness, reciprocally and alternately are seen in their full Power when in the same Representation and at the same time; the Fire, Robustness; and Strength of the Warrior is seen, mixt with the Softness, and Delicacy of Love; Boldness and Vigour, in one, and a coy, and complying Reluctance in the other.

This would seem to be not only a *pas d'action* similar to Petipa's Rose Adagio, but also clearly to define the difference between the male and female dancer, an essential part of any *pas de deux* where a conversation in movement takes place. In fact, Weaver's description suggests that Mars and Venus (M. Dupré and Mrs. Santlow) were performing a very different *pas de deux* from those used in opera-ballets, which were little more than a gracefully brilliant display of steps based on a well recognized type of court dance.

In the second scene Weaver seems to have had a *scène d'action* in mind when he writes—

> This last Dance being altogether of the Pantomimic kind, it is necessary that the Spectator should know some of the most particular Gestures made use therein: and what Passions, or Affections, they discover, represent or express.

He then gives an analysis of fourteen gestures used when Venus repulses Vulcan.

There are other clearly distinguishable *pas* and *scènes* as well as purely danced passages, which are essential to create the proper atmosphere for the development of action. Amongst these are the Pyrrhic dance of Mars and his Followers which opens the ballet, and a *passacaille* danced by Venus, the Graces and others to introduce the heroine and her retinue.

As far as it is possible to judge from the libretto, Weaver only indulged in one set of variations as a grand finale, an economy forced upon him by the management's reluctance to spend money on what was an experimental production, as Colley Cibber, the manager himself admits. It should also be remembered that *The Loves of Mars and Venus* was only one item on a bill whose main attraction was *The Maid's Tragedy* by Beaumont and Fletcher.

The Music and the Continuity

As further evidence that Weaver considered that a difference existed between the *pas* and the *scènes* is the fact that he employed two composers to write the music and each had a different task. Weaver obviously felt the need for some other type of composition to accompany the *scènes* than the purely "Dancing Airs" composed by Mr. Firbank, himself an accomplished dancer. He therefore employed Henry Symonds, member of the King's Band of Musicians, to compose the "Symphonies," which "introduced the Subjects and adapted his Sounds to the Passions and Affections of the Characters."

Technique

Because economic circumstances did not allow him to use expensive sets and costumes, Weaver had to rely principally on his dancers' own qualities to communicate his ideas. But he admits they were not equal to the task because it was so entirely foreign to their manner of dancing although he had "endeavour'd to enter into the Characters and describe their Manners and Passions by proper Actions and Gestures, suitable to the Fable; yet I must confess that I have in this Entertainment too much inclin'd to the Modern Dancing." Thus Weaver, like most later choregraphers, accepted contemporary technique as a basis on which to frame his choregraphy.

The Loves of Mars and Venus was a success, as were Weaver's later ballets, one proof being the production of a burlesque at the rival theatre in Lincoln's Inn Fields where John Lun (Rich) was quick to follow Drury Lane's example by staging similar types of serious and comic ballets. These new kinds of entertainment were staged principally by Messrs. Weaver, Lun and Thurmond using Greek and Roman themes for their serious works, and the antics of Harlequin and his colleagues for the comedies. There was thus a uniformity of style and content in the productions as well as in the dancing, for although the dancers did sometimes change theatres, if they were English, they would seem to have possessed the same technical equipment.

This sharing of technical knowledge was largely due to the work of John Weaver as writer and teacher. Each book of his was subscribed for by his fellow dancing-masters in London, the provinces and the colonies. His translation of Feuillet's technical work on the analysis of the steps (1706) ensured that English and French practice came from the same source.

Weaver then wrote an original *Small Treatise of Time and Cadence in Dancing* (1706) designed to help in the recording of dance, which is a valuable guide to the timing of steps and musical phrasings. Both his *Essay Towards a History* (1712) and the *History of Dancing* (1728) contain much valuable information about style and expressiveness in dance as well as the historical side. But his *Anatomical and Mechanical Lectures* deserve greater attention.

These were delivered to his fellow teachers and dancers at the Academy in Chancery Lane and were the first attempts to relate anatomy and the movements of bones and muscles to the technique of dance and were as well an attempt to state the principles by which the dancer could perfect the technique of the four movements of dance. Weaver describes these as "Sinking, Rising, Turning and Springing," which, he says, are to dancing "as Light and Shade are to Painting."

He gives an analysis of the true and false positions, describes the physique and divides his dancers into their various categories. He also suggests their need for a proper understanding of "Music, Painting and Rhetorick," the last was understood as the art of gesture. But by this Weaver did not mean a purely mechanical performance of conventional gesture. Throughout his book he insists that the dancer must convey expressiveness through the movements of the whole body. In fact these lectures are the first textbook on the technical and artistic requirements of a dancer.

FOREIGN ARTISTS IN ENGLAND

John Weaver paved the way for both the proper technical and artistic training of a dancer and the construction of a classical *ballet d'action*. Yet, although his English colleagues were fully aware of his activities, and English dancers, often led by the enchanting Mrs. Santlow, usually played all the roles in his ballets, an English school of dance did not develop.

At this period the connexion between the English and continental theatres was very close. After the Restoration foreign artists were welcomed and they further developed ballet as a medium of expression, influenced possibly by what they had learnt from working with Weaver, or on the same stage as English dancers, who were active abroad, particularly at the Parisian *Opéra Comique*, where the English pantomime dancer, Roger, was *compositeur des ballets* for several years and had with him several compatriots.

LE GRAND DUPRÉ (1697–1774)

One of the first links between English and continental practices was Le Grand Dupré, who played Mars and other leading roles for Weaver as well as dancing Harlequin in dances specially arranged for him in England. He does not seem to have made so formal an approach to dance as other virtuosos. Gardel told his pupil Blasis that Dupré "Used to dance extempore to familiar airs by which means he rendered his imagination more creative in the forming of steps, and accustomed his ears to catch the measure and rhythm of the music with greater rapidity."

This anecdote suggests several interesting ideas. Firstly in Du Manoir's attack on the new academicians (1664) he is emphatic that "A dance was always composed to an air and not an air to a dance" (*see* page 20). Dupré was, therefore, feeling for the intimate relationship between the two arts, which dancers tended to forget in their search for virtuosity. He was also accustoming himself to other types of music than formal dance tunes, a practice he had first encountered when dancing and miming to Mr. Symonds' "Symphonies" in *The Loves of Mars and Venus.*

Secondly, was not Dupré practising methods of the Commedia dell'Arte players, whose art of extemporization he would have to emulate when dancing Harlequin. It is hard to believe that Dupré did not pass on some of his experiences of dancing with Weaver when appearing in the *ballets d'action* staged at the *Opéra Comique* by Jean Monnet and when teaching his famous pupils Gaetano Vestris and Jean-Georges Noverre.

MARIE SALLÉ (1707–56)

Marie Sallé is a second link between English and continental ballet. She was dancing at the Lincoln's Inn Fields theatre when *The Loves of Mars and Venus* was produced. *The Daily Courant* announced that she and her brother were pupils of M. Balon (she was also a pupil of Mlle. Prévost), but as she came from a family of travelling players, she used a far freer form of movement through which she could express the emotions, moods and actions of the characters she played. Riccoboni (*see* page 33) mentions that much of her natural expressiveness was learnt from the English Harlequin (John Rich or Lun) for whom she was later to dance Mrs. Booth's part in his most successful ballet-pantomime *Apollo and Daphne.*

Some indication of Sallé's particular qualities can be gleaned not only from Voltaire's poem in which he compares this sensitively expressive dancer with the brilliant Camargo, but also from descriptions of their first performances in *Les Caractères de la Danse* (*see* page 23). La Camargo, also a pupil of Prévost, made the sequence an excuse for a brilliant display of virtuosity, changing her steps of elevation and *batterie* to suit the technical requirements of each dance. Sallé, however, performed the *pas* with a cavalier and in a simple ball-gown instead of the usual elaborate ballet costume, and brought to each passage the dignified elegance and charming grace of a lady at court. This course was taken because she was dancing at *L'Académie royale de Musique* and not at a popular theatre, where she suited her style to the national, character and other dances. She possibly felt the need of impressing her aristocratic audiences that she was equal to this important occasion.

The sense of dance style which Sallé showed rose partly from her feeling for the music. This was noted by Handel, who invited her to join his season at Covent Garden in 1734, after the success of her ballet *Pygmalion*. He composed a new prologue to his opera *Il Pastor Fido*, which subtly drew attention to her importance. The success of this item resulted in Sallé's appearing and arranging dances in others of Handel's operas which were held by most critics to be masterpieces, aptly fitting to the music.

Sallé's greatest contribution to the ballet lay in her expressive movement, which was the notable feature of every ballet she arranged for herself. *Pygmalion* (14th January, 1734), the most important of these, was staged at Covent Garden and given no less than thirty times before the end of the season. The London correspondent of the *Mercure de France* went into raptures about her performances and described the action thus—

> Little by little the statue comes to life, showing astonishment at her new existence and everything round her. Amazed and enchanted Pygmalion takes her hand leading her from the pedestal. Step by step she feels the way, gradually assuming the most graceful poses a sculptor could possibly desire. Pygmalion dances before her as if to teach her to dance. She repeats after him the simplest as well as the most difficult and complex steps; he endeavours to inspire her with the love he feels and succeeds.

Reading this and descriptions of Sallé's other ballets, it seems as if she concentrated principally on creating a *pas de deux* through which she could develop a conversation in dance with a sympathetic partner because it gave larger scope for expressive gesture than any solo. It was a practice to which she had been accustomed since her first appearance with her brother; the difference was that her later works were based on classical technique and not on the national, character and other idioms of her early performances.

When *Pygmalion* was produced in Paris this lack of words was an innovation because there the distinction between an opera and a ballet had still to be made. The dancers were only allowed the stage to themselves for interludes and *divertissements* during the total action of operas by Lully, Rameau and others, and although they did attempt to be expressive, especially when Sallé herself appeared and staged an episode, it still had to be explained by actor or singer.

Sallé also dared to appear in *Pygmalion* in the simplest of Greek draperies, with her hair down. But again this was only an innovation in Paris, where the dancers wore elaborate wigs and panniered dresses. In England a simpler form of dancing costume had already been introduced by Inigo Jones for some of the English masques, and by 1722, when Mrs. Santlow (Mrs. Booth) appeared in Thurmond's *Masque of Deities*, her hair was loose, a deer-skin was fastened to her breast and her "purple gown was tuck'd up to the knee."

Pygmalion is the link between London and so many later reformers because it became a ballet to be revived seemingly whenever a certain style and type of dancer wished to make a debut in a new town. It is perhaps significant that in each case the *danseuse* playing Sallé's role of the statue came, like Sallé herself, from a Commedia dell'Arte or similar company. Catherine Rolland in Riccoboni's production at *Le Théâtre Italien* in Paris closely followed Sallé herself in 1734. Then came La Barbarina (Barbara Campanini) in Fassano's beautiful production in Berlin in 1745 when Noverre danced as a figurant. Favart writing about Antonia Veronese (Camille) dancing in 1760 might have been writing about Sallé herself "The art of her pantomime is beyond praise . . . one might say of Camille that she dances even with her thought."

THE BALLET D'ACTION IN PARIS

LE THÉÂTRE ITALIEN

Although Luigi Riccoboni, the Italian comedian, was not a dancer, except that as a "serious lover" he performed contemporary court dance, he helped to link French and English ballet. Firstly he placed on record his impressions of certain English actors, particularly those of Garrick to whom he dedicated his *History of the Theatre*. Because of his eminence, his writings were studied by other players anxious to profit from his experiences, and to learn about the influence "things English" had on many continental thinkers and reformers in all fields during the eighteenth century. The most outstanding features of the English theatre for Riccoboni were the naturalness of the acting, the lack of official directives which narrowed theatrical art elsewhere thus driving it into conventional channels, the direct approach to human problems, particularly as shown by Shakespeare, and the more tolerant attitude of the audience towards innovations. The last point was of vital importance to such reformers as Noverre, Dauberval and Didelot, and later Diaghilev, because any experiment was at least allowed to proceed, even if it were finally given an adverse verdict.

Secondly although Riccoboni was firmly grounded in the traditions of the Commedia dell'Arte, he also believed in the value of contemporary ideas. It was perhaps his sense of the need for experiment which led him to persuade his son, François, to introduce Sallé's *Pygmalion* to Parisian audiences, feeling no doubt that the inclusion of a serious work in the otherwise comic ballet repertoire of his company would enhance their reputation and make his *Théâtre italien* an even stronger rival to the *Opéra comique*, who staged somewhat similar items (*see* page 34).

This introduction of a serious *ballet d'action* into the repertoire of a more or less permanently settled company helped to develop the expressiveness of their classical dance, because its success led to other productions in a similar vein. One of these, produced by François Riccoboni, *Les Filets du Vulcain* (1738), seems to have been based on Weaver's libretto and contained similar dances. For example "Mars and Venus dance to a light melody, a kind of well-expressed dialogue which outlines the inception of their mutual tender feelings." Vulcan dances a monologue of "raging jealousy," and there was a "*pas de trois*" of infidelity (*see* pages 28–29).

Further innovations were made at the *Théâtre Italien* by Jean Baptiste de Hesse, a dancer from the Netherlands, who joined the company in 1734, dancing as a figurant in *Pygmalion* and later becoming ballet-master. Many of his ballets were of the same comic genre as earlier works based on the Commedia dell'Arte characters, but he also staged several tragic *ballets d'action* and some lighter pastoral pieces which greatly influenced other choreographers, because of their dramatic unity and well-balanced action. It seems that from 1740 De Hesse initiated a firm system of artistic training which ensured that his entire cast and not merely the leading players, were able to dance not only with technical facility, but also to give expression to their movement. There was thus a uniformity of emotional quality in the dances of both soloists and *corps de ballet*, which made such a work as his *Acis and Galatea* (1753) appear to his contemporaries as a "genuine tragedy pantomime" with a unity of action and purpose.

OPÉRA COMIQUE

The Paris *Opéra comique*, which rivalled the *Théâtre italien* also produced several serious works among the usual pantomime ballets. Because these *ballets d'action* were considered to be unusual they were always announced as *ballets qui représentaient en scènes muettes* and for some years after 1727 were produced by Roger, a dancer from London, who, with other pantomime dancers in the company, introduced certain of their native productions, judging from the titles and librettos of such works. The taste for these entertainments grew when Jean Monnet took charge and called on such importantly expressive dancers as Dupré and Lany from the *Opéra*, and Marie Sallé, who reproduced for him her famous *Ballets des Fleurs* in which Noverre danced (1743).

VIENNA — HILFERDING (1710–68) AND ANGIOLINI (1723–96)

It was while the first classical *ballets d'action* were being staged in Paris that the Viennese dancer, Franz Hilferding, came to study and on his return to Vienna, began to experiment, staging such highly dramatic works as Racine's *Britannicus*, Crébillon's *Idomenée* and Voltaire's *Alzire* in the form of ballets in which the entire action was expressed through gesture. These works were on the same lines as the scene performed by M. Balon and Mlle. Prévost. But he also presented other ballets of a lighter, more lyrical nature, where dance took precedence and was reinforced by expressive movement, following the example of Weaver and Sallé.

Hilferding, like De Hesse, did not confine his serious and more lyrical works to strictly classical themes, but frequently introduced pastoral subjects, and in his comic ballets rejected the usual stock Commedia dell'Arte characters and used instead themes drawn from real life, preferably from the countryside. This enabled him to design dances characteristic of threshers, charcoal-burners and the like that became an important feature in the ballets he and his pupil, Angiolini, were to produce during their long service in St. Petersburg, where the latter attempted and succeeded in giving stylized form to some of the highly expressive Russian folk dances (*see* page 49).

When Gasparo Angiolini took over the leadership of the Viennese ballet on Hilferding's departure for St. Petersburg (1757) he made further efforts to integrate dance, gesture and music. At this time the Viennese State Theatres were under the direction of Count Durazzo, whose wide study of the European theatres and anxiety to further the arts of opera and ballet led him to promote whatever would eliminate the senseless conventions and artificialities into which the *opera seria* and opera-ballet had fallen. His was greatly influenced by his friend, Count Algarotti, whose writings and lecture to the English Royal Society (1750) on the reform of opera served as a theoretical basis for many other contemporary writers on similar subjects; notable among them was Noverre who sometimes used Algarotti's own ideas, merely substituting the term *ballet* for the term *opera* in his *Letters on the Dance* (1760).

Angiolini's first works, apart from some national ballets intended to reveal the spirit of certain peoples in whose customs and dances he was interested, were little different from those of Hilferding. These met with such success that he produced his first important dramatic *ballet d'action*, *Don Juan* based on Molière's play *Le Festin de Pierre* with music by Gluck (1761). In this he was clearly trying to create a dance-drama instead of the mimodramas or pastoral idylls of his master. It was also in essence different from the strong dramas with their realistic gestures then being produced by Noverre at Stuttgart, following that master's study of Garrick in Shakespeare's plays, which broke all the academic rules to which Noverre had been accustomed during his training in Paris.

In his preface to *Don Juan*, written in collaboration with the librettist Raniero Calzabigi, Angiolini states—

> If we can stir up every passion by a mute play, why should we be forbidden to attempt this? If the public does not wish to deprive itself of the greatest beauties of our art, it must accustom itself to being moved by our ballet and brought to tears.

Don Juan was a success and was played more frequently than any other dramatic ballet staged during the latter half of the eighteenth century.

It is not possible to discover the details of Angiolini's choregraphy for *Don Juan*, yet from contemporary writings it is clear that Count Durazzo presented this "drama expressed through dance" as a protest against the senseless artificialities or merely sensuous succession of dance *divertissements* strung together by vocal explanation of the usual state theatre ballets. The music too was unlike that used elsewhere. Gluck's score did not consist of the usual academically formed dance numbers. Doctor Burney mentions that after Gluck's visit to England (1745) he "Endeavoured to write for the voice more in the natural tones of the human affections and passion than to flatter the lovers of deep science and difficult execution." These remarks are equally true of the music for *Don Juan*, where Gluck emphasized the varying emotional content of the three acts by setting each in a different key and so phrasing the different phases of each episode that they arrived at a proper climax.

This same sense of the vitally descriptive power of music to enhance the emotional content of the dance is equally obvious in Gluck's later score for *Sémiramis*, Angiolini's next important work, and in the dances for such operas as *Orpheus* which Angiolini also arranged.

ANGIOLINI'S WRITINGS

Angiolini, like his master Hilferding, worked on the theory of choregraphic design and has left on record some valuable comments on the production of a dramatic *ballet d'action* in his introduction to *Sémiramis* (1765), and in two letters to Noverre (1772), written when his anger was roused by Noverre's personally made claim to be the "unico riformatore della danze pantomima"; a claim repudiated because Angiolini believed Hilferding had a right to this title, not only because he had staged dramatic *ballets d'action*, but also because he had entirely dispensed with the crude comic ballets and had done away with the conventionally elaborate costumes and masks.

Angiolini's first letter to Noverre is a criticism of the latter's *Agamemnon*, a vindication of Hilferding's position in history, and a refutation of Noverre's argument that ballet should not be governed by the same rules as drama. His second letter is a criticism of Noverre's *Letters*.

Angiolini attacks *Agamemnon* and incidentally other Noverre ballets, because the unity of action is disrupted by the introduction of a second action as well as unnecessary *divertissements*. He also accuses Noverre of neglecting the other two unities. Angiolini makes his own viewpoint on this difficult problem clear in his libretto for *Sémiramis*: "One's first thought is that the three unities of time, place and action are almost as necessary to *Danse-pantomimes* as to comedies and tragedies." By the unity of place he understands the action occurs in one place, in one town; by the unities of time and action he believes it is difficult to prolong the action and not keep it within twenty-four hours; firstly because it is tiring, if not impossible for the main characters to dance for any length of time; secondly because it is impossible to include other episodes without confusing the audience; and lastly because—

> The art of mime tells the story so succinctly that before they are aware, the dénouement has come. The choregrapher can make use of the *corps de ballet* to lengthen the action and allow the principals some rest,

but these dancers must be part of the action so that they assume the role of the chorus in the Greek tragedies, which should be the example to follow.

Angiolini then condemns the ways of the *Opéra français* which weakened the dramatic impact of the action by including transformation scenes and "episodes," saying—

It is with a convex lens which gathers all rays into a single focal point that we ought to examine the subject used; the slightest deviation and we lose sight of those characters by whom we wish to touch the feelings of the audience.

This singleness of purpose seems to have marked all Angiolini's work as choregrapher and may have been the reason why his *Sémiramis* did not meet with immediate success. It was too closely based on Voltaire's drama from which he eliminated all but the main action and principal characters. This proved to be too dramatic and too little relieved by dance to please the Viennese public, although they came to appreciate its merits later when Noverre's own ballets appeared to them to be top-heavy with action and *divertissements*. Noverre's works also seemed to lack that sensitive feeling for the music, which had been obvious when Angiolini worked with Gluck. Mozart noted Noverre's insensitivity when he complained to his father that the great man, having commissioned *Les Petits Riens*, added "Six old miserable ariettas written by others," to pad out the action.

Angiolini was inspired to create *Sémiramis* for the English dancer, Nancy, after seeing her dance for Noverre in Stuttgart. She had acquired "The art of speaking through dance." This was something that Angiolini believed was only possible after the dancer—

Had studied the steps or alphabet of our language and given them grace, nobility, elegance, attitudes, a sense of design and purpose . . . The dancer should himself be affected by what he wants to portray; he should even feel and communicate to the audience those inner tremors with which horror, pity and terror speak inside us and force us to go pale, sigh, to start and weep tears; in spite of our knowledge that that which makes us so sensitive is nothing but an artificial being, an imitation, without any of the force and eloquent truth which nature employs in reality.

JEAN-GEORGES NOVERRE (1727–1810)

Weaver, Sallé, De Hesse and Hilferding paved the way for Angiolini and for Noverre, whose claim to be the only reformer of ballet seems to have been based on his own terms. He was a man of his own times and not an isolated figure. His great merit is that he had the ability to collect and collate the ideas and practices put forward by his predecessors and contemporaries for the reform of the theatre and ballet in particular and, even if he did neglect to acknowledge his debt to others, his first *Letters on the Dance* (1760) mark a turning point in the history of ballet. Angiolini, although working independently, was quick to realize this and only began to criticize fifteen years later when he obviously felt that although Noverre's theories were sound, his practices were questionable (*see* page 36).

One important reason for Noverre's claim to fame lies in his careful nursing of his own reputation by making contact with the famous people of his day. Amongst these was Voltaire, whose influence was enormous on all art-workers of that time. It was on reading *Letters on the Dance* specially sent to him by the author that he recommended Noverre to go to England, where he believed "Your merits will be appreciated . . . because there they love nature." And it was after working with Garrick, the great English actor, and on sending Voltaire a libretto for a ballet based on that author's *Henriade*, Noverre wrote: "The English theatre has given me the beauties most suitable for the pantomimic action."

There can be no doubt of the tremendous influence that Garrick's personality, realistic methods of acting and attention to the historical details of costumes had on Noverre. The actor's talent is one of the very few acknowledged by the choregrapher, who sings Garrick's praises and analyses his methods. It was in Garrick's library that he must have collected much of the material for his *Letters*, for on its shelves were books by some of the leading thinkers and workers in the theatre, including those of L'Abbé du Bos, Algarotti and Riccoboni. In conversation with the famous people met there, and perhaps with Garrick's wife, Mme. Violette, he may even have learnt something of Hilferding's methods, whose pupil she had been.

Noverre's *Letters on the Dance* were published from Lyons and Stuttgart where the Duke of Wurtemberg afforded him every facility, giving him the services of his composer Jomelli, of the scenic artist Servandoni and of Bocquet for the costumes, and allowing him to invite some of the leading Paris *Opéra* dancers such as Gaetano Vestris, who doubtless enjoyed dancing in Noverre's experimental works and such an unusual artist as Mlle. Nancy (*see* page 37). Such ballets were different from those at the *Opéra* in which they usually performed their own type of solo and were unable to express any kind of emotion owing, firstly, to the Director's reluctance to do away with verbal explanation (the *Opéra* held the sole performing rights for all such entertainment with speech presented in Paris), and secondly to the entirely inappropriate costumes. The cult of antiquity originated by De Baïf had reached such dimensions that the performers wore real armour, heavy helmets, plumes, shields, *tonnelets* and masks, all of which made any natural or expressive movement an impossibility. Even the pastoral ballets were similarly affected. The very name rococo, applied to this period, comes from the French word *rocaille*, meaning artificially made rock and pierced-shell work, and indicates that the style of everything in state ballet, as in court art and life, was centred round the art of decoration.

That such pastoral works appeared at all was due to the superficial interest taken in the work of the Encyclopedists led by Diderot and Rousseau, and the latter's idea of going back to nature for theatrical themes. This suggested to the artists working to entertain the pleasure-loving court that it might be fun to play at being shepherds and shepherdesses and the pastoral gods, goddesses, nymphs and satyrs.

Exactly how much reform Noverre was able to accomplish in Stuttgart or elsewhere is not known. In his second set of *Letters* (1807) he suggests he did not do without words until he produced *Les Caprices de Galathée* in Lyons (1758). Later he states he could only put a few of his reforms into practice largely because his audiences, who were mostly in state or court theatres, expected his *grands ballets* to be on the same spectacular scale as those of the court of Louis XIV. Therefore he had to compromise, and in compromising frequently changed his opinion. He states also that only his principal dancers could fulfil his demands for expressive movement. This was not so when he worked for Count Durazzo in Vienna, staging both his ballets and the dances in Gluck's operas. Here he found dancers trained by Hilferding and Angiolini, who were so expressive that when Gluck despaired of getting the opera chorus to express any emotion at all, Noverre placed the singers behind the scenes and arranged movements of such expressiveness for the *corps de ballet* that the audience believed the dancers were singing.

The fact that Noverre was not always able to obtain an entire company grounded in the same type of dramatic movement used by Garrick, which was what he needed for his heavily blood-stained dramatic ballets, may account for his overloading of the action with extraneous episodes and *divertissements*. His interpretation of Aristotle's statements on the construction of a play that "Ballet must have a beginning, a climax and end," seems to have led him into the same trap as some modern choregraphers, whose ballets are full of climaxes, not always pertinent to the main action. It is difficult not to reach this conclusion after reading some of his libretti, which he admits were borrowed from other authors. For example, *The Jealous Man Without a Rival* has no less than seven scenes with a climax to each borrowed from a different source: (1) Diderot; (2) his own; (3) Mahomet; (4) Molière's *Le Dépit Amoureux*; (5) Molière's *Tartuffe*; (6) his own; (7) Racine's *Andromaque*; and the unravelling of this tortuous action came from Crébillon's *Rhadamiste et Zénobie*.

It was during his second and third visits to London (1782–9) that Noverre was able to experiment more freely and stage those of his works that relied more on the expressiveness of his dancers than on the magnificence of the costumes and scenery. This period in Noverre's career was perhaps the most fruitful, not for himself, but for those who worked with him, particularly Jean Dauberval and Charles Didelot and their wives, who were to become the leaders of their profession and develop their art at the end of the eighteenth and beginning of the nineteenth centuries. Noverre perhaps realized this because their ballets and those of other choregraphers were staged alongside his. He complains somewhat bitterly in his last *Letters* that his works are neglected by those for whom they were written and who now produce ignoble themes. He retracts his statement that "Ballet should show the passions, actions and manners of all people of the globe," stating that only noble characters and themes are suitable subjects. He then praises Maximilian and

Pierre Gardel, who preserved the aristocratic style of ballet, not only as the true technique of dance, but also its theme and form.

The question whether all the stars were so wonderful as Noverre asserts cannot be proved. The Russian ballet-master, Valberg was sent to Paris to study and in 1802 wrote of Auguste Vestris, the so-called "god of the dance": "He dances paying no attention to his arms, revolves like a mad man and sometimes even puts his tongue out." But by this time Valberg had seen something of the work of Noverre's followers, Dauberval and Didelot, who had made many innovations. Their ballets were not heavy mimodramas of conventional gesture interspersed with accomplished but expressionless *divertissements*, nor were they great spectacles. Their ballets introduced a more expressive form of danced-mime and mimed-dance.

FURTHER READING

ANGIOLINI, GASPARO, *Dissertation sur les Ballets pantomimes des Anciens, publiée pour servir de programme au ballet pantomime tragique de "Sémiramis"* (Vienna, 1765).
ANGIOLINI, GASPARO, *Lettere di Gasparo Angiolini.*
BEAUMONT, C. W., *Three French Dancers of the Seventeenth Century* (London, 1934).
BEAUMONT, C. W., *Complete Book of Ballets* (London, Putnam, 1939).
BEAUMONT, C. W., *Supplement to the Complete Book of Ballets* (1942).
BLASIS, CARLO, *The Code of Terpsichore* (London, 1830).
BLASIS, CARLO, *Traité élémentaire et pratique de la Danse* (Milan, 1820).
CAHUSAC, LOUIS DE, *La Danse ancienne et moderne, au Traité de la Danse* (Paris, 1754).
FOKINE, MIKHAIL, *Manifesto to "Daphnis and Chloe"* (1904).
FOKINE, MIKHAIL, *Conversations with Edwin Evans* (1923–4).
HUEFFER, FRANCIS, *The Troubadors. A History of Provençal Life and Literature* (London, Chatto & Windus, 1878).
LAWSON, JOAN, *European Folk Dance* (London, Pitman, 1953).
LAWSON, JOAN, *Mime* (London, Pitman, 1957).
LAWSON, JOAN, *Classical Ballet, its Style and Technique* (London, A. and C. Black, 1960).
MAURICE, ALBERT, *Théâtres de la Foire* (Paris, 1900).
NOVERRE, C. E., *Letters on the Dance* (trans. C. W. Beaumont) (London, 1930).
NOVERRE, C. E., *Lettres sur les Arts imitateurs en general et sur la Danse en particulier* (Paris, 1807).
RICCOBONI, LUIGI, *An Historical and Critical Account of the Theatre in Europe* (London, 1751).
RICCOBONI, LUIGI, *A General History of the Stage from its Origin* (dedicated to David Garrick) (London, 1754).
WEAVER, JOHN, *Essay towards a History of Dancing* (London, 1712).
WEAVER, JOHN, *A History of the Mimes and Pantomimes* (London, 1728).
WEAVER, JOHN, *The Loves of Mars and Venus* (1717).
WEAVER, JOHN, *Orchésographie* (translation of Feuillet's book) (1706).
WEAVER, JOHN, *Small Treatise of Time and Cadence in Dancing* (1706).
WEAVER, JOHN, *Anatomical and Mechanical Lectures* (1721).

CHAPTER 4

Towards the Romantic Ballet of the Nineteenth Century

Variety is one of the great charms of nature, nor can you please the beholder for any length of time, but in changing your compositions.

(DAUBERVAL)

IT was the great theorist of classical dance, Carlo Blasis, who noted the importance of Bordeaux when he was on tour and who believed it to be the fountainhead of ballet production as opposed to Paris, where, he asserted, every dancer must go if only to perfect his technique. From before the French Revolution and for some years afterwards the Bordeaux ballet was under the leadership of Jean Dauberval, who had studied and worked with Noverre, and whose inability to gain permission for experiment at the Paris *Opéra* had sent him to the provinces. In Bordeaux he produced many different kinds of ballet about which Parisian critics complained that sentimentalism and melodrama had replaced the tragic nobility of Noverre. But it would seem that although Dauberval did utilize such themes, he was working towards a more flexible type of technique, which could be adapted to suit the style of each work instead of basing it, like the older ballet-masters, upon the strict formulas of classical dance, conventional gesture and an occasional use of some folk or Commedia dell'Arte idiom.

JEAN DAUBERVAL AND THE DEMI-CARACTÈRE BALLET (1724–1806)

Dauberval's famous ballet, *La Fille mal gardée* (1789), is one of the oldest and one of the first purely *demi-caractère* ballets in the repertoire. Like Galeotti's *Les Caprices du Cupidon*, which is the oldest ballet and was produced in Copenhagen (1786), it has passed through the hands of many ballet-masters and has lost its original choregraphy. Yet its importance should not be minimized for in its original form it helped to establish a new and important type of ballet, which allowed choregraphers more scope to design dance styles of their own.

La Fille mal gardée was based on Egidio Duni's comic opera of that name produced in Paris and introduced to the ballet stage some real-life village characters seen through the eyes of authors and players for the popular theatres. They were part of the Commedia dell'Arte traditions, but were shown in a contemporary setting. The original score, compiled by an amateur, consisted of folk-dance tunes supplemented by popular airs.

DAUBERVAL'S CHOREGRAPHY

Until *La Fille mal gardée* was produced by Perrot in 1848 Dauberval's choregraphy seems to have remained practically unchanged except for the introduction of the *pointes* for the 1828 Paris production by Aumer (Dauberval's pupil). According to contemporary accounts, Dauberval's choregraphy fell into three distinct categories: it was a character dance, or dances of character, or it was a special type of dance based on classical technique, an important distinction which became of the utmost value to Dauberval's pupils.

Character Dance

Dauberval seems to have understood character dance to be one in which the dancers changed their own nationality or status into that of some other country or environment, and used the characteristic gestures, steps, rhythms and qualities found in a particular type of folk dance—a definition which also included the court and social dances he arranged to create local colour in other ballets. Thus in *La Fille mal gardée*, Dauberval arranged dances based on the dances of Southern France and the Basque Provinces for the *corps de ballet* playing the roles of peasants and villagers.

Dances of Character

A dance of character Dauberval understood to be one in which the dancer changes his or her personality and presents instead the portrait of some clearly defined individual derived from the study of his character, idiosyncrasies and specialized movements. In these dances Dauberval's characters had descended from the old Greek comedies by way of the Commedia dell'Arte and included a scheming old woman (mother or nurse), traditionally played by a man *en travesti*; a cunning and wealthy villager with a simpleton son (foolish zany, or clown) and a marriage broker, for whom Dauberval used some of the stock tricks of the Harlequinade.

Demi-caractère Dance

But the two categories described above did not completely satisfy Dauberval's need to establish a style for all the characters. His heroine and hero, Lisa and Colin, were descended from Columbine and Harlequin, who had become the real dancers of the Commedia dell'Arte. He therefore devised a specific form of classical dance which he himself termed the *demi-caractère*.

This *demi-caractère* dance was based on the classical formulas of his day and had gradually been making its appearance in the dances of the nymphs, shepherds and other rustic characters in the pastoral scenes of ballets and operas by Lully, Rameau, Gluck and the ballet-masters mentioned earlier.

But with Dauberval, this softly graceful form of *demi-caractère* work was greatly developed and became strongly characterized by the use of special *ports de bras*, in which the strict rulings of the academic school were very frequently ignored. Arms were not kept rounded, nor did they move in one piece, so to speak. They could be bent at wrist or elbow, or used in movements borrowed from the typical attitudes of a peasant in some dance or work process. Dauberval is said to have used the false positions described by Weaver and Noverre for both arms and feet in order to make his dancers look more natural.

With the success of Dauberval's *La Fille mal gardée*, the habit of borrowing a theme from opera or drama became more widespread among choregraphers probably because they realized that an audience who came to the theatre already knowing the action would follow the ballet more readily.

The choice of a well-known theme possibly rises from the fact that whenever a ballet-master originates a new type of ballet, dance itself lags behind and the action tends to be worked out and developed in dramatic gesture, thus depriving the stage at some points of dance movement.

But as the dancers grow accustomed to this new type of ballet, they develop expressive qualities, thus enlarging their technique, so that the themes tend to lose their melodramatic elements and impact and become more lyrical or more characteristic in the dance content.

Weaver felt that his dancers were not able to express themselves as fully as he wished in his ballets, so he incorporated purely mimed episodes. Sallé and others working with her, De Hesse, Hilferding and Angiolini had developed a more flowing expressive style of movement, which acquired great emotional qualities, through working with the dramatically naturalistic gestures of Garrick, as seen by Noverre. Dancers who had acquired this style performed for Dauberval in Bordeaux, and he was thus able to dispense with the so-called rhetorical or formal gestures and steps, and pave the way for further innovations by his pupil, Didelot.

CHARLES DIDELOT AND THE DEVELOPMENT OF MIMED-DANCE OR DANCED-MIME (1767–1836)

> The ballets of Didelot are carried out with vivacious animation and unusual charm. One of our writers has found in them greater poesy than exists in all French literature.
>
> (PUSHKIN in a footnote to *Eugene Onegin*)

The French Revolution (1789) sent many of the leading dancers from the Paris theatres into the provinces and abroad, where they were able to dance for those ballet-masters whose works were not acceptable to the Directorate of the Paris *Opéra*, which now ceased to act as arbiter of taste to the fashionable world elsewhere: this dispersal of artists was, however, entirely beneficial to the art of ballet.

London became an important meeting ground for artists of all schools and it was here that Charles Didelot, a student of Dauberval, gained his experience dancing in ballets by his master, Noverre, Gardel and others during the 1788–9 season. He thus assimilated much valuable and varied material before setting out on his own creative journey on which, firstly, he paved the way for the Romantic ballet and, secondly, founded a distinctive school of Russian classical dance.

Didelot took the initiative in the staging of a romantic style of dance when he produced his famous ballet *Zéphyr et Flore* at the Theatre Royal, Drury Lane (1796), where he designed unusual dance movements for a classical legend. His introduction of a fantastic element into academic dance arose from his desire to present Greek myths in a form more acceptable to the London audience, by no means all of whom came from similar aristocratic circles to those frequenting the classical ballet theatres on the continent.

The three innovations which Didelot made in *Zéphyr et Flore* to give his dance its fantastic and expressive qualities were—

1. The first use of the *pointes*.
2. The development of the *pas de deux* as a conversation between two dancers.
3. The introduction of simple lifts and more lyrical groupings.

The last two innovations were particularly important in his creation of mimed-dance or danced-mime (*see* page 104). He also made a thorough reform of costume, which the London Press continually noted; he appeared as Zéphyr in the briefest of Greek tunics and flesh-coloured tights, and both he and Flore wore wings as they flew away together.

THE POINTES

It is curious that the introduction of simple lifts and the use of the *pointes* may have developed from the use of the improved flying machine invented by the English mechanics for *Zéphyr et Flore*, by means of which the dancers were able to fly the length and breadth and even circle the stage instead of merely ascending and descending in the older *gloire*, which had hoisted the gods and goddesses up and down Olympus since the days of *Balet comique de la Royne*.

Admittedly the dancers had been rising higher on to the tips of their toes in their desire for speed and more spectacular feats of balance, but it is not certain that the *pointes* were actually used before this ballet, when the rise to the tips was made possible because the dancers, using the flying machines, momentarily held that position as the machinists took their weight before beginning their flight.

There is plenty of evidence to prove that the *pointes* were first used by Didelot in *Zéphyr et Flore*. Pushkin mentions how Istomina's feet scarcely touched the floor when this ballet was produced in St. Petersburg (1822). The Moscow ballet-master, Glouzhkovsky, had said the same about the tragic Danilova, who lost her life through an accident in this ballet (1808).

Castile Blaze writing in the *Journal des Débats* (1827) recollects the 1815 production in Paris: "Everyone remembers the elder Mlle. Gosselin and the astonishing flexibility of her limbs, that muscular strength which enabled her to remain *sur les pointes* for one or two minutes." (*See also* BARON'S *Letters to Sophie*.)

THE DEVELOPMENT OF THE PAS DE DEUX

The development of mimed-dance or danced-mime was Didelot's most important contribution to ballet. He did this firstly by distinguishing between the physical qualities of the movements (i.e. bending, stretching, rising, jumping, gliding, darting and turning); secondly by defining the difference between the male and female dancer; and thirdly by exploiting the dancers' natural ability to express themselves through movement. All this enabled him to make the conflict in the action more clearly defined whenever it was necessary.

The Difference Between the Male and Female Dancer

Until *Zéphyr et Flore* it seems both dancers performed the same steps, the only difference being each dancer's ability to display a certain type of movement. With the introduction of the *pointes* and simple lifts, however, Didelot made it possible to define more exactly which steps are best danced by a woman and which best by a man. The one accentuates the *danseuse's* lightness and daintiness, the other the *danseur's* strength. This distinction is an essential element of any *pas de deux* (or any dance) where the man dances equally with the woman and is not merely a porter. When this fact was lost sight of during the late nineteenth century, in every European country except Denmark and Russia, the male dancer became effeminate and his part was often played by a woman *en travesti*.

Didelot's need to emphasize this difference probably arose from his realization of his own limitations in style and a need to distinguish it from that of his wife, with whom he usually danced. His dancing seems to have been more in the style of the *danseur noble*, but as he was short, broad-shouldered, and not good-looking, Noverre and Dauberval usually cast him for such roles as Cupid or Mercury, or in *demi-caractère* works such as Colin in *La Fille mal gardée*. However his pupil, Glouzhkovsky, says that despite his looks he was a most graceful dancer with great purity and flow of line, as well as impeccable technique. Since he did not possess great elevation he arranged dances for himself based on gliding steps, which displayed his easy *ports de bras*, his excellent poses and lively *pirouettes*. He possessed great speed and lightness, and these qualities were of particular importance when dancing Zéphyr, because he heightened their effectiveness by utilizing the flying machine to give height and length to his jumps.

The Introduction of Simple Lifts

Didelot's introduction of simple lifts into the *pas de deux* of *Zéphyr et Flore* doubtless rose because he wished Flore to appear as if swept up in the gentle wind's embrace and then, as she gradually reciprocated his love, a climax would be reached, and they could fly away together. By thus enlarging the dancers' sphere of movement, he also enlarged their means of expression, and this type of mimed-dance would make the argument more convincing when set in a dramatic context than it would be if dancers reverted to passages of conventional gesture.

Although Didelot did not do away with the *scènes d'action* in his "dancing tragedies," he tried to create these of danced-mime only. That is, he endeavoured to dispense with conventional gesture as such, and used a more fluid and natural type of mime. But he presented such scenes only when they were justified by the development of the plot. Similarly he has left it on record that any purely dancing episodes also had to be in accord with the action. It is perhaps notable that in the few works where the spectacular nature of the ballet demanded a grand finale, he left the arrangement of such *divertissements* to others, usually his assistant, the first soloist August.

Nevertheless he did not starve his ballet of dance as De Hesse and Noverre seem to have done in some of their tragic works. Didelot used mass dance to paint the background and create atmosphere in the same way as Dauberval had done, but, because of his wider experience and perhaps greater appreciation of style, he was not afraid to design dances more strongly characteristic of their setting. These dances were not seen in isolation. The soloists and *corps de ballet* were expected to maintain their characteristic movement throughout. For this reason he sometimes broke the rigid formulas of *corps de ballet* dance where every member performed identical steps as they wove through the set figures. Instead he allowed a certain amount of individual movement which helped the action to unfold more realistically, an important element in those ballets based on contemporary themes (e.g., *The Hungarian Hut, see* page 49).

This individual freedom of movement was very important for the purely pictorial element of Didelot's work. It allowed the dancers to fall into more picturesque groupings and something of their value can be seen in the sketches by his pupil, Feodor Tolstoy, for two of his own projects, *The Golden Harp* and *Echo*, which he based on his master's principles. These are of great importance in showing how lyrically flowing a line Didelot had achieved before he retired in 1831.

DIDELOT'S EXPLOITATION OF THE DANCERS' NATURAL ABILITY TO EXPRESS THEMSELVES

His First Stay in Russia (1801–11)

Didelot's main work in developing the expressiveness of dance lay in Russia where he went as principal dancer and ballet-master in 1801. The Imperial St. Petersburg School was just emerging from a period of utmost frustration and in order to understand his importance in the development of Russian ballet, a brief summary of its history seems necessary (*see also* page 88).

The school was founded by the decree of the Empress Anne in 1738 by Jean Baptiste Landé, who had originally been commanded to Russia to teach the cadets at the Shliakhetny College "the delicate art of the French court dance." He had, however, been so inspired (according to the story) by the dancing of some peasants on the quay as he arrived that he ultimately persuaded the Empress to allow him to train a selected number of children of the court serfs to dance in ballets presented at the palace. His place was taken by other Italian, Austrian, French and German dancing-masters. Amongst those who made important contributions to the development of the school were the Italian Fassano (*see* page 26), the Austrian Hilferding (*see* page 34) and the Italian Kanziani. The last named was the first systematically to work out a syllabus of training necessary to develop an artist in all aspects of the dance as well as to ensure the student's general education. Unfortunately before his plan could demonstrate its worth, the mad Tsar Paul I came to the throne and his lack of interest in the Russian theatre, together with the Imperial Treasury's lack of money caused Prince Youssopoff, director of the Imperial Theatres, to economize. He approved a plan for the reorganization of the school presented by one of its inspectors, an Italian Kazzacci, which so drastically curtailed Kanziani's activities that he resigned.

Plan for a School (1793)

After the death of Paul I, a new Director of the Imperial Theatres was appointed, who immediately invited Didelot to Russia and the St. Petersburg ballet-master, Valberg, who had tried to carry on his master, Kanziani's work, was sent abroad to study (*see* below).

One of Didelot's most important acts on arrival was to fight for the right of any dancer, having been so trained, to a place in the ballet. He also lengthened the period of study (it had hitherto been only two or three years). He then began to teach mime as well as dance, and insisted on a study of music.

Throughout his first stay of ten years he made few attempts to experiment. The audience's taste for virtuosity meant that visiting stars preferred *divertissements* in which they could display their own particular feats. Didelot was no exception and staged the fashionable anacreontic ballets in which he could show his ability to turn and beat, but by including his new type of *pas de deux* with its simple lifts, he was able to introduce some of his Russian pupils such as Istomina, with whom he himself danced, and Danilova, who danced *Zéphyr et Flore* with the great dancer Louis Duport (1808).

Didelot was the forerunner of Fokine, who believed that everything began in the classroom, therefore his main work at this period lay in the school, and he had so prepared the ground, that when he was forced to leave Russia because of the Napoleonic invasion his pupils, led by his favourite Kolossova, developed his teaching in the school and, because of the difficulty of obtaining stars from abroad, began to play leading roles in all the ballets presented.

Didelot's Second Stay in Russia (1816–31)

> At last ballet offers a genuine drama taken from real life with all its disturbances and passion and here mimetic art attains its highest point of development.
>
> (F. Koni on Didelot's *The Hungarian Hut*, 1817)

When Didelot returned to Russia after the defeat of Napoleon the taste of the Imperial audiences had changed. Their interest lay in "dancing tragedies" which had gradually been introduced into the repertoire, following the work of Angiolini, by Valberg, the St. Petersburg ballet-master, who produced the first ballet on *Romeo and Juliet* (2nd November, 1809). Didelot now worked to stage those ballets he had already shown in London dealing with more heroic subjects and utilizing themes with plenty of action which would give him an opportunity of presenting strong conflicts of characters and differing styles of dance. Some of these had already been staged by Hilferding, Angiolini, Noverre. Dauberval and others because in those days no theme was exclusive to one choregrapher. In addition, he devised others of a strong dramatic, even contemporary basis, or having a contemporary interest. For example two of his most successful works were *The Hungarian Hut* (1817) and Pushkin's *The Prisoner in the Caucasus* (1823).

The success of such ballets lay not only in their topicality but also in the expressive dancing of the Russian cast led by such artists as Kolossova of whom Lermontov, the poet, wrote: "Every movement of her face was so natural and clear that it was absolute speech for the audience."

Expressive dance is part of the Russian ethos and comes from the native folk dance which has never been entirely absent from the repertoire of the Russian State theatres. Didelot seized upon the natural expressiveness of the Russian dancers, as Angiolini had done before him, and utilized it to develop their technique so that he helped them to create their own national school of classical dance, whereby they always spoke through their movements no matter in what style they were dancing. It was the continued existence of national dance, music and costume in the Russian court ballet that undoubtedly helped to preserve their classical dancing from the absolute stylization found elsewhere when the Romantic ballet got under way.

Needless to say the Russian expressiveness was seen at its best in *The Prisoner in the Caucasus*, where Didelot exploited both the Russian form of western court dance and the more fluid exotic style of the Caucasian folk dance. The theme was heavily censored by the Tsar himself in order to eliminate any element of Pushkin's poem which might be considered revolutionary (the poet had been exiled to the Caucasus). Nevertheless, enough of the poem's lyricism and dramatic conflict remained for contemporary critics to realize that Didelot was establishing a new type of mimetic drama in ballet. He had assimilated the necessary technical elements of dance, drama and music, imparted these to his dancers, and then designed his choregraphy so that it displayed their own native talent for expressing emotion, mood and action through danced-mime or mimed-dance. This convinced their audience of the actuality of their performance, no matter whether the theme dealt with the Gods of Olympus, a tale of the Crusades, a purely contemporary theme (*The Hungarian Hut* appeared fifteen years after the events which inspired the theme), or a deeply felt romantic poem. Glouzhkovsky, the Moscow ballet-master, explains that the dances were woven into the action—

> They always appear to the point and in the right place; the dying feet are not compelled to dance before death, heart-felt grief is not expressed by *battements*, heroes do not skip about like wild chamois.

DIDELOT AND MUSIC

Didelot did not confine his activities to the dancing side of his work, he took a personal interest in every detail of the production and was particularly attentive to the musical side.

It seems he always worked in the closest collaboration with the composer, defining the phrasing, tempos and other details so that the score was illustrative of the action. The score usually conformed to the same principles as Gluck's *Don Juan*, that is each scene was broken up into numbers and was not written as a continuous movement. In *Don Juan*, however, Gluck had not entirely dispensed with the formulas of the court dance, the last item was written in the form of a *chaconne*, even though it was not suitable for the court dance, nor yet for the stage version performed by some virtuosos because it had expression and was descriptive of the Furies. Gluck broke away from the formal dance patterns in the dances for *Orpheus* and it was this type of music that Didelot wished to obtain from his composers, whilst insisting that it maintained a dance rhythm throughout.

DIDELOT AND STAGECRAFT

The last important aspect of Didelot's work was the use he made of the technical resources of the theatre to create the necessary illusion and fantasy. But like all the other items mentioned, he only used these when justified by the action and not merely to add spectacular glory. His use of the flying machine has already been cited. Another interesting effect was the storm in the shipwreck scene of *L'heureux Naufrage*, which was apparently brilliantly worked out by his English machinists to whom he paid tribute.

Perhaps Didelot's choregraphic principles are best summed up in his own words—

> I do not wish the fame of this production to be referred to as something other than my own work. No audience should be able to say "Yesterday I was at the theatre and saw charming décor, wonderful machinery, rich costumes"—but as to the ballet—not a word.

In other words everything Didelot needed to create a ballet was a means to an end and not an end in itself.

SALVATORE VIGANO AND THE DEVELOPMENT OF THE DRAMATIC ACTION (1769–1821)

> His ballets contained no conventional gestures as were taught in the state opera schools, but natural gestures which were moving and expressive, at times rather stylized and resembling familiar attitudes found in ancient statuary. But he made great use of facial expression and made me believe in what he was doing.
>
> (STENDHAL, about the great artist Salvatore Vigano)

For all the applause given to Salvatore Vigano the "Shakespeare of the Dance" during his lifetime and all the innovations he made in Italian ballet at the beginning of the nineteenth century, nothing remains of his work. He does however merit a place in any history of ballet, because of his strong personal influence on such musicians as Beethoven and Wagner, who in their particular fields made many important innovations. Moreover his vivid personality inspired every dancer and ballet-master coming into contact with him, causing them to pay far more attention to the total aspect of a production, instead of concentrating on the technical side of dance.

As a student and dancer under Dauberval in Bordeaux and Madrid, Vigano learnt a great deal about *demi-caractère* work and expressive movement, which in his own performance became more dramatic owing to his Italian temperament. But because he also appeared in the more lyrical ballets of Didelot and others, his dancing could be gracefully flowing also, like that of his wife, Maria Medina. It was their simple and beautifully elegant movement which attracted Beethoven's attention when he saw them dance in Vienna and composed, firstly, some dance numbers and, later, the ballet *Prometheus* (1813) specially for Vigano to produce at La Scala, Milan.

Vigano, like Didelot, wished to eliminate the purely mimed, or danced episodes. The two arts had to be fused and he believed that a ballet-master could express his theme entirely in terms of dramatic dance movement that harmonized exactly with the rhythmic and emotional content of the music. It seems from Stendhal that Vigano had a genius for developing his subject and the action with the necessary feeling of tension and relaxation. That is, he realized the value of quiet passages of lyrical movement or groupings even in the most lurid dramas and built his scenes into a climax, allowing *divertissements* only when justified so that the action flowed.

It was this continuity of action that Beethoven tried to supply in his score of *Prometheus*, showing to later composers of ballet the way in which the choregraphy requires continuity and distinctive themes illustrative of the characters and the action. Although Beethoven's score differs little in formula from those written by earlier composers, it is vastly different in content and quality. Its themes might be said to have epic qualities because Beethoven himself believed that man's struggle against fate, as he saw the struggle of Vigano's *Prometheus*, was a valid problem to express musically. It was one to which he returned again and again, utilizing themes from the ballet to express his meaning (e.g. in the Fifth Symphony, etc.) and only finally resolved in his great Choral Symphony, the Ninth.

These themes in *Prometheus* gave the choregrapher space to develop both character and action, which may make some of the passages seem too long now that dancers can express themselves through their dance and do not have to slow down to make each gesture clear, or make a definite pose as Vigano seems to have demanded. He saw his ballet as a grand classical subject and required his dancers to achieve something of the grandeur, breadth, and ordered form of the ancient statuary he loved. Nevertheless, despite the break between each dance and scene, Beethoven's score creates the impression of a symphony rather than a suite of dances merely in formal relationship to each other.

It was probably the feeling of continuity permeating the ballet that caused one critic to say—

> There was a constant interplay between the separate groupings, so that they became silent poetry, each one forming a part of an expressive and harmonious whole.
>
> (Stendhal)

Unfortunately Vigano never again had the opportunity to work with another major composer. In order to obtain the scores he required for his highly dramatic works, he was forced, like Dauberval before him, to compile them of extracts taken from music by Haydn, Mozart, Beethoven, and others, and when nothing was suitable, composed something himself, a task for which he was fully equipped having had a proper musical training from his uncle, the composer Boccherini.

It was only Vigano's personal genius however that enabled his heavy mimodramas with their heterogeneous music, magnificent scenery and effects to become popular with the pleasure-loving audience of La Scala, Milan. But they were popular and were considered in a very different category from those of the usual Italian ballet-master. Vigano was a great student of Shakespeare and possibly earned his title of "The Shakespeare of the Dance" by actually staging *Coriolanus* and *Othello* as ballets, instead of acting like Noverre, who merely promised to do so when coming as ballet-master to London for the 1781–2 season.

Two criticisms of Vigano's Shakespearean ballets demonstrate something of his methods. On *Coriolanus* (1804) his biographer Ritorni writes—

> The dance was so explicit that the audience could follow it without the libretto, without which the usual historical Italian ballet would have been quite incomprehensible.

Stendhal compares *Othello* (1818) with Rossini's opera—

> Vigano displays much more genius in his ballet, which he has the hardihood to begin with a *Furlana*. In the second act he again has the wit to place a big scene in the quiet and noble style—an evening festival, which Othello gives in his gardens. It is during this Festival that Othello becomes jealous . . . So on reaching the last act of Vigano's ballet we did not experience a satiety of the dreadful and shocking, so soon tears filled every eye. I have rarely seen anyone shed tears at Rossini's *Othello*.

Vigano's ballets were not all so carefully balanced between the tense and relaxed scenes as in *Othello*. His later works seem overloaded with dramatic episodes, scenes and scenic effects, perhaps because the Milanese audiences demanded their money's worth of spectacle. In fact, Vigano's vast *I Titani* with its multiplicity of characters, scenes and actions is thought by some to be the origin of Wagner's series of operas, *Der Ring der Nibelungen*. This supposition may be true as Wagner himself comments on Vigano's "musical dramas in movement," and *I Titani* might well have been termed a mimodrama for all the purely dancing episodes it contained.

The reason why no trace of Vigano's work remains is possibly because he founded no school and, therefore, took a long time to rehearse, since dancers had to be taught each tiny movement and detail. He frequently took so long over a new work that on two occasions he was thrown into prison by La Scala authorities for failing to produce a ballet on time.

The other reason why no work remains, save in the writings of such prominent authors as Stendhal and Wagner, may well be the absence of a proper score. Beethoven had clearly demonstrated that a worthwhile score, conceived in epic and continuous form was of the utmost value to dancers conveying their meaning solely through dance movement.

FURTHER READING

BEAUMONT, C. W., *Three French Dancers of the Seventeenth Century* (London, 1934).
BEAUMONT, C. W., *Complete Book of Ballets* (Putnam, 1939).
BEAUMONT, C. W., *Supplement to the Complete Book of Ballets* (1942).
BEAUMONT, C. W. (with SITWELL, S.), *Romantic Ballet* (Faber & Faber, 1937).
BLASIS, CARLO, *The Code of Terpsichore* (London, 1830).
BLASIS, CARLO, *Traité élémentaire et pratique de la Danse* (Milan, 1820).
BORISOGLEVSKY, Y., *Materials for a History of Russian Ballet, 2 vols.* (in Russian) (Leningrad, 1938).
BOURNONVILLE, AUGUST, *Mon Theatreliv* (Copenhagen, 1858).
BOURNONVILLE, AUGUST, Études chorégraphiques dediées à mes élèves et mes collègues (Copenhagen, 1861).
DIDELOT, CHARLES, Libretti for *Zéphyr et Flore*, *Psyché et l'Amour*, *The Hungarian Hut*, *The Prisoner in the Caucasus*.
LAWSON, JOAN, *European Folk Dance* (London, Pitman, 1953).
LAWSON, JOAN, *Mime* (London, Pitman, 1957).
LAWSON, JOAN, *Classical Ballet, its Style and Technique* (London, A. and C. Black, 1960).
RITORNI, CARLO-REGGIANI, *Salvatore Vigano* (Milan, 1838).
SLONIMSKY, YURI OSSIPOVITCH, *Masters of the Ballet* (Moscow, 1937).
SLONIMSKY, YURI OSSIPOVITCH, *Didelot* (Moscow, 1958).
SLONIMSKY, YURI OSSIPOVITCH, *La Fille mal gardée* (Moscow, 1960).

CHAPTER 5

The Romantic Ballet

Dramatic ballet must have continuity and can show development of character through the conflict of personalities, who can be defined by contrasting styles of dance.
(PERROT in a note on *La Esmeralda*)

THE ghosts, wilis, sylphs and fairies who drove the gods and goddesses, the noble heroes and heroines of classical ballet from the stage at the beginning of the nineteenth century were all manifestations of the imaginative use made by certain choregraphers of earlier material. This had been collected by learned men in their efforts to preserve and interpret something of the rich heritage of the medieval period when the acts and deeds of the noble knights and squires who went to the Crusades and who rescued ladies in distress gave rise to legends, myths, ballads and folk-lore traditions. The Romantic movement had started in England as a reaction to too much classicism and had inspired the mysteriously fantastic, or Gothic novels, the poems of chivalry, the strange adventure tales and poems written by Sir Walter Scott, Mrs. Ratcliffe, Lord Byron and others. Such imaginative works, which often described the unrequited love of knights for an unapproachable lady and upheld the sanctity of marriage, influenced most of the art forms on the continent, particularly that of ballet, where choregraphers and dancers began to enlarge the scope of their activities in two different ways.

The Romantic movement helped them to develop classical dance as a more expressive medium, because they were no longer able to stylize the movements of their heroines and heroes by using a single type of classical dance. They had to draw the portrait of a particular character who lived in one ballet only and had, therefore, to be distinguished by certain movements, or a certain style of movement descriptive of that role.

This particularization ultimately led to the production of ballets centred round the personality and distinctive qualities of one *danseuse*. In many ways this was limiting because only those dancers possessing "star" quality were used and the rest of the dancers were considered merely as background to her talents; and because it led to the writing of libretti whose contents varied very little from each other (*see* page 57). Nevertheless limiting the libretto to a few basic plots did help to consolidate the technical and expressive progress made through the introduction of the romantic theme. Moreover, by concentrating on the need for exactly defining a role by appropriate movement, some choregraphers learnt how to show development of character and thus achieve a more logical continuity of action.

Eventually the cult of the individual *danseuse* led to the development of technique through the careful analysis made by certain ballet-masters of the movements of the body in relation to dance-steps. They applied this study to the training of *danseuses* able to fulfil the demands of choregraphers who were unable to work in the purely Romantic style, but who wished to exploit a talent which while it lacked the gift of expression was yet equipped to display virtuosity in a spectacle of dance, costumes, scenery and brilliant effects.

FILIPPO TAGLIONI (1778–1871)

The principal theme of most serious literary Romantic works was man's search for his own soul as he battled against mysterious forces and tried to reconcile his life as he lived it in reality with that of the spirit to which he aspired. The first choregrapher successfully to develop this in terms of ballet was Filippo Taglioni in *La Sylphide* (1832). It was by no means the first Romantic ballet and borrowed heavily from Romantic operas, nevertheless the struggle between the world of the flesh and the world of the spirit was stated more clearly than ever before and the popularity of *La Sylphide* made it a pattern for later ballets. It was not, however, a deeply felt, significant work like Goethe's *The Sorrows of Werther* or Wagner's great opera cycle *Der Ring der Nibelungen*, which derived from similar sources and had a deeply philosophical basis. Nor was "Truth cloaked in myth and image" (*see* page 13) as in the classical *ballets du cour*. *La Sylphide* had a superficial bearing on problems of the day and was in keeping with the fashionable world's interest.

The libretto of *La Sylphide* is based on a novel by Charles Nodier (*Trilby ou Le Lutin d'Argäil*) and was written by Alfred Nourrit, a leading tenor of the Paris *Opéra*. It pandered openly to the fashionable tastes of those who were then taking a superficial interest in the conflict between the world of the spirit and the world of the flesh, particularly when it was described by such imaginative novelists as Sir Walter Scott. But the contemporary success of the ballet was due primarily to the exquisite dancing of Marie Taglioni. It was specially designed to display her somewhat unusual qualities which had attracted Parisian audiences when she made her appearance in Didelot's *Zéphyr et Flore* (1828), although this work did not display them entirely to their best advantage since it had been designed for a *terre à terre* dancer. Marie Taglioni's particular gifts for *ballon* and elevation had been shown to better advantage in the dances arranged for her by her father in Meyerbeer's opera *Robert the Devil* (1831), in which he followed Didelot's example, using both the *pointes* and the flying machine to enhance the effectiveness of his daughter's dance when she was rising from the grave as a ghostly nun.

THE CHOREGRAPHY FOR LA SYLPHIDE

Taglioni's choregraphy for *La Sylphide* no longer exists, but that of Bournonville, who produced it four years later in Copenhagen (1836) is still in the repertoire of the Royal Danish Ballet. Some parts of Taglioni's work can perhaps be traced because Bournonville seems to have followed his original style and quality of movement. A score was specially composed by Løvensksjold, which closely resembled that of Schneitzhoeffer's original music with its hints of favourite Scottish airs contrasted with the sweetly sentimental melodies illustrative of the sylphs and the friends. Both scores were divided into the usual dancing numbers. The libretti of the two versions are identical.

Taglioni (and Bournonville) saw the conflict of the world of the flesh and the world of the spirit in terms of two distinct styles of dance. Both choregraphers had made a study of the dances of Scotland and used the features special to the male dancers of that country as well as its more generalized social dancing as the basis for their dances in the world of reality—the interior of a Scottish farmhouse. In this way they established James in his own environment and as a dancing hero having equal rights in the performance with La Sylphide, for whom they created dances of ethereal lightness by the subtle use of the *pointes*, *grande élévation*, simple lifts and the flying machine. This clear distinction in style was further emphasized by the division of the action into two acts, each with an atmosphere of its own. The first was very much the world of reality with its solid looking set, realistic furniture, costume and behaviour. The dancing too was in true character with the exception of several male variations, where the juxtaposition of Highland male and classical steps stressed even more the affinity of these two types of dance. The entrance of La Sylphide into this "down-to-earth" scene, immediately made an impression. Not only was her newly invented *ballet* dress with its long full, diaphanous skirt entirely different, but so was everything else about her.

The prelude to the second act resembled the Witches' scene in *Macbeth*, which had inspired other ballet-masters of this period, but it soon faded into the reality of a Scottish glen; from this natural-looking set the world of fantasy quickly took shape as the glow-worms and dew began to glisten in the moonlight. The ghostlike Sylphide flew first through the trees (a double was used for this effect), and then across the grass with her feet scarcely touching the ground.

From pictorial evidence it can be seen that Taglioni and Bournonville after him were not content to design a new type of *enchaînement* from the classical steps merely to create the illusion of a spirit lighter than air who was apparently able to poise on a leaf or the branch of a tree. They also changed the form of the *ports de bras* so that as La Sylphide felt the pressure of the air on her arms, she was able to use them more naturally and express something of her emotions and feelings as she danced. Thus not only was the footwork of the Scottish characters in contrast to that of the sylphs, but also their *ports de bras*, which followed either a character style closely based on the correct Scottish forms or else moved more prosaically in conventional gestures whenever they had to tell some part of the story.

THE PLACE OF THE POINTES

Although Taglioni, like Weaver and Didelot, was an innovator and developed a particular style of romantic *enchaînement* and *ports de bras* expressive of the moods, emotions and actions of the fairylike creatures interpreted by his daughter and her imitators, he also, perhaps unwittingly, introduced an element into ballet which has frequently hindered its development. His type of ballet encouraged the cultivation of dancers who worked only for themselves and acquired technique merely for technique's sake. He based *La Sylphide* on his daughter's particular style of movement and continued to produce similar ballets round that style. (Moscow critics complained that Taglioni danced *La Sylphide* in every ballet she performed.) Similarly Fokine shaped *The Dying Swan* round the lyrically dramatic yet frail qualities of Anna Pavlova, of which he had been made aware originally by her teacher Volkov. She continued to exploit these in all the miniatures created during her career. Yet, lovely though they were, they added nothing to the progress of ballet as a whole.

Nevertheless for Marie Taglioni and Anna Pavlova as well as People's Artist Galina Ulanova, Dame Margot Fonteyn and similarly expressive dancers, the *pointes* were and are only incidentals to give the finishing touch to the portrait of some character of ethereal qualities or dramatic subtlety. When the *pointes* were first introduced by Didelot (*see* page 44) they were not obligatory, but after Taglioni's success in *La Sylphide* they became essential for every *danseuse*. It was the discovery of what could be done *sur les pointes* that finally led to the *ballerina's* domination of the spectacle and the relegating of the male to the position of a mere porter.

CARLO BLASIS AND THE REQUIREMENTS OF THE DANCER (1797–1878)

The development of the classical technique of dance during the nineteenth century was primarily due to the work of Carlo Blasis (1797–1878), an Italian pupil of Dauberval and Pierre Gardel; who stated: "I work with pantomime and dance, all honour of the success of my ballets, I wish to attribute and give to these two arts." Yet nothing remains of his ballets, which were not so important to posterity as his teaching, which, when he became Director of the Imperial Academy in Milan in 1837, revolutionized the technique of the Italian dancers. By this time his methods had become firmly fixed for he had first stated them in writing in his *Treatise on the Dance* in 1820, a book that had very great influence on most European dancing-masters. This book recapitulates the methods of the great masters with whom Blasis had studied and danced in many Western European theatres, the most valuable aspects of Noverre's *Letters*, as he felt they should be applied to the contemporary scene, and his own intensive study of anatomy and music as well as other subjects which appertain to ballet.

Blasis concentrated on the technique of movement, paying particular attention to the principles of balance, or equilibrium. This undoubtedly helped his pupils to perform more difficult feats of balance *sur les pointes* and the *danseur* to spin multiple *pirouettes* whilst in *attitude*, *arabesque* or similar pose.

Yet despite his concentration on technique Blasis made a valuable contribution to the textbooks on the art of ballet. In certain passages of his book he sometimes seems to be looking forwards to innovations which were made later by Fokine. This occurs particularly when he makes an analysis of the spectacle, describing its essential features and how they all play a part in the making of a whole. That is, he helps a reader to understand how to build characters through the art of mime and a special dance style appropriate to each theme, and points out how important it is to compose the right type of step. He makes interesting comments on the part to be played by the ballet-master in linking dance and mime to the action with the help of illustrative music. For this he recommends a study of the works of famous composers, especially if the libretto has a serious subject. He is equally emphatic that such a ballet must point a moral. This idea arose from his study of classical drama, and shows how the broadly-based education Blasis had received coloured his work in the theatre.

Although Marie Taglioni was a contemporary of Blasis, the Romantic movement seems to have influenced him in only one way. He was, however, aware of the important part played in the ballets of his day by the star dancer and he gives a list of the qualities that he expected from her.

They were the following—

1. Steadiness and equilibrium.
2. Natural ease and facility. Like Weaver and Noverre he analyses the various types of dancer and their physique.
3. Keen observation and an analytical mind.
4. Worship of beauty and no deviation from classical principles.

This precept, Blasis himself practised in his teaching and handed to his pupil Lepri, who passed it on to Cecchetti, who by his maintenance of the classical standards prevented the technique of the Diaghilev company from deteriorating even though no classical ballet remained in their repertoire, and who achieved this at a time when *ballerinas* elsewhere tended to perform steps and poses in any way that they thought suited them best.

5. A knowledge of how to discriminate between the various types of dancer and a knowledge of one's own limitations.
6. An interest in dance composition in order always to make it seem that the performance was a spontaneous interpretation.

   This he learned from Gardel and Dauberval (*see* page 30).
7. A study of drawing and music.

He had thoroughly studied both these arts as can be seen by referring to the drawings with which he illustrated his *Treatise* and which give a wonderful idea of the line and placing of the movements performed in his time and today in ballets where a certain type of classical or *demi-caractère* dance is demanded.

AUGUST BOURNONVILLE AND THE ARTISTIC QUALITIES OF THE DANCER (1805–79)

It was August Bournonville, the great Danish ballet-master who exactly described the needful qualities of an artist of the dance as opposed to a brilliant technician. Writing for his pupils and colleagues at a time when the cult of the individual dancer was at its zenith, his list is of the greatest importance because it clearly states all those qualities which today should be, or are possessed by that handful of artists recognized in the Western world as the leaders of their profession. They also belong to a very great extent to all those dancers of the Royal Danish Ballet, who consider the part they play in the ballet as a whole as far more important than their status as individuals in the organization, once they are on the stage.

Bournonville's list is so comprehensive that it is best presented in his own tabloid form as follows—

Physical Qualities	Intellectual Qualities	Artistic Qualities
Beauté	*Goût*	*Grâce*
Vigueur	*Energie*	*Légèreté*
Souplesse	*Persévérance*	*Aplomb*
Vivacité	*Imagination*	*Moëlleux*
Oreille	*Harmonie*	*Précision*

Dramatic Qualities	Technical Qualities
Stature	*Placé*
Physionomie	*En dehors*
Marche	*Pointes*
Port	*Ballon*
Geste	*Brillant*

Bournonville was an extremely accomplished dancer and mime. He had studied widely before he settled in Copenhagen to create his major ballets and to found what became the firm basis of the style of the Royal Danish Ballet. It was inspired by the teaching of such great French masters as Vestris, but coloured by Bournonville's own happy temperament and personality. He states—

> I danced with a manly *joie de vivre*, and my sense of humour and my energy have always made an impression in every theatre. I seemed to make the audience happy and before they admired me, they liked me.

That *joie de vivre* and energy is still typical of the Royal Danish Ballet and its particular classical style is nowhere better stated than in *Conservatouri* (1849) one of the first ballets to be based on the daily lessons of a dancing school. It gives a very clear idea of Bournonville's choregraphic design and his brilliant flair for creating unusual *enchaînements* out of the steps used at that time, that is before the *pointes* had become so important, and when a precision of pose and position were vital.

The interest in these *enchaînements* lies firstly in Bournonville's use of the various placings of the body so that the sudden turns and twists in the line of the dance become immediately visible. Secondly there is his rich use of *grande élévation* and *batterie*, as well as his practice of suddenly bringing the dancers from the back to the front of the stage in great leaps, as if they were about to throw themselves into the audience's arms through their sheer enjoyment of the dance. Thirdly there is the clear distinction he makes between the male and female dancers, the former with their strength and breadth of movement and the latter with their dainty, graceful *ports de bras* and exquisite lightness, which show how much the Romantic style of dance became part of Bournonville's particular school. This distinction between male and female dancer was possibly Bournonville's great merit as a choregrapher working at a time when the male dancer elsewhere was rapidly being banished from the stage. He undoubtedly understood the technique of the male dancer better than any of his contemporaries and handed this knowledge to his pupil, Christian Johannson, who was to do so much in training the St. Petersburg dancers, those magnificent warriors of Fokine's *Prince Igor* and other ballets, by which means Diaghilev restored the man to his rightful place on the ballet stage.

Bournonville's most important ballets are however those based on the rich materials he collected when on tour. He was a keen observer of the dances, customs, behaviour and characteristics of the people whose country he visited and, by using the elements that were appropriate to the style and action of his libretto, he coloured and brought life to his type of classical dance by turning it into a vivid *demi-caractère* medium. His choregraphic range in this type of work was wide and embraced Scottish (*La Sylphide*), Flemish (*The Kermesse in Bruges*), Italian (*Napoli* and others), Norwegian (*A Wedding at Hardanger*), Danish (*A Folk Tale*), Spanish or South American (*Far From Denmark*), as well as Eastern, Russian, Czech and other countries.

THE STRUCTURE OF A BALLET

Bournonville planned both his Romantic and *demi-caractère* ballets along the same lines as those of Dauberval or Taglioni. But he made some interesting comments on the actual structure of a dramatic ballet when visiting St. Petersburg to see his pupil Johannson and some of Petipa's ballets, which he found extremely poor—

> I could not discover with all my efforts a work of dramatic interest, of logical continuity, of anything that would suggest a sound idea. If ever I did succeed in discovering a trace of interesting material, then it was immediately obscured by an endless number of monotonous *bravura* performances. . . . When I asked about this both Johannson and Petipa declared they were forced to go with the stream and pleaded the blasé taste of the public and the decisive orders of higher authorities.

But Bournonville hints that he feels Petipa did not understand how to construct a dramatic ballet. He himself believed that a two-act ballet was better than a three-act ballet if a tragic tale is to be clearly told and brought to its proper denouement. He takes for his examples the two Romantic ballets *La Sylphide* and *Giselle* and analyses them thus—

> *Act* 1 states the facts, establishes the characters and their relationship to each other. This sets the action going to the inevitable conflict, which will lead ultimately to the climax, but brings a logical curtain to a first act.
>
> *Act* 2 reaches onwards to the proper denouement because it deals with the result of the conflict and thus brings the climax needed to close the action.
>
> *Act* 3 can, therefore, only be a *divertissement* denoting a happy end, which is not needed in a dramatic, tragic work if it is to make its proper effect.

Bournonville however considered it was legitimate to stage three-act ballets when they had a happy conclusion, as his list of works clearly shows.

Bournonville's findings are interesting because Didelot had noted that the London public of the late eighteenth century did not like long ballets. They preferred a ballet, if it had a strongly dramatic theme, to be short and replete with action, which had to unfold without sub-plots and extra episodes.

JULES PERROT AND THE USE OF THE LEITMOTIVE (1810–92)

ARTISTS IN COLLABORATION

The construction of a tragic ballet was clearly understood by the four men who created *Giselle* (1842), the greatest Romantic ballet. Like *Balet comique de la Royne*, it was inspired by the research of literary men, but, unlike the *Pléiade* the poet-journalist, Théophile Gautier, and the librettist, Vernoy Saint-Georges, were content to let dance speak for them. They did not dictate, but played an equal part with the composer, Adolphe Adam, and the choregrapher, Jules Perrot, in producing a whole in which the arts of drama, music and dance subordinated themselves to each other for the purpose of telling a story through movement. Giselle comes to life only when the *danseuse* interpreting this difficult role brings to her performance unusual dramatic expressiveness as well as strong technical ability, and when her partner can match her simple yet ethereal grace and elevation with a firm, masculine, noble and flowing style.

The unity of purpose shown by the four authors of *Giselle* was rarely to be found in nineteenth-century ballet, where the ballet-master dominated the production because of his need to show off either the talents of a particular dancer or his own in devising a brilliant spectacle. Admittedly *Giselle* was no exception to the first part of this rule, but the unusual qualities of Carlotta Grisi inspired all four men, so that each perhaps realized the limitations of his own medium for displaying her talent and relied on the others to supply those elements lacking in his own contribution.

The Libretto of Théophile Gautier and Vernoy Saint-Georges

It was in the course of his journalistic activities that Théophile Gautier encountered both the *danseuse* and the ideas which inspired *Giselle*. Having reported on Grisi's Parisian début and other performances Gautier felt impelled to produce her in a work of his own choosing. The story of the wilis, or ghosts of betrayed maidens rising from their graves at midnight to dance any unwary traveller to his death had caught his attention when reviewing *D'Allemagne*, a collection of German legends by the poet, Heinrich Heine. He was also attracted to Victor Hugo's poem about the young girl whose love of dance led to her early death and whose ghost haunted the ballroom.

But Gautier realized that these themes lacked sufficient substance to support a two-act ballet, which seemed essential to display the simple charm and sympathetic nature of the woman, Carlotta, with whom he was in love, and the ethereal grace and dramatic expressiveness of the dancer, Grisi, as he saw her on the stage. He enlisted the help of Vernoy Saint-Georges, whose flair for inventing plots with interesting episodes and local colour ultimately made him one of the most popular librettists of the nineteenth century with some twelve ballets and eighty serious and comic operas to his credit. He had the ability to seize upon topics popular with his fashionable contemporaries and utilize them so that his works were much to the taste of those audiences who "go to the opera because of fashion and are fully satisfied when beautiful décor, costumes and dance arrest attention; they quite overlook the splendid music." (STENDHAL).

Although Saint-Georges' libretto for *Giselle* is built on the same lines as *La Sylphide* with its two acts firmly fixed, the first in the world of the flesh and the second in the world of the spirit, it has greater substance and continuity. Giselle lives as a peasant amongst other peasants for whom she is the natural leader of the vintage because of her unusual dance ability and sympathetic personality. Her mother provides one link between the two worlds because she realizes the fate which will overtake Giselle if she dances so much. The woodcutter, Hilarion, provides another link, for, being suspicious of Albrecht's identity and intentions towards the one he also loves, he becomes the one to bring about the climax of the first act, the confrontation of Albrecht with his fiancée, Bathilda. This results in Giselle's madness and death.

Saint-Georges also gives Albrecht a proper background of wealth and aristocratic behaviour, so that the conflict between the two worlds is also viewed as a conflict between rich and poor, another favourite topic of novels, dramas and operas of the mid-nineteenth century.

ADOLPHE ADAM AND THE SCORE

The skilful way in which Saint-Georges links together the threads of his narrative is impressive. The episodes rise so easily from each other that the action unfolds without unnecessary *divertissements* (several used today are later additions, e.g. the peasant *pas de deux* Act I) and the smooth unfolding of the story is enhanced by Adolphe Adam's eminently suitable score.

Adolphe Adam was already an experienced composer of theatrical pieces when he was invited to provide the score for *Giselle*. He too had been inspired by Grisi's talents and he composed music which illustrated the action, created the necessary atmosphere and provided a firm rhythmic base on which to deploy the dance. But what is more important is his use of some five leitmotives. These short themes help the *danseuse* interpreting *Giselle*, because, as they are repeated throughout the ballet, sometimes in a slightly changed form, she is able to show through the movements associated with these passages, how the events of the story are moulding her character.

By using the leitmotives in this way Adam provides continuous links of music and dance, sight and sound, throughout the ballet thus helping the audience to understand the plot more clearly. This had not been done before in ballet and preceded Wagner's use of similar motives in his opera cycle *Der Ring des Nibelungen* by some twenty-eight years. Adam was instrumental in breaking down the strict formulas of writing ballet music in set numbers, something that Wagner was quick to recognize and an example to be followed by later important musicians.

Jules Perrot and his Choregraphy

Upon Adam's five short leitmotives Jules Perrot based certain dancing movements through which Carlotta Grisi could interpret the changing dramatic content of the role.

Like Marie Sallé, Jules Perrot was born into a family of travelling players, making his début at the age of four playing the role of a monkey. His wonderful dancing talent was quickly appreciated by Auguste Vestris, who, having trained the boy for the sheer love of a talented student, arranged for Perrot's début at the Paris *Opéra.* Here he sometimes danced with Marie Taglioni in Didelot's *Zéphyr et Flore* (among other ballets) where a critic writes: "They danced as if a puff of wind had swayed them, as if in one exalted moment they would soar forever upwards." Such eulogies however did not please Taglioni who, so the story goes, refused to dance with him again. Perrot certainly failed to obtain a permanent post at the *Opéra* and was forced to tour, meeting success wherever he went not only for his brilliant dancing but also for his interesting productions. These displayed his unusual ability to introduce meaning into dance by his sensitive use of expressive movement and by his ability to develop the talents of young dancers both as technicians and artists. Carlotta Grisi was the greatest of his pupils and the one for whom he created two of his finest works, *Giselle* and *La Esmeralda.* (He created *Ondine* for Fanny Cerrito.)

THE LEITMOTIVES OF GISELLE

It is now recognized that Perrot was responsible for the dances of Carlotta Grisi in the role of Giselle, having been invited to undertake this task by Adolphe Adam, and it would seem that his choregraphy remains much as he created it, presumably because the movements are so pertinent to each situation as it arises. Undoubtedly they have changed a little with the development of the *ballerina's* technique, her *arabesques, attitudes* and *pointe-work* have become fuller and stronger, but the five leitmotives are always recognizable and can be summarized.

The Dance Leitmotive

This consists of two *ballonnés* and a *pas de basque*. The latter has a special form, the *danseuse* stretching her leg forwards through the air instead of gliding it past the leading foot in the second movement. The *enchaînement* is used to describe Giselle's love of dance and opens her first solo, establishing, as it were, this particular facet of her character. She dances it later when arm in arm with Albrecht; when Albrecht's fiancée asks her what she enjoys most; uses it in a sadly distorted form in the Mad scene; and in a more elevated version in her dance as a Wili shortly before Albrecht falls exhausted.

The Second Love of Dance Motive

This is joined to Giselle's love for Albrecht and appears when the couple first dance arm in arm during the opening scene. It is repeated in the general dance number and, with some *ballerinas*, when Giselle tries to re-live those happy moments in the Mad scene. It consists of a *ballotté en avant* and *en arrière* (repeated twice in all) and a *grand jeté en avant*, and although the *enchaînement* is not repeated in Act II, the two movements form a major part of the choregraphic design for Giselle's dance in that Act and appear as well in the dances of the Wilis.

The Flower Motive

This motive has two musical forms; the first is heard when Giselle tells the daisy petals to find out if Albrecht loves her. An episode of flowers is introduced in Act II, when Giselle throws her lover some to prove she has tangible form. The second musical motive is allied to the dance and is repeated several times. Both motives are found in the Mad scene where Giselle sadly retells the petals and tries to recapture her first moments of love. They are repeated again when she calls Albrecht to join her in the dances of Act II.

The Wili or Fear Motive

This is predominantly a musical phrase; it is first heard in the overture and several times in Act I (if the original score is being used) but it is not associated with any movement until Act II, where it accompanies the *posés* and *petits battements sur le cou-de-pied* opening the dance of the Wilis. This movement has already been introduced by Giselle in her first-act solos, as if stressing her unusual qualities as a dancer, qualities which cause her Mother to predict her death and being as a Wili, and during the miming of this scene, the Fear motive should be heard.

The Hunting Call

This, with the musical phrase which follows it, is associated with Hilarion and is not danced; each time it occurs it presages a dramatic development of the action: Hilarion seeing Albrecht dismiss his servant Wilfrid, which arouses his suspicions; the entry of the ducal party with Albrecht's fiancée; Hilarion finding Albrecht's sword and summoning the Duke in order to disclose Albrecht's proper identity. This leads to the confrontation of Bathilda, Albrecht and Giselle and to the Mad scene. In Act II the musical phrase announces the entrance of Hilarion and later of Albrecht before the Queen of the Wilis commands their death.

The very fact that these leitmotives occur in both acts gives the interpreter of Giselle an excellent opportunity to show her mastery of style and mimetic action. In the first act she can frame them with *demi-caractère port de bras* as befits her peasant origin, yet allow enough grace and unusual lightness to her movements to make her seem different from the *corps de ballet,* thus making her transformation into the Wili of the second act seem logical. The lyrically flowing line of her romantic style of dance can then acquire greater depth of meaning, because one can see how the tragic betrayal and madness have drained her delicate framework of all passion.

Perrot undoubtedly used these brief leitmotives of movement because he felt that his choregraphy must not rely on a single vocabulary of academically formed steps but that such steps must develop with the character. Moreover he felt the need of wrapping conventional gestures into his *ports de bras* so that, while not completely repudiating the conventional *scènes d'action* of his predecessors, he was able to allow the action to flow onwards during the purely danced passages. This was a great step forwards and one to be developed still further by Ivanov and later Fokine, who was the first entirely to eliminate these formal scenes.

PERROT AND THE CORPS DE BALLET

La Esmeralda did not have the same lasting success as *Giselle* possibly because the score by Cesare Pugni was of little interest, being not much more than a time-keeper. Nevertheless the ballet is important as it marks the first occasion in which the *corps de ballet* were used as individuals. Perrot composed mass dance so that—

> For every Group and even single members of a group, he created an independent course of movement leading them from the depth of the stage in continuous succession.

He did this because *La Esmeralda*, and others of his ballets, dealt with real-life characters in a realistic setting and they had to be seen in their proper environment before they could rise to be the heroine or hero of the action. This was particularly so in *La Esmeralda* (produced in London, 1844) where his heroine had to rise from the raggle-taggle band of homeless beggars, vagabonds and the like, sheltering under the great shadow of Notre Dame. Once his heroine had been established in all her innocence and her sympathetic nature had been proved, she could be seen to grow in importance as the action unfolded. Perrot's wide experience of life and work in all kinds of towns and theatres gave him the necessary inspiration to design such convincing scenes that critics were quick to point out the authenticity and originality of his crowd work. This was specially so in Russia, where he gave wonderful opportunities to almost unknown members of the *corps de ballet* to shine for a moment at some essential point in the action without detracting from the principal players, because that moment was only one part of a whole to which all had to contribute.

THE ROMAN THEATRE AT POMPEII
(*Collection of Vittorino Ottolonghi*)

PLATE I

Salome Dancing
(From a Spanish MS. in The British Museum)

Dance of the Wildmen, Masking of the Fifteenth Century
(From Froissart's Chronicles in the British Museum)

PLATE II

BALET COMIQUE DE LA ROYNE, THE SCENE
(*Collection of P. J. S. Richardson, Esq.*, O.B.E.)

PLATE III

The Four Virtues from Balet comique de la Royne

The Sirens with Two Tails from Balet comique de la Royne
(*Collection of P. J. S. Richardson, Esq.*, O.B.E.)

PLATE IV

A COMMEDIA DELL'ARTE BALLET
(Collection of Vittorino Ottolonghi)

COSTUME FOR NANCY

COSTUME FOR M. VESTRIS

Both designed by Bocquet for Ballets by Noverre
(Lunacharsky Library, Leningrad)

PLATE V

DANCE TO THE MUSIC OF TIME BY POUSSIN
An example of French official art
(Wallace Collection)

THE MINUET IN "LE BAL CHAMPÊTRE" BY WATTEAU
(Dulwich College Picture Gallery. By kind permission of the College Governors of Alleyn's College of God's Gift)

PLATE VI

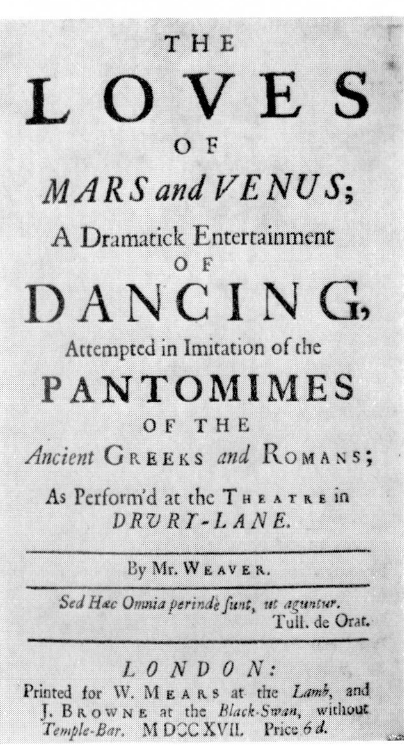

THE

LOVES

OF

MARS and VENUS;

A Dramatick Entertainment

OF

DANCING,

Attempted in Imitation of the

PANTOMIMES

OF THE

Ancient GREEKS *and* ROMANS;

As Perform'd at the THEATRE in *DRURY-LANE.*

By Mr. WEAVER.

Sed Hæc Omnia perindè sunt, ut aguntur.
Tull. de Orat.

LONDON:
Printed for W. MEARS at the *Lamb*, and J. BROWNE at the *Black-Swan*, without *Temple-Bar*. M DCC XVII. Price 6 *d.*

THE LOVES OF MARS AND VENUS,
TITLE-PAGE

xv

DRAMA.

Mars, ——The God of War, was Son of *Juno*. The Ancient *Latins* gave him the Title of *Salisubsulus*, from Dancing and Leaping; he intrigued with *Venus*, was discover'd in his Amour by *Vulcan*, and taken by him in a Net.

Danc'd by Mr. *Dupré*, Senior.

Vulcan, ——Son of *Jupiter* and *Juno*; for his Deformity *Jupiter* threw him down from Heaven; he fell on the Isle of *Lemnos*, and broke his Leg in the Fall; he kept a Forge there, and work'd for the Gods; he was Husband to *Venus*.

Danc'd by Mr. *Weaver*.

Venus, ——The Goddess of Love and Beauty, was Daughter of *Jupiter* and *Dione*; she was Wife of *Vulcan*, and Mistress to *Mars*.

Danc'd by Mrs. *Santlow*.

Aglaia,

THE LOVES OF MARS AND VENUS,
CAST

(*Collection of P. J. S. Richardson, Esq.*, O.B.E.)

ILLUSTRATION FROM LIBRETTO OF PERSEUS AND ANDROMEDA, ANOTHER ENGLISH BALLET SUPPOSEDLY BY WILLIAM HOGARTH

ILLUSTRATION FROM ESSEX'S TRANSLATION OF THE DANCING MASTER

(*Both from collection of P. J. S. Richardson, Esq.*, O.B.E.)

PLATE VII

Maria Medina Vigano
(Collection of Vittorino Ottolonghi)

Zéphyr et Flore by Didelot (1828)
The first type of lift
(Lunacharsky Theatre Library)

Two Sketches by Didelot's Pupil F. Tolstoy for The Golden Harp
(Collection of Yuri Slonimsky)

PLATE VIII

L'Épreuve Villageoise, a Dauberval Demi-caractère Ballet
(Collection of Peter Revitt)

PLATE IX

Demi-caractère Dance by
Carlos Blasis

Character Dance from Denmark
From an old Danish newspaper
(*Collection of Peter Revitt*)

Napoli by Bournonville
The Royal Danish Ballet with Margot Lander and Borge Ralov
(*Photo Mydtskov*)

PLATE X

Carlotta Grisi and Jules Perrot in Giselle

Carlotta Grisi and Jules Perrot in Esmeralda

Lucille Grahn, the Great Danish Dancer

Carlotta Grisi and Jules Perrot in Giselle

(All from collection of Peter Revitt)

PLATE XI

MARIE TAGLIONI IN LA SYLPHIDE
A CHALON PRINT
(*Collection of Peter Revitt*)

FANNY ELSSLER
An ORIGINAL PORTRAIT
(*Collection of Peter Revitt*)

PLATE XII

THE SLEEPING BEAUTY: ENTRANCE TO THE CASTLE, ORIGINAL PRODUCTION, MARINSKY THEATRE (1890)
(Lunacharsky Theatre Museum)

THE SLEEPING BEAUTY: THE PROLOGUE, LILAC FAIRY—ZOUBKOVSKAYA IN THE KIROV BALLET
(Photo, Anthony Crickmay)

PLATE XIII

Sketches by Paul Gerdt of what became the Grand Pas Classique, The Sleeping Beauty Finale

(*Bakroushine Theatre Museum*)

Paul Gerdt, the Original Prince Charming of The Sleeping Beauty

(*Lunacharsky Theatre Museum*)

The Little Hump-backed Horse by Saint-Léon, "Under the Sea" by Roller (1867)
(*Lunacharsky Theatre Museum*)

PLATE XIV

THE LANGUAGE OF FLOWERS, PART OF A SERIES OF PHOTOGRAPHS POSED BY DAME ADELINE GENÉE (1907)

PLATE XV

SWAN LAKE BY PETIPA–IVANOV: ORIGINAL LAST ACT, MARINSKY THEATRE (1895)
(*Lunacharsky Theatre Museum*)

SWAN LAKE BY IVANOV, WITH DAME MARGOT FONTEYN AND MICHAEL SOMES, C.B.E.
(*Photo Roger Wood*)

PLATE XVI

PERROT IN RUSSIA (1848–59)

There is little doubt that at Perrot's hands, the personnel of the Imperial St. Petersburg ballet was once again given opportunities to display their expressive talents as a corporate whole. After Didelot had been forced to retire, new German and French ballet-masters had reverted to the old mythological and heroic ballets using greater spectacular effects and the technical virtuosity of French and Italian stars. When the audience tired of such shows the Imperial Theatres bought a circus and, in order to augment the performers, the dancers were commanded to learn "Equestrian Riding," sometimes with disastrous effects on their dancing career, although some unfortunate enough to suffer accidents were able to turn to the drama, opera or music, because they had received a comprehensive education.

Perrot was invited to St. Petersburg after Marius Petipa and his father had failed to revive the audience's interest in ballet by their productions, which had been either borrowed directly from other choregraphers or were based on the novelties fashionable in London or Paris (*see* page 74). For a time Perrot did hold the interest of the Marinsky ballet-goers.

Such an audience demanded novelty and Perrot's productions of *Giselle*, *Ondine* and *La Esmeralda* with Carlotta Grisi in the leading roles won their applause. But the court censor soon became suspicious of the choregrapher's intentions. His use of the *corps de ballet* as individuals with a right to solo roles seemed revolutionary. His choice of themes became suspect. The censor complained that: "In *Esmeralda* Perrot has presented an officer as the villain, an unforgivable offence. It is also inadmissible that Esmeralda should be ruined by a clergyman." His staging of *Catarina, Daughter of the Bandit,* based on a supposedly true incident in the life of Salvatore Rosa and his revolutionary affairs, and of *Lysistrata, the Strike of the Wives*, was also considered dangerous.

Like Didelot before him, Perrot fell into disfavour through his desire to treat contemporary and other themes seriously and realistically. Like Didelot he was forced to retire; but not before both dancers and audiences realized the value of a choregrapher who sought to make each member of his cast into an active participant in the development of the plot, and not before the dancers under him had learnt to distinguish between the classical, romantic and *demi-caractère* styles in such a way that they could, when necessary, link two of these together in order to show continuity of action and development of character. He also taught his dancers that all, from the most minor member of the *corps de ballet* to the star were equally important in the production of any ballet which was an artistic whole and not a mere spectacle. A vital lesson also taught by Diaghilev and Dame Ninette de Valois.

Was it perhaps his ability to make each dancer feel as important as the other that made the four great *danseuses* of his era dance so amicably together in the famous *Pas de Quatre* produced in London (1845)? Or was it his ability to seize upon the particular qualities of Taglioni, Grahn, Elssler and Cerrito, and display these to the best advantage so that none of them felt she could be outshone by the others? An answer to that question may never be given. It is enough to know that these four great artists and many others besides did shine in any ballet Perrot created for them, and that each time he re-rehearsed his work for a new *ballerina*, something in his choregraphy was altered to bring out the various aspects of her particular talent. It is also important to note that Perrot, dancing his Romantic ballets in Moscow with Fanny Elssler, had a greater success than in St. Petersburg. His dramatic approach was akin to that of the Moscow artists and he helped them to develop these qualities still further as actors (*see also* page 89).

FURTHER READING

BEAUMONT, C. W. (with SITWELL, S.), *Romantic Ballet* (Faber & Faber, 1937).
BLASIS, CARLO, *The Code of Terpsichore* (London, 1830).
BLASIS, CARLO, *Traité élémentaire et pratique de la Danse* (Milan, 1820).
BLAZE, CASTILE, *Le Danse et les Ballets* (Paris, 1932).
BORISOGLEVSKY, Y., *Materials for a History of Russian Ballet*, 2 vols. (in Russian) (Leningrad, 1938).
BOURNONVILLE, AUGUST, *Mon Theatreliv* (Copenhagen, 1858).
BOURNONVILLE, AUGUST, Etudes chorégraphiques dediées à mes elèves et mes collègues (Copenhagen, 1861).
KRAAGH-JACOBSEN, SVEND, *The Royal Danish Ballet* (London, A. and C. Black, 1955).
PERROT, JULES, Libretti for *Giselle*, *La Esmeralda*, *Lysistrata*, *Ondine*, *Catarina*, and others.
SLONIMSKY, YURI OSSIPOVITCH, *Giselle* (Leningrad, 1930).

CHAPTER 6

Changing Tastes in Ballet

These Dances were compos'd according to the Genius and Manners of Countries and their Inhabitants. (JOHN WEAVER)

BY the 1860s audiences had lost interest in Romantic ballet. Their attention could only be held by novelty. Producers of ballet, in despair at the lack of interest, began to depend heavily on stage tricks and on inventions based on the scientific discoveries then being made. Aquariums with real fish, horses and other animals, fireworks and even choral singing vied with the *ballerinas* and enormous casts who sometimes appeared in patriotic episodes. Operas and operettas too had to be enlivened with smartly dressed pseudo-national dances, cancans and the like. And the ideas that were fashionable in Paris had to be produced elsewhere.

ARTHUR SAINT-LÉON AND CHARACTER BALLET (1821–70)

Arthur Saint-Léon seems to have been very successful in satisfying these demands. Where and when he was born is still unknown. He was first "noticed" in the German theatres as a pupil of his father and was immediately recognized as a "star." He was a brilliant dancer, an excellent man of business, he was realistic in his approach to his art, talkative, adaptable and enterprising.

His accommodating nature may be explained by the contemporary conditions under which he made his début in Paris. A dancer there had no chance of success unless he or she was a pupil of Vestris (or some other popular dancer), or was a foreigner.

Saint-Léon was sensitive to public demands and expended so much energy to secure engagements that he was always busy. (During the years 1859–69 he acted as chief ballet-master in St. Petersburg and Moscow, as well as at the Paris *Opéra*, where he worked from 1863 to 1870.) A letter to the St. Petersburg management explains how this was done—

> In recommending my ballet, I should explain the production is not expensive although it has many different effects. If you wish, you could change the title. If you do not alter much—I should be able to set four scenes in fifteen days. I offer my services—free.

Saint-Léon was a good linguist and quickly found his bearings. Soon after entering a theatre he recognized those artists upon whom he could rely, just as, shortly after arriving in a city, he seemed able to sum up what would most please the audience and management.

This versatile Jack of all trades intrigued everyone. He could compose music as well as dance and fiddle. One of his posters reads—

> Today, Saint-Léon's Violin Concert; Tomorrow, Musical Evening, the Compositions of Maestro Saint-Léon; The Day After Tomorrow, Saint-Léon will dance the principal role in a ballet composed by himself.
>
> (*Le Violon du Diable* in which he also played the fiddle)

The range of subjects Saint-Léon treated in his ballets is astounding. But if his libretti are closely examined it will be found that many of them are adaptations of each other or of older productions. For example, in Paris a work was called *Némea*, in St. Petersburg *Fiametta*; the plot of *Alma* is almost identical with that of *La Fille de Marbre*, and both of them stem from Sallé's *Pygmalion*. This happened because Saint-Léon carefully adjusted his choregraphy to the talents of successive *ballerinas*. In essence his ballet was intended for a given dancer and company, and, when he moved to the next town, it had to be adapted to suit and find places for the local cast.

THE LITTLE HUMP-BACKED HORSE

Saint-Léon's claim to a place in choregraphic history lies in more than the excellence of his spectacles. He himself claimed (but this was self-advertisement) that *The Little Hump-backed Horse* was the first national ballet. Didelot had already attempted to create national ballet in St. Petersburg (*see* page 49) and his pupil Glouzhkovsky, on becoming ballet-master in Moscow, had continued his master's work. There he produced *Russlan and Ludmilla* (1821), thus anticipating Glinka's opera by twenty years, and *The Black Shawl* (1831) using traditional themes and dance. Saint-Léon's ballet was based principally on nationally characteristic dance in the sense that Dauberval understood that term (*see* page 42). But although Dauberval defined character dance as dance belonging to one nation, that designed by himself and his pupils (with the possible exception of Didelot in Russia, *see* page 49) seems to have relied principally on classical formulas and steps, and to have made its characteristic elements apparent only in the costumes and certain typical poses and arm movements. Saint-Léon strengthened these native characteristics, and was able to do so because of his interest in the national art forms then being manifested in so many of the countries he visited to stage ballets.

Saint-Léon's creation of a purely character or pseudo-national ballet probably arose from his flair for seizing upon matters of moment. By 1864, when he produced *The Little Hump-backed Horse*, that group of Russian composers known as the "Mighty Little Heap" (*Kutchka*) was beginning to be known in St. Petersburg, an important event because this city, "the window to the west," was very cosmopolitan in its outlook and had hitherto shown little interest in things Russian. Balakirev, Borodin, César Cui, Rimsky-Korsakov and Mussorgsky were attempting to establish a national style in music following the initiative taken by Glinka in his *A Life for the Tsar* (1836). The Russians' belief in their own art forms had been awakened by the publication of Pushkin's poems at the beginning of the nineteenth century, an event which had inspired Didelot's *The Prisoner in the Caucasus* (1828). But Pushkin's work to establish the use of colloquial Russian as the basis of all literary and dramatic work and the development of a native musical or dance idiom for opera and ballet was shunned by the aristocratic audiences filling the St. Petersburg theatres. All national life seen on the stage in any medium was called "mud and abomination." (A term incidentally used by the late Sophie Fedorovich when commenting in her brilliantly economical way, on settings designed to capture the glory of the Imperial theatres in a modern work). Saint-Léon's ballet however won them over. One critic wrote—

> Not until *The Little Hump-backed Horse* has all the rich resources of Russian ballet been revealed, a whole arsenal of character and of classical dance has been disclosed.

Despite such eulogies, certain of Saint-Léon's contemporaries maintained that although the theme and certain elements of the original *The Little Hump-backed Horse* were essentially Russian, it was not national ballet in the proper sense of that term. The reasons are simple: firstly Saint-Léon had not enough knowledge of Russian folk dance to base his choregraphy entirely on such sources, therefore a great many of his dances were based on a brilliantly imaginative use of the few elements he had noted in his visits to Moscow or had seen among the few folk dancers in St. Petersburg; secondly his ballet was built according to the old formulas whereby his long series of *divertissements* were linked by brief *scènes d'action* and thirdly, the music by Cesare Pugni possessed few of the typical characteristics of the Russian musical idiom (*see* page 117).

Nevertheless the ballet was of value. The journalist who suggested the staging of Ershov's popular children's story realized that it would give Saint-Léon enormous scope to stage dances of great variety because the hero, Ivanoushka, had to travel through air, water and fire in his efforts to find the Tsar-Maiden and the magic Ring with which to wed her. At each place visited there was a court, the members of which were given opportunities to dance solo or group items inspired perhaps by some Russian dance or by material

Saint-Léon had collected in his many journeys throughout Western Europe. If these sources failed, then the choregrapher himself had abundant imagination and used fantastic or comic ideas as they suited the situation. But above all, Saint-Léon knew how best to display the talents of his cast and it was this which brought out the particular Russian qualities of his ballet. The cast was entirely Russian, led by Martha Muravieva (the Tsar-Maiden), and they were given an opportunity to display their native talents in a story of vivid characters well known and loved by them all, a thing which had not happened in St. Petersburg since Didelot's *The Prisoner in the Caucasus*. It was, therefore, the cast themselves working under Saint-Léon's direction, who supplied the truly Russian spirit, expressiveness and quality of movement, which gave *The Little Hump-backed Horse* its air of authenticity.

COPPÉLIA

Coppélia, produced at the Paris *Opéra* in 1870 was Saint-Léon's last ballet and remains a favourite item in the repertoire. Although his choregraphy has not been retained the libretto and score afford sufficient evidence to discuss his methods of producing character dances which can still be of value to modern choregraphers. In addition, it is known that Petipa and Ivanov (who is usually credited with the present choregraphy) both learnt from Saint-Léon, firstly, how to transfer national dance to ballet without diminishing its native richness and, secondly, how to reveal and use the talents of each dancer.

Coppélia is another example of Saint-Léon's flair for staging works of contemporary interest. The libretto is based on a story by E. T. Hoffman, whose imagination had been fired by the making of the first automata around which he built a collection of fantastic tales (*see also* page 82). Such objects had also given rise to much talk in the fashionable world.

The scene of the action is Galicia, a part of the world selected no doubt because Saint-Léon felt it would give him an opportunity to stage lively Hungarian and Polish dances as the boundaries of these two countries were then joined, and they too were much in the news because of their fierce struggle to revive and maintain their national customs, language and traditions after long suppression by others. *Coppélia*, however, is not a plea for nationalism: it is meant to entertain by a variety of means and to display the talents of a *comédienne danseuse* and her partner, who is not a *danseur noble* but a man of some character, and both were expected by Saint-Léon to show a broader range of style than was usual in *demi-caractère* ballet. *Coppélia* contains broad and subtle comedy, pathos and tenderness hinged round a charming love story, which gives plenty of scope for gay dances of many types.

The production is built according to the old formulas of *pas* and *scènes d'action* to link the *divertissements* and although Delibes in his lively score used several leitmotives to characterize Franz, Coppélia (the doll with whom he is in love), and Doctor Coppélius, there is little indication that Saint-Léon used these in the same way that Perrot had utilized Adam's leitmotives in *Giselle*. The music is, however, much more than a time-keeper.

Delibes already had several operas, operettas and ballets to his credit when he composed *Coppélia* for the Paris *Opéra*. His success as a writer of such scores lay in his gift for illustrating the action as well as for creating the appropriate atmosphere for the unfolding of the plot because he was a master of orchestration. He seemed always to sense the instrumentation most suitable to describe the necessary effects. His provision of local colour was always interesting and in *Coppélia* he was not afraid to borrow directly from the Polish composer, Monszuiko, and from the Hungarian folk tunes used for the newly invented dance of the nationally minded Hungarian aristocracy in Budapest, the *czardas*, which Saint-Léon staged for the first time in any theatre.

The two items, the Polish "Mazurka" and the Hungarian "Czardas" together with Swanhilda's Spanish and Scottish solos in Act II, demonstrate the methods by which Saint-Léon and, following his example, Petipa and Ivanov transferred folk dance to the stage. This strengthened the impression given to an audience that they were watching some real-life characters performing an "authentic" national dance, which displayed all the characteristic traits of the country in question.

Firstly, Saint-Léon stylized the traditional steps used, classified them under the terms in the classical vocabulary, but confined them to that category of dance he termed character. For example, the so-called *bell-step* of Russian and the *harang* of Hungarian dance became *pas de bourrées*; the *goat's leap* and similar jumps of several countries became *pas de chat*; the Polish *holubetz*, Czech *pritukavany* and other beaten steps became *cabrioles*; the Russian walk became a *pas de basque*.

Secondly, he brought out the type and quality of the movements by emphasizing those elements which he felt were exclusively characteristic of one country, and drew attention to these factors by limiting each dance to certain steps, so that the audience could quickly appreciate its specifically Russian, Hungarian, Polish, Spanish, Scottish or other national quality. For example, in the Hungarian *czardas* he stressed the "down to earth quality," the couple's concentration on each other, the clipping of the heels; in the Polish *mazurka*, the accenting and travelling of the steps and the boys' particular handling of their girls; in the Spanish he emphasized the typical poise of the body known in Flamenco dancing, and the easily recognizable *ports de bras* and poses; in the Scottish, he made great show of the swift, brilliant footwork and arm positions; in the Russian, the unending flow of movement for the girls and the spectacular feats of the boys.

Thirdly, in order to stress these native features he carefully designed the pattern of his dances and set each step according to the classical formulas. That is, he broke up the traditional circle, chain and couple dance formations and saw that each step or particular feature was seen at its best from the audience's point of view.

Fourthly, he paid great attention to the accenting and phrasing of the steps so that the intimate relationship between each dance and its music became apparent, thus strengthening the authenticity of its style and quality within the framework of the ballet.

MARIUS PETIPA AND THE REVIVAL OF THE CLASSICAL BALLET (1822–1910)

Of the forty ballets which were his original design and the many others he claimed for his own, only three works by Petipa have endured. It is perhaps significant that these have scores by major composers, Tchaikovsky (*The Sleeping Beauty* and *Swan Lake*), and Glazunov (*Raymonde*). Yet the lack of permanence of his other works was not entirely due to their generally humdrum music. A study of the content of Petipa's particular type of ballet reveals that, despite their spectacular nature, they were lacking in dramatic continuity of action and character.

Marius Petipa was famous throughout Europe for some sixty years, originally as a dancer and then as chief ballet-master of the Imperial St. Petersburg Theatres, a post he held for thirty years. He went to Russia as first soloist in 1849, when his father, Jean, was appointed chief ballet-master. The ballets these two men first produced were borrowed from other choregraphers for whom they had worked, and were either staged in entirety and given greater spectacular effects or else with slightly altered plots and action and under a different title. Their lack of success as producers did not however worry Marius, who was glad to work under Perrot and later under Saint-Léon, both of whom cast him for the leading roles in their ballets. He thus learnt a great deal of their methods and was able to send glowing accounts of his dancing to his brother, Lucien, in Paris who seduously spread the news of Marius' increasing fame as "soloist of the Tsar."

Petipa owed his first success as a choregrapher to the librettist Saint-Georges, whose flair for seizing upon a theme has already been noted (*see* page 62). *The Daughter of Pharaoh* (1862) was inspired by Théophile Gautier's novel, *The Romance of a Mummy*, and was produced when interest in the excavations taking place among the Egyptian pyramids was at its height. The libretto is an excellent example of the spectacles Petipa continued to produce for the rest of his career. They were always built upon the old formulas of *scènes* and *pas d'action* padded with brilliant *divertissements*, through which Petipa could display his masterly control over both classical and character dance, in particular Spanish and semi-oriental dance which he had studied during the four years he had worked in Spain.

The Daughter of Pharaoh contained many of the melodramatic elements introduced by Perrot into his more realistic works, so that the plot was always full of action. But the ballet contained nothing new in choregraphy, and Bournonville was not the only critic to notice Petipa's reliance upon spectacle and other people's ideas (*see* page 61). He was frequently accused of plagiarism. One critic wrote of *The Beauty of Lebanon* (1863)—

> I know of no other ballet which surpasses it by such interminable borrowings from other choregraphers. All the groups are either unsuccessful or a reminder of things already seen.

However in 1864 Petipa had a success with a dance arranged for his wife, Marie Surovchikova, *The Little Moujik*, for which she wore a national coachman's costume and performed some of the characteristic steps of Russian male dance. This was the first time an Imperial *danseuse* had appeared *en travesti*, a thing which had been becoming increasingly common in all other European theatres except the Danish. The item aroused great controversy between those balletomanes who regarded it as an amusing novelty and critics who felt Petipa had found his *métier* and others who felt their national dance and music were being degraded. Petipa's further attempts to create pseudo-Russian dances were failures and the Directorate discussed sending him to Moscow which to them was of minor importance as a theatre. Petipa demanded such a substantial increase in his salary if this step were taken, that the Imperial St. Petersburg Theatres found it more economical to retain him in St. Petersburg and allow him to stage minor works and revivals of ballets by Perrot and others, under the supervision of Saint-Léon, in which he frequently rearranged the dances (i.e. the *grand pas des Wilis* in *Giselle* as now performed in Russia).

This re-editing of another person's choregraphy undoubtedly strengthened Petipa's inventiveness and when Saint-Georges provided him with the libretto of *Le Roi Candaule* (1868), Petipa produced another magnificent spectacle replete with the most fantastic details based on discoveries made during the excavations taking place in Lydia, home of the mythical King Gyges, hero of the ballet.

The work was a huge success for the subject was topical and had captured the interest of the fashionable world. Largely as a result of its success Petipa was engaged as chief ballet-master when Saint-Léon departed (1869). Immediately a large field of choregraphy was opened before him because he had to provide for both St. Petersburg and Moscow theatres and schools, as well as five small court theatres. His contract stipulated that he had to create one long ballet at the beginning of each season and between 1869–79 he staged fourteen major works in addition to thirty revivals and dances in several operas.

Despite Petipa's efforts, the fashionable audience upon whom the Imperial Theatres relied, gradually lost interest in these huge spectacles and he, remembering Saint-Léon's advice "to know one's audiences," made friends with Khudekov, the balletomane and editor of *The Petersburg Gazette*, who realized that Petipa's salvation lay in following the news. Khudekov then began to write or suggest scenarios based on current topics and the immediate result of this collaboration was *La Bayadère* (1877); *Roxana* (1877) at the time of the Russo-Turkish war; *The Daughter of the Snow* (1879) when the Northern Scheldt froze over; *Mlada* (1879) which aroused patriotic feelings after certain Russian victories. But the dramatic side of the action in all these was neglected. Bournonville wrote—

> The artistic side of contemporary ballet, that is to say grace, plasticity, mime, harmony and picturesque groupings, has been pushed into the background . . . the dancers have now run to technicalities and effects, choregraphy to décor, fountains and panoramas. All Petipa does is to try and devise new difficulties for the dancers.

These virtuoso feats were performed by the visiting French and later by Italian stars, who had been brought in at the command of the Directorate in their efforts to revive interest in ballet. The importation of these virtuosos was a blow to Petipa's pride, particularly when they, in their turn, failed to hold the public with the "wind raised by their diabolical *pirouettes*." It seemed that Petipa would have to retire, but the new Director of the Imperial Theatres, Vsevelozhsky, decided to make one more attempt to recapture public interest by reverting to the grand classical ballet as it had been shown in the days of Louis XIV. Moreover, he felt that if he could persuade Tchaikovsky to provide the score, such a venture would almost inevitably be successful because the composer was then at the height of his fame and could command an audience for any of his compositions.

THE LIBRETTO OF THE SLEEPING BEAUTY (15TH JANUARY, 1890)

"*The Sleeping Beauty* is a pearl of great price." So wrote Laroche, the St. Petersburg critic. Like *Giselle* before it and many Diaghilev ballets after it, it was the result of a collaboration between three artists all of whom loved the theatre and were prepared to work together to produce a single work of art, although Petipa's colleagues ultimately accepted his dictates because he had greater experience. His knowledge of the French court ballet and academic technique assured that he alone could fill in the framework supplied by the others.

Vsevelozhsky was, like Diaghilev later, a highly cultured man and somewhat of an artist, who actually designed the costumes for the ballet. He realized that the production of a classical theme as presented in the seventeenth-century court ballet was impossible, because his audience would tolerate neither explanations of the action by singers or actors nor the interminable series of court dances performed by amateurs. Moreover the allegory and symbolism essential to those early works would not be understood. Yet something of these elements had to be introduced if the style of the ballet were to emerge correctly. His choice of *The Sleeping Beauty* by Charles Perrault, one of the first Frenchmen to examine and exploit in fairy-tale his country's rich folk lore, did allow Petipa to disclose something of the significance of his theme, the death of winter and the coming of spring, even though at first glance the ballet appears as a charming fantasy.

Vsevelozhsky wrote out the original plan of the action, allowing each act to develop an appropriate climax which would lead easily into the next scene and give continuity to the action. This logical development of plot had not been a strong point in many of Petipa's ballets and must have forced the choregrapher to economize on the style of dance created. But Tchaikovsky would not accept the commission until he had received a detailed libretto from Petipa, an understandable precaution because his first attempt at ballet-making for the Imperial Moscow Theatres (*Swan Lake* 1877) had not been wholly successful.

Tchaikovsky had never shrunk from providing music to order as the following extract from his letters to Jurgensen, his publisher, should prove—

> You seem to believe that to compose pompous pieces for the Exhibition is a species of sublime delight to which I will hasten, pouring out inspiration without having an idea what it is all about, how, why, when, etc. I will not lift a finger until I have a definite commission.

Petipa was at first reluctant to accept a task which he himself had not initiated. He, the Tsar's soloist, was not used to being dictated to by a director. However, he gradually warmed to his task, realizing it would at last give him the opportunity he had always wanted to display the wealth of pure classical dance which had hitherto been impossible in ballets, whose actions were located in countries unsuitable for so refined a medium. He finally provided the composer with so vividly descriptive a plan that Tchaikovsky wrote—

> It seems to me that the music of this ballet will be one of my best productions. The subject is so poetic, so adaptable to music that I am composing it as one would write with warmth and abandon always, if the production merited it.
>
> (In a letter to Mme. Von Meck)

Petipa and the Music

Petipa's libretto for *The Sleeping Beauty* is the work of a master. Like all other choregraphers trained in the French academic principles, he thought that music had to be in accord with the action and assist in achieving the denouement, but above all be the firm time-keeper and background to the dance. He frequently created dances before he received a score, because he knew in advance exactly what he intended by way of movement and bowed to no one in his domination of the production; whoever the composer, whether a worthless dilettante or the great Tchaikovsky himself, Petipa refused to yield precedence. If the score did not meet requirements, it had to be adjusted to meet his demands.

The Rose Adagio and the End of Act I

There is no doubt that Tchaikovsky found such vivid pen pictures as the following a fascinating source of inspiration—

(The original libretto was written in a hand-sewn exercise book of twelve pages, each item had two sections, the *régisseur's* section in black and the musical section in red ink. The items are bracketed and numbered identically.)

9, 10, 11, 12, 13. (*The régisseur's plan.*) What happens during the Adagio and *pas d'action*?

The Four Princes surround her (Aurora J.L.) and beg her to dance for them as they have been told she is the most graceful dancer in the world.

Aurora with her natural kindness agrees to grant their request with pleasure. She dances whilst her friends and pages play on their flutes and violins. The Four Princes in turn come up to her, pay her compliments and express their admiration. She redoubles her graceful and easy movements.

Not only the Princes and the court are captivated by her, but also the townsfolk and villagers, young and old, follow her changing aerial flights with curiosity. General movement and dance. (*Petipa's remark in brackets*: It will be necessary to make groups of old men, women and little children.)

14. (*Musical suggestion.*) Suddenly Aurora notices an old woman who is beating the time of her dance with a spindle 2/4—which develops. It is beaten out all the time into a 3/4 gay and flowing. When the 3/4 begins Aurora seizes the spindle, which she waves like a sceptre. She expresses her delight to everyone—twenty-four bars valse. But suddenly, pause, the pain, blood flows! eight bars 4/4 broadly. Full of terror, now it is not a dance, it is a frenzy as if she has been bitten by a tarantula. She turns and falls senseless. This will require from twenty-four to thirty-six bars. A few bars *tremolo* with the sobbing and cries of pain. "Father! Mother!" Then the old woman with the spindle throws off her disguise. At this moment the entire orchestra must play a chromatic scale.

Everyone recognizes the Fairy Carabosse, who laughs at the sorrow of Florestan and the Queen. Short masculine-like music, culminating in a diabolical laughing tempo, when Carabosse disappears in a flurry of flame and smoke. The Four Princes run away in terror. At this moment the fountain in the centre stage is illuminated—as the Lilac Fairy appears in the streams of water. Tender, fantastic, magical music.

It was Tchaikovsky who realized that the Lilac Fairy was the one character linking the various scenes and provided the ballet with its only leitmotive, the "tender, fantastic, magical music" accompanying her every appearance. It was he who brought out in his music the vivid contrast between the good and evil fairies, the difference between the court dances of Act II (Act III Royal Ballet version); and the charmingly human and humorous touches Petipa added from time to time, such as in Puss in Boots and the White Cat, for which he required: "Character dance, The miaowings and mutual caressings and pattings with their paws. For the finale, the scratching and shrieking of the cats. At the beginning—an amorous 3/4, but for the end quickening miaowings. The whole dance must not be long."

It is perhaps worth noting that Tchaikovsky and Petipa seldom met as the latter was on tour whilst the ballet was being composed, therefore Tchaikovsky had to rely on the choregrapher's libretto and the few hints that arrived from time to time by letter.

SYMBOLICAL AND OTHER DETAILS

A story runs that Charles Perrault wrote *The Sleeping Beauty* at an inn, whilst waiting for his carriage to be repaired after an accident when returning from the Hautes Pyrénées. Perhaps he had visited Briançon, where a charming May Day drama used to be enacted, relic of an old death and resurrection rite: the boys wrapped in leaves one whose sweetheart had left him. The Green Man (who personified the dead year), lay down by the river and feigned sleep; a girl, who would marry him, approached, kissed him awake and then led the May Day dance with him.

It seems that Petipa and Vsevelozhsky were aware of the old custom because of their request to the five artists designing the scenery that Aurora's embattlemented castle should be seen from afar, perched in the mountains, and that the Lilac Fairy should always emerge through the jets of a fountain or down a river. They were also aware of the significance of kissing the "dead year" awake by insisting that, as the Prince sailed down the "River of Dreams" to find the Beauty, the scenery should appear to change as summer, autumn, winter and finally spring coloured the trees and horizon.

Petipa undoubtedly studied Perrault's story very thoroughly as well as court ceremonials and old theatrical practices, and brought his knowledge to bear upon props, costumes and his choregraphy and let it colour some of his dances. By thus introducing a subtle expressiveness within the classical medium he gave it greater descriptive qualities.

The Fairies at the christening in Perrault's original story brought a gift which could have been symbolized by some prop, as did the Four Ladies representing the Virtues in *Balet comique de la Royne* (*see* page 17). Petipa, however, gave each Fairy certain movements which described their gift, and symbolized their property by giving each a symbolical name borrowed from another source. The first two fairies, Candide, *who is flowing*, and Fleur de Farine, *who weaves and intertwines*, brought beauty and grace. As they danced, the former made the conventional gesture for beauty and smoothed her arms with her hands during her *ports de bras*; the latter slightly turned her back and glanced downwards as she raised her arms in the traditional gesture for grace. Both names were associated with the language of flowers frequently used in the seventeenth and eighteenth centuries to express ideas to a lover. The third fairy Kroshka, *breadcrumbs*, was a particularly Russian fairy, bringing plenty, and derived from the custom of the godmother breaking bread over a child's cradle. The fourth fairy, Canary, brought the gift of language with her gestures of singing and twittering. The fifth fairy, Violante, brought energy and is said to have been introduced because Petipa was so impressed by the invention of electricity, that he wished to show its sparkling power and darting nature. The Lilac Fairy brought knowledge.

The Rose Adagio was inspired by the traditional practice of the Serious Lovers in the Commedia dell'Arte, which also evolved from the language of flowers, in which the lover sent his belowed a rosebud when his love first awakened, and later a full-blown rose when he wished to declare it.

Another important point in the Adagio was Petipa's insistence to Tchaikovsky that each passage had to be repeated four times because there were Four Princes. But the *pas* never becomes monotonous because of this repetition. Both composer and choregrapher allow sufficient variation in their music and dance to keep interest alive, and it is those slight variations which allow the *ballerina* playing Aurora, sufficient licence to draw the portrait of a human being and not to be a mere technician. So do Petipa's hints that in Act I Aurora is a happy Princess never having known pain, in Act II she longs to be awakened and in Act III she has now come into her kingdom, happy in her love.

Petipa introduced court dances and pastimes into Act II to show the passage of time, for they showed exactly one hundred years' difference in style from those performed in the Prologue before Aurora falls asleep. This is not to say that they were authentic court dances. Petipa had no intention of reproducing the real thing, but only such vital elements of the respective types which would be theatrically and pictorially effective in creating the realistic atmosphere of a court, and serve as contrast to the fantastically classical dances of his nymphs and fairies. In the same way he introduced a valse and farandole for the peasants.

PETIPA AND CLASSICAL CHOREGRAPHY

The Sleeping Beauty was Petipa's greatest and last wholly successful ballet. It looked backwards because it was based on the old formulas of the court ballet and French academic principles. But it also looked forwards because, by allowing subtle characterization to appear within the classical medium itself, he gave it not only greater expressiveness, but also greater freedom. Until this ballet, the dances created for the Italian and French virtuosos had concentrated mostly upon those "stunts" which they personally had mastered. That is, instead of being expert in one type of dance like the eighteenth-century virtuosos, who rarely appeared in anything but their own style, nineteenth-century virtuosos kept either to long series of jumps *sur les pointes*, or *relevés développés*, or *pirouettes* and so on.

Petipa changed all that. He examined each step of the classical vocabulary, assessing its merit and quality as it were, and allotting it to one of the seven categories of movement so that it could—

1. Be a preparation or provide a link between one movement and the next. (The auxiliary or preparatory steps.)

2. Add lightness, height, depth and breadth to the dance. (Steps of *grande* and *petite élévation.*)

3. Add brilliance and sparkle, even wit. (*Grande* and *petite batterie.*)

4. Lend continuity to the flow of line, help to the movement and complete the total pattern of the steps. (The *ports de bras.*)

5. Add speed and excitement. (*Pirouettes.*)

6. Become the highlight or finishing point of an *enchaînement* or dance. (Poses.)

7. Lend the finishing touch to the total picture (*Pointes* which he always used with the greatest discretion and finesse.)

He then amalgamated these in such a way that they became a fascinating picture of movement drawn with subtle nuances of colour, expression, quality and pattern filling the framework of his stage and displaying the particularly personal quality and ability of his dancers.

Slonimsky, the great Soviet critic, has said—

> To Petipa every dancer must owe that wealth of dance in which is found the mark of well-accentuated phrases, the finish of a picture, the sharply underlined quality and completion of each body movement; in fact—dance perfection. Without a complete mastery of technique, no artist can attempt his roles, because the slightest nuance of expression in the movement itself must be conveyed with crystal clarity.

FURTHER READING

BORISOGLEVSKY, Y., *Materials for a History of Russian Ballet*, 2 vols. (in Russian) (Leningrad, 1938).
KRASSOVSKAYA, VERA, *Russian Ballet* (in Russian) (Leningrad, 1958).
PLESCHEYEV, A. A., *Our Ballet* (in Russian) (St. Petersburg, 1899).
SAINT-LÉON, ARTHUR, Libretti for *The Little Hump-backed Horse, Coppélia, Alma, Le Violon du Diable.*
SLONIMSKY, YURI OSSIPOVITCH, *Masters of the Ballet* (Moscow, 1937).

CHAPTER 7

The Search for Expression: I

First seek the impression heard through the music, later seek to express the emotion felt through the style and qualities of the movement.
(The late EDWIN EVANS in a conversation on choregraphy)

THE success of *The Sleeping Beauty* suggested to Vsevelozhsky that another ballet from the same collaborators would be equally popular with the audience. He had been intrigued by E. T. Hoffmann's fantastic, slightly macabre tales, which had already inspired Saint-Léon's *Coppélia* (1870) and Offenbach's opera *The Tales of Hoffmann* (1881), and worked out a plot, *Casse-Noisette* (12th December, 1892), based on three tales about a Nutcracker Prince and Drosselmeyer, a magician and maker of dolls, supposedly told by a godfather to a little girl, Clara, in bed after an accident. But Petipa did not take the same interest, and had great difficulty in making up his mind how he could develop logically in classical dance the complicated action proposed by the Director. Eventually, after Petipa had placed two or three variants of the plot before Vsevelozhsky, the latter asked for an enrichment of the dances as the second act seemed feeble. Petipa immediately decided to "vulgarize" his action, and injected into it the Sugar Plum Kingdom with its pink sea, fountains of lemon and orangeade, almond milk, coffee, chocolate, tea and the like, with all the various dances this implied. He then triumphantly concluded the libretto with the words: "J'ai affranchi. J'ai écrit cela. C'est très bon," and sent it to Tchaikovsky.

The composer could not return the compliment and in a letter to his brother, Modeste, wrote: "The subject of Casse-Noisette pleases me very little. I am very tired and in reality suffer a great deal. . . . Is it wise to accept the offer of the Imperial Theatres? My brain is empty." However, on his return to Russia after his American tour, he reluctantly reconciled himself to the subject. The second act was particularly unattractive to him as it showed no development of action and he once again wrote to Modeste: "I am groping in the dark, finding it impossible to express musically the Sugar Plum Kingdom." Just before rehearsals commenced he wrote again: "And now it is finished, *Casse-Noisette* is all ugliness."

Tchaikovsky's score, like Petipa's libretto for *Casse-Noisette*, is unequal in quality. The music for the first act is based on symphonic methods. The composer had been instructed "to make transparent the intrigues." This allowed him to develop and counterpoise certain leitmotives, and describe the characters expressively so that, in his treatment of the older people, the music sounded ironical, was gaily simple for the children and fantastically impressionistic in the scenes with Drosselmeyer and the Battle between the Mice and the Toy Soldiers. But after giving Clara's journey through the snow a lyrically danceable treatment, the score finishes unexpectedly with a witty picturesque series of *divertissements*, which only differ in pure musical quality from those supplied for other ballets by "composers of special ballet-music."

LEV IVANOV AND THE CLASSICO-ROMANTIC BALLET (1834–1901)

At the commencement of rehearsals Petipa fell ill and the choregraphy fell into the hands of Lev Ivanov, his assistant, who had to choose between a conscientious fulfilment of his master's orders and his own artistic conception of Tchaikovsky's music. Ivanov had begun his career with the last stars of the Romantic school and was out of sympathy with the wave of virtuosity sweeping the theatres. His diary states—

> I was so good a soldier that I went through every step of the "service." I have been in the *corps de ballet*, *coryphée*, first soloist, played character roles, was a teacher of dancing, and finally they made me a ballet-master.

This last advancement came when Petipa needed an assistant who would be modest and obedient enough not to develop into a rival. Lev Ivanov answered that description, and it became Petipa's habit to place his own name on the posters for Ivanov's ballets, although he had only acted as Artistic Director.

Ivanov was a talented musician. His aim throughout his career as ballet-master was to interpret the music and transmit its sound choregraphically. Dance to him was the "blossoming of the music." The creative process for Ivanov began when, after being inspired by the music he began the choregraphic design. All things which were in process earlier, which to Petipa were of vital importance, because he was the absolute dictator of a production, to Ivanov were merely technical requirements and by occupying himself with the dull mechanics of plots, libretti, scores, scenery, costumes and props, he felt he lost the enthusiasm of creation.

It was not surprising, therefore, that the many contradictions and diversities of Tchaikovsky's score and Petipa's libretto faced Ivanov with a problem he had not the strength to overcome, because he had not the courage to demand a clarification of both action and music from persons he considered of more importance than himself. A tiny note in his *Diary* reads "Never be too self-loving, do not regard yourself as better than the others, be modest."

The best pages of Tchaikovsky's score did however inspire Ivanov to create some exquisite items such as the Dance of the Snowflakes, for which Petipa demanded from Tchaikovsky a first act finale—

> The Fir Forest in Winter. Snow begins to fall. Suddenly a snow-storm occurs. Light, white snowflakes blow about (sixty dancers). They circle everlastingly to a 3/4 valse. They form snowballs, a snow-drift, but at a strong gust of wind, the drift breaks up and becomes a circle of dancers.

Ivanov's choregraphy closely followed this description and was very far from Petipa's usual *corps de ballet* number with its straight or diagonal lines and circles, and every dancer moving identically at the same time. Another exquisite item was "The Dance of the Sugar Plum Fairy" which, although technically brilliant, did not in the least deviate from the quiet yet clear tones of the music.

SWAN LAKE (ST. PETERSBURG VERSION 27TH JANUARY 1895)

Chance placed the initiative for re-creating *Swan Lake* in Ivanov's hands. The Imperial Theatres wished to pay homage to Tchaikovsky and a year after his death, gave a concert in his memory for which Ivanov staged The Flight of the Swans (Act I, Scene ii). It was a triumph, one critic going so far as to say—

> Ivanov and Tchaikovsky have so closely interwoven their scenes that one might say there was a choregraphically musical union. The dances of *Swan Lake* are lyrically symphonic. Lev Ivanov has created an example of a choregraphic symphony, which is an expression of elegiac grief, continuing sorrow and the illusion of love.

The success of Ivanov's effort convinced the Director of the Imperial Theatres of the wisdom of restaging the entire ballet. The task was entrusted to Petipa and the conductor, Drigo, with the stipulation, on orders from above, that Ivanov's scene be left intact. The original Moscow version now underwent drastic revision (*see* page 85). Drigo edited the music, omitting about a third and using other compositions by Tchaikovsky (e.g. Odile's dance in Act III was a piano solo, "The Playful Girl") as well as making a few additions of his own. Petipa reset the action, reserving for himself the Prologue and Act II, and allowing Ivanov to set the last act, so that the scenes of the Swans would be in a uniform style.

It is obvious that the ballet is the work of two choregraphers, one who felt the music intensely, and the other who, because he was not the real instigator of the ballet, had to fill up so many bars. It is on record that Petipa said at one point "Listen to the music again," and on completing the finale of the last act "Can I include a solo or not?" Then, when he had completed the final variant of this scene to send to Ivanov, he wrote out the list of characters participating and said—

> The music gave absolutely no opportunities for staging solo dances. If I had been able to dispense with these dancers, it would have been excellent. It would have conformed to the music.

In other words, Petipa realized that the symphonic structure of the music could not be broken by the introduction of *divertissements* with which he always concluded his work and which Tamara Karsavina so aptly sums up—

> His productions were all founded on the same formulas. An inevitable *divertissement* brought his ballets to an ever happy conclusion, while those of his heroes for whom anything but a tragic end was an historical impossibility, found themselves crowned in an apotheosis.

Petipa's arrangement of the Prologue and Act II of *Swan Lake* differed in no way from any other ballet which had gone before. The plot is unfolded by *scènes* and *pas d'action* generously sprinkled with *divertissements* and variations of classical and *semi-caractère* dance. Some of the former are brilliantly designed, Odile's dances in particular. They offer a challenge to any *ballerina*. Not only do they contain the famous thirty-two *fouettés*, which Petipa introduced because his star, Pierina Legnani had mastered this difficult feat, but also because the choregrapher, in order to strengthen the expressiveness of the character, was wise enough to borrow certain elements from Ivanov's choregraphy and so disperse them through his dances, that the magician's daughter Odile, could be seen to be simulating the part of the tragic Swan Princess. It was this aspect that Gorsky was to emphasize in his production in Moscow (*see* page 92).

The Leitmotives of Swan Lake

The choregraphy of the two acts in *Swan Lake* created by Ivanov is of a different style and quality from that of Petipa. When the Moscow production of *Swan Lake* (1877) failed to win full approval because some of the music was *undanceable*, this was surely due to the fact that the choregrapher, a German, Reisinger, was not capable of understanding Tchaikovsky's symphonic methods, his use of leitmotives and far from ordinary structure of ballet music. Only one earlier score had been composed in something the same style and with a similar continuity of action, Adam's *Giselle*, which although invaluable in its context, was not of the same calibre as Tchaikovsky's score. Long before the St. Petersburg production, suites from the ballet had been published (one incidentally, arranged by Debussy), which won universal acclaim from both audiences and serious critics. It has already been noted that Petipa found the music difficult (*see* page 84), and both he and Drigo edited it sufficiently to bring the Prologue and Act II into line with the usual run of ballet music. But they could not do the same with Acts I and III because the nature of Tchaikovsky's writing prevented much, if any, alteration in the sequence of events which occurred mostly whilst the dancing was taking place, not as was usual between dances, each with its beginning, climax and end.

It was this symphonic continuity of action that inspired Lev Ivanov's choregraphy and gave it expression through various leitmotives of movement. These are not associated with particular musical passages as are those of *Giselle*, because Tchaikovsky created only one leitmotive and this runs like a thread throughout each scene. It symbolizes The Flight of the Swans either passing over the Prince's head, or away from his sight, until that last moment when he and his beloved sail away together. Moreover, Ivanov's leitmotives have a different purpose from those of Perrot in *Giselle*.

Ivanov wished to characterize some favourite figures of Russian fairy-tale, the Swan Princess and her friends, who have lost their human shape through the craft of a magician.

They could only regain their human shape for a few moments, unless they could find a lover who would swear to be true to them. At that moment when they first appear in Petipa's libretto, Odette, the Swan Princess, has had no time properly to regain her human shape before being captured by the Prince, and it was this detail which inspired Ivanov to see his Princess also as a Swan. To do so he based his choregraphy on pure classical dance to give her a regal dignity, but emphasized certain elements to describe her being as a Swan. There are five of these leitmotives of movement—

1. The *arabesque* in which Odette appears to be floating through the water, her body and arms breasting the waves as she turns from side to side.

2. The movements of the head, which sometimes quivers, like the hands and arms, as if shaking off the drops of water; and the *ports de bras* in which the hands are often slightly turned outwards from the line of the arm to represent the tips of a swan's wing.

3. The *pas de chat* which moves from an open to an open position with the legs raised behind the body on the jump, to symbolize the Swan alighting on to or rising from the water.

4. A movement where the arms are drawn from the head downwards by the side of the body and then pressed outwards to symbolize the Swan's shape, and as if smoothing the feathers.

5. A movement where the upraised hands are gradually floated downwards as the body is lowered and then circle upwards and round the head, which represents the long curving line of its neck as the swan floats along the river.

Such specialized movements as these would not, however, have been so effective if Ivanov had not given them emotional overtones. Perhaps the most beautiful example of his choregraphy is the "Love Duet" after the Prince has sworn to marry Odette and thus save her. Its melodious structure is partly explained by the original structure of the music which is based on a vocal duet Tchaikovsky had written for a projected opera, *Ondine*. Several times Odette and the Prince, who are dancing to the duet played by violin and 'cello, are interrupted by the *corps de ballet* of Swans coming to life and performing one of their leitmotives.

The first phrase is based on tranquil loving poses during which Odette scarcely looks at the Prince, afraid that he may see the love in her eyes. The second phrase has another meaning. As the music soars, so does the *ballerina* and after a momentary pause, swiftly descends and turns. The sudden change in the character of the movements gives the impression of a rush of passion, then sudden fear. Later a new idea arises as the Swans, moving in a diagonal line, slowly echo Odette's movements. As she glides forwards in a series of *arabesques* and is then lifted high by the Prince, so they gradually incline their bodies into their particularly characteristic curtsy and rise to their toes. This echoing of movement resembles the way in which the chorus will echo a *prima donna's* notes after she has sung them, and seems to emphasize Odette's passionate hope that the Prince will save them all.

Ivanov paid great attention to the patterning of these general dances so that they, too, would lend emotional expression to the action, such as creating movements which would thrust upwards and outwards during those happier moments when the swans hope to be saved, and downwards and inwards when all seems to be lost at the sad opening of the last act.

Petipa seized upon Ivanov's five leitmotives and used them in his dances for Odile, but he insisted they be performed with unyielding strength and without that same flow of line which allows Odette to express her innermost feelings through the movements. Petipa's Odile imposes expression deliberately on each movement as it arises such that the falsity of her nature is visible throughout.

Swan Lake was Ivanov's greatest and last achievement, he continued to work in the theatres producing, amongst other ballets, "The Polovtsian Dances" in Borodin's *Prince Igor* (23rd October, 1890) in which both Fokine and Gorsky were to dance. This probably made a great impression on both of them and undoubtedly influenced their own productions given in 1909 and 1914 respectively. But Ivanov was saddened and humiliated by the insulting behaviour of Petipa and others. Nevertheless his ideas of lyrically symphonic dance were of the utmost value. He was the first choregrapher to open the pathway to the vast possibilities of uniting dance and music more closely, and enlarging the expressive scope of classical dance. Out of his exciting formulas and creative fantasies came the first great masterpieces of Fokine in *The Dying Swan* for Anna Pavlova (22nd December, 1907), and the first version of *Les Sylphides* produced under the title of *Chopiniana* for his students at the Imperial School (1907), and the first purely symphonic ballets produced by Alexander Gorsky in Moscow to music by Glinka (1901), and to Glazunov's Fifth Symphony (1916).

Had Ivanov realized how much the future of ballet rested upon his sensitive feeling for music and dance, perhaps he would not have felt it so bitterly necessary to repeat to himself the aims he had always held and thus justify his life and work. Just before he died he wrote in his *Diary*—

> To have wished that you should not become one such of the idols, to have wished that there should enter into you the spirit and energy so that you did not look upon your vocation as a trade, but that you loved your art with all your soul and as a banner held it constantly aloft.

ALEXANDER GORSKY AND THE REFORM OF RUSSIAN BALLET (1871–1924)

Alexander Gorsky is a name that is rarely mentioned in histories of ballet, yet he occupies an important place not only for his influence on those Moscow dancers joining the Diaghilev company, but also upon some of its choregraphers and on the Bolshoi company itself, perhaps only now putting into practice ideas originated during his leadership of that company.

BALLET IN MOSCOW*

The history of Russian ballet properly begins in Moscow, where the Tsar Alexis (father of Peter the Great) established a theatre and dancing school at the Kremlin Palace in 1672. Its first dancer, teacher and producer was Nicholas Limm, a military specialist in fortification, who was probably a Scottish and Stuart emigré, and had studied at a French military academy where dancing was compulsory. By 1675 the company consisted of forty Russian male dancers, and he had produced a ballet, *Orpheus*, in addition to the usual *entrées* of any court ballet. After the Tsar's death the theatre was temporarily closed, but was reopened by Peter the Great as a popular theatre which functioned until 1707 when the court moved to the new capital. It was not until the Trustees of the Moscow Orphanage decided to set up a dancing class for its children in 1773 and the Theatre of Drama, Opera and Ballet began to give regular performances in 1776 that the history of the Bolshoi company and school can be said to begin.

Its repertoire, style of performance and performer have always been different from those of St. Petersburg (Leningrad). This is due to the fact that it was always essentially free from court directives and catered for a more democratic audience of Russians and not the cosmopolitan St. Petersburg aristocracy (*see* page 71). It always employed more actors and dancers from among former serfs, who had been sent for training to the Imperial schools by their masters and their practices, together with the tastes of the audience, led to the development of distinctive features, which were reflected in its ballets.

At the beginning of the nineteenth century a new form of entertainment was staged, consisting of dance scenes suggested by folk festivals, games, Yuletide and Shrovetide customs and the like, which were not only popular in essence but led to the development

*This passage is based on material suggested by Yuri Aleexevich Bakroushine.

of a specifically theatrical form of Russian dance. These scenes became exceedingly popular and originally inspired Didelot to produce some Russian dances for his 1812–14 London season, and later the *genre* dances for his *The Prisoner in the Caucasus*. This introduction of pure character work was fostered by Didelot's pupil, Glouzhkovsky, when he took over the leadership of the Moscow ballet in 1812, and was the first to adapt works by Pushkin for the stage, *Russlan and Ludmilla* (1821), followed by the Didelot, *The Prisoner in the Caucasus* (1827), and *The Black Shawl* (1831).

The creation of a particularly Russian form of character ballet continued to be fostered by the various ballet-masters throughout the nineteenth century. But in addition, Moscow audiences were introduced to ballets with far greater dramatic depth when Bernadelli, a pupil of Vigano, produced *Othello*, 23rd August, 1828). This greatly influenced the trend of Moscow ballet and its performers. One of the first to be so influenced was Ekaterina Sankovskaya, who incidentally was Stanislavsky's first dance teacher. The so-called "Russian Taglioni," who was "A herald of truth, beauty and goodness . . . a plastic interpreter of a new word" (SALTYKOV-SHEDRIN, the Russian satirist and essayist). The *new word* was Romanticism. But the Romantic ballet did not become so overwhelmingly successful in Moscow as elsewhere, although it did much to develop the expressiveness of the *danseuses* and develop the dramatic content of the ballet (*see* page 55). The Moscow audience seemed to prefer character ballets and, in order to develop their dancers' technique, the Directors of the Bolshoi Theatre invited Carlo Blasis to become chief choregrapher and teacher. His three years' stay in Moscow (1861–4) ensured that many of the peculiarities of his own particular school became part of the Bolshoi style of classical dance. But his efforts did not bring the audiences into the theatre, and in 1882 the Directorate of the Imperial Theatres decided to abolish the Moscow ballet on the grounds that it was too expensive. The Tsar would not accept this plan and demanded a "Reform of the Bolshoi company," an action which resulted in the dismissal of one hundred and ten dancers and a halt to the development of its repertoire. Nevertheless the teaching at the school under Mendes (a pupil of Blasis), and particularly Tikhomiroff (a pupil of Johannson, Gerdt and Petipa) was so successful that when Gorsky was appointed *régisseur* in 1900 he had a well trained company with which to work. From this date onwards the Bolshoi ballet began to build up its world-wide reputation.

EARLY INFLUENCES

Alexander Gorsky originally studied at the Imperial St. Petersburg School under Karsavin (Tamara Karsavina's father) who, in addition to classical, taught character dance and instilled a love of this medium into his students by his brilliant demonstration, and by his methods of illustrating his lessons with his drawings of appropriate costumes in order to make his dancers appreciate the effect these had on movement. It was this introduction to the need for authenticity, which later made Gorsky insist upon historical and geographical accuracy in décor and costume designed for those of his ballets requiring greater realism of atmosphere.

Gorsky also worked under Volkov, that sensitive teacher who realized Anna Pavlova's particular qualities. From him Gorsky learnt how to think and revalue the plastic form of classical dance practised by the Romantic choregraphers, and dare to give it greater emotional expression and that closer *rapport* with the music which Ivanov had shown in *Swan Lake*. It was as a result of lessons learnt with Volkov that Gorsky later made so many innovations in the methods of training used in Moscow. One of his first tasks there was to banish the fiddle played at class by the master himself and to introduce instead a piano and musician able to appreciate the relationship between the two arts. Gorsky also worked under Petipa and finally became assistant to Paul Gerdt, the great *danseur noble*. From these masters he learned the strict principles of the old French school and this meant that even when he appeared to be breaking entirely away from academic dance, when influenced by Lois Fuller, and to be becoming infatuated with the ideas of Isadora Duncan, he never completely dispensed with it as the foundation for his choregraphy.

Gorsky was first sent to Moscow to stage Petipa's masterpiece, *The Sleeping Beauty* (1898), which he had notated according to the system of Stepanov. The success of this Moscow reconstruction (17th January, 1899) and its faithful adherence to the many details of the intricate choregraphy led to further engagements to stage other St. Petersburg ballets, and finally to his appointment as chief *régisseur* of the Bolshoi Ballet. (1900).

GORSKY AND THE DRAMATIC CONTENT OF BALLET

Gorsky lived through one of the most interesting periods in the development of Russian, as opposed to Western, art. Moscow, on his arrival as permanent leader, had become the artistic capital of Russia. At Sava Mamontov's private theatre, which opened in 1885, the operas of Rimsky-Korsakov and other nationalist composers were being staged with wonderful décor and costumes by young artists of the calibre of Vroubel, Serov, Korovin, Golovin and others. It was a theatre which spoke or sang truth, because its producer, Mamontov himself, entirely broke with the old Italian opera conventions. He required his singers, led by Chaliapin, to live their roles in the most realistic way possible within the framework of score and libretto. In this he was giving a tremendous lead to Stanislavsky at the Arts Theatre where altogether new and realistic methods of production and the training of actors would later completely alter the audience's conception of the theatre. In addition to these major theatrical enterprises lively discussions upon realism in art were taking place in literary circles led by Gorsky and other important authors, and among artists working at the Moscow School of Painting, Architecture and Sculpture.

This search for new ways in art and the struggle against the routine of the Imperial

Theatres and official Institutions undertaken by so many different artists, inspired Gorsky to develop many of the ideas he had begun to formulate when producing, and later modernizing some of the older ballets such as *Don Quixote* which he produced in Moscow (6th December, 1900) and in St. Petersburg (20th January, 1902). He was a profound admirer of the Moscow Arts Theatre and wanted his dancers to live their parts in the same way as did its actors, otherwise there could be no real characters in ballet. For this reason, from the beginning of his work in Moscow, he introduced something of Stanislavsky's methods into the training of his artists, so that with the help of an authentic style of costume and impressionistic décor they could, within the period and status of the characters and plot, more closely approximate to real life. This was something new in the Imperial Theatres and quite unlike its routine academic realism.

He did not however starve his ballets of dance when developing them on more dramatic lines as Angiolini and others had done (*see* page 37). He urged that every production should have its own style of movement, and that subordinated to the creation of an image, which in detail, either by way of folk-lore dance, "local colour" of his own imagination, or mere gesture, had to be true to the subject and rise out of the needs of the plot.

His choregraphy was much more complex than that of any earlier choregrapher because, in order to achieve "realism," he gave each member of his *corps de ballet* an individual dancing role, thus his crowds, with their contrapuntal dance patterns, became a picture of living people and created the necessary realistic atmosphere and background to the logical development of the dramatic action. Moreover, in his two finest works, *Gudula's Daughter* (1902, a version of *The Hunchback of Notre Dame*, which was closer to the original Hugo novel than Perrot's *La Esmeralda*) and *Salammbô* (1910, based on Flaubert's novel), his heroes and heroines were seen to emerge gradually from the crowd and the action grew more and more tense as attention was increasingly focused on their personal drama.

It was not enough for Gorsky to subordinate his own choregraphy to the dramatization of plot, character and action. He believed that the artist, musician, dramatist, choregrapher, dancers and producer should each serve the same cause and seek together the best way to present the ideological and artistic content of every new ballet. In other words, he believed, unlike Petipa, that ballet must be a collaboration between artists, each giving to the other to serve one aim. It was for this reason that when he produced *The Little Hump-backed Horse* (1902) in Moscow, he entirely reset the libretto, bringing it more closely into line with Ershov's original story; moulded a new score from music by Tchaikovsky, Rubinstein, Liadov, Dvořák and others to make it more Russian and folk-like in content; based his dance more closely on the native medium; and invited the Russian artist Korovin to design décor and costumes.

GORSKY AND PLASTIQUE

Mikhail Gobovich, who worked under Gorsky and later became artistic director of the Bolshoi school, has stated that during his twenty-five years' work in Moscow, Gorsky went through many phases, some that were rashly experimental, others of the utmost value. Perhaps the most important of these, after his search for greater dramatic reality, was his striving to express emotion through a fuller dramatic plasticity of line within the classical style.

To achieve this aim he experimented whilst reconstructing the Petipa–Ivanov *Swan Lake* and other ballets by introducing a form of *plastique* which was greatly influenced by the teaching of André Delsarte. This he began to teach in all his classes of the Bolshoi School when he tried to make his students express the content of symphonic music through dance movement. For this purpose, and following Ivanov's example in *Swan Lake*, he introduced new forms of *ports de bras* and established the so-called sixth and seventh positions of the feet. The very fact that in both these positions the feet were placed, either together or apart, in a perfectly natural position with both feet and knees facing forwards, gave freedom to the entire body and allowed the dancers greater fluidity of movement. His first ballet in this new *genre*, the *Valse Fantaisie* of Glinka (5th September, 1901), was without theme or story. It attempted to show, in plastic form only, the content of Glinka's music. This short work was immediately recognized by critics as showing a new sense of form, mode of expression and quality of movement.

He continued further along these lines after he became infatuated with the ideas of Isadora Duncan and better acquainted with the theories of Jacques Dalcroze, whose book was published in Russia in 1907. Gorsky finally produced a first ballet to be danced to a symphony, Glazunov's Fifth (1916), which was also without theme or story. It was at this point, if some of the leading teachers of classical dance had not taken a firm stand, that the particular form of technique practised in Moscow would have been lost, his choregraphy had deviated so far from its basic principles.

Nevertheless it was Gorsky's original and careful analysis of the theories of *plastique* and dramatization of movement within dance, worked out and applied both in Moscow ballets and classrooms before Isadora Duncan appeared in St. Petersburg (1905) that did so much to give artists like Mordkin, Novikov, Volinine, Sophie Fedorova, Vera Coralli and Leonide Massine their greater understanding of the art of acting out the life of a character within the framework of the dance. It was to these great dancers and to the forward-looking artistic movements taking place in Moscow that Diaghilev was to owe much when he came to start his company. Moscow, the despised "provincial" capital, was the place where so many of his artists, dancers and composers had already been allowed to sow the seeds of Russian ballet in its truly national sense in the works of Gorsky and in the operas at Mamontov's private theatre.

SERGE DIAGHILEV AND HIS RUSSIAN BALLET

The history of the Diaghilev Russian Ballet has been told many times and from many different angles, but only Arnold Haskell has mentioned the important part played by Moscow in the development of this great enterprise. The fact that Serge Diaghilev, its inspired director, was a "provincial," possibly helped him more clearly to appreciate the particular nature of the formulation of national art in the ancient capital of Russia, and relate its trends with the ideas shown in the pictures by modern Western artists, avidly being collected by enterprising Moscow merchants. That he was a "provincial" also helped him to look upon the conventional outlook of cosmopolitan St. Petersburg and its Imperial Ballet with different eyes from those of his colleagues when working with them upon the famous magazine *The World of Art*. They had had a westernized education and were fully aware of the other progressive movements taking place in Western European circles, which were of a different nature from the Moscow ventures. To some extent it is possible to say that Western art was running towards abstract forms, impressions seen and heard, and experiments in light and shade, whilst Moscow artists were seeking for more realism and the projection of real-life tragedy through the medium of play, opera, music and ballet. It required the genius of a Diaghilev to unite these elements in the one art of ballet.

When Diaghilev began to be tolerated by his cousin's coterie of friends, he was still undecided wherein lay his *métier*. Although studying music with the hopes of becoming a composer, he was also constantly being made aware of the technical and aesthetic problems of pictorial art, or the theatre, or literature and philosophy discussed by other members of the circle who were professional workers in one of these fields. Therefore, when he finally set about the creation of a ballet company, he had a wide knowledge of all the elements needed to create a single work of art in balletic form. He understood, right from the initial stages in the working plan of a ballet, the approximate value of the parts to the whole and had the genius to unite the right artists with each other so that each was prepared to subordinate his materials to the needs of the other, and particularly to the dance forms envisaged by the choregrapher.

Diaghilev's desire to present to the Western world a peculiarly Russian Ballet and not that of the Imperial Theatres, despite his love of so much that was presented in St. Petersburg, had gradually been developed since the first issue of *The World of Art* (1899), when to the surprise and not altogether the approval of all his colleagues, he compiled a section on Russian Peasant Art. To some of them it seemed as if he were rejecting that part of their manifesto which stated: "Above all, our efforts will be turned in the direction of improving taste in all branches of our national art." But this preliminary excursion into the value of Russian art was followed by his increasing interest in and exposition of other aspects of his country's artistic genius. Amongst his activities were the organization of the exhibition of historical Russian portraits at the Tauride Palace (St. Petersburg 1905), of the Russian Exhibition in Paris (1906), of a series of Russian Historical Concerts at the Paris *Opéra* (1907), the production of *Boris Godunov* at the Paris *Opéra* (1908), and finally the first Paris season of Russian opera and ballet (in 1909).

That the ballets in his repertoire did not conform to the generally accepted pattern of the two or three long acts shown at the Imperial Theatres arose firstly through Diaghilev's desire to show the immense and varied wealth of Russian dance and ballet; secondly, because economic circumstances did not allow him to stage the great spectacles of an Imperial Theatre even if he had wished to do so; thirdly, the Russian choregrapher, whom he had chosen to provide his first repertoire, had already shown that it was possible to create a short one-act ballet from carefully selected material which would be a perfect whole in itself, and this in no way diminished its importance in relationship to other longer works. The fact that the choregrapher chosen was a man of infinite talent, meant that the three ballets presented at each programme were varied in style one from the other. But no choregrapher, no matter how great a genius, could possibly supply enough of these shorter ballets of a consistently high artistic calibre to satisfy an ever-increasing audience. Moreover, Diaghilev's own taste and ideas changed with the political changes taking place through wars and revolutions and with the changing tastes of those members of his audience with whom he was most in contact. Even though it has been said that Diaghilev produced only those works in which he himself was interested, he drew his ideas from the varied movements in art and music, and was always aware of the interest these aroused in fashionable circles.

The history of the Diaghilev Ballet falls into three distinct phases, in each of which his company was dominated by one major choregrapher, all of whom made a vital contribution not only to the repertoire of his company, but to the development of ballet as a whole.

These three phases can be roughly outlined as follows—

1. When he relied almost entirely upon Russian sources for dancers, artists and composers, and when the main choregraphic works were designed by Mikhail Fokine.
2. When he sought inspiration from the traditional and historical sources of other European countries and his main choregrapher was Leonide Massine.
3. When he sought the new for the sake of its being new, when his choregraphers were George Balanchine and Serge Lifar.

Between these three main phases there were brief interludes of interest, when works by Vaslav and Bronislava Nijinsky made some contribution to choregraphic development.

FURTHER READING

BAKROUSHINE, Y. A., *A. A. Gorsky* (Moscow, 1946).
BEAUMONT, C. W., *The Diaghilev Ballet in London* (London, Putnam, 1944).
BENOIS, ALEXANDRE, *Reminiscences of the Russian Ballet* (London, Putnam, 1941).
BORISOGLEVSKY, Y., *Materials for a History of Russian Ballet*, 2 vols. (in Russian) (Leningrad, 1938).
GRIGORIEV, S. L., *The Diaghilev Ballet* (London, Constable, 1953).
HASKELL, ARNOLD H., *Diaghilev* (London, Gollancz, 1935).
LIEVEN, PRINCE PETER, *The Birth of Ballets Russes* (London, Allen & Unwin, 1936).
LIFAR, SERGE, *Diaghilev* (London, Putnam, 1940).
SLONIMSKY, YURI OSSIPOVITCH, *The Bolshoi Theatre Ballet* (Moscow, 1956).
ZAKHAROV, ROTISLAV, *The Art of the Ballet Master* (in Russian) (Moscow, 1948).

CHAPTER 8

The Search for Expression: II

He needs above all to possess the power of selection and the power of adaptation.
(SIR ALBERT RICHARDSON on the origins of an artist's work in a BBC Radio talk)

IT has sometimes been said that if there had been no Fokine the Diaghilev ballet would never have come into being. Whether that statement is true no longer matters. What it is more pertinent to ask is: if there had been no Diaghilev would some other far-seeing impresario have recognized Fokine's choregraphic genius and have given him the same opportunities to work with equally great artists and composers of his own generation and enthusiasm, in order to develop the composite art of ballet that Fokine himself envisaged? The fact that no less than seven of Fokine's ballets, created during the first three years' existence of that company, still continue to be revived by one or another organization is sufficient proof that the Diaghilev-Fokine period was the most fruitful (*see* page 94).

MIKHAIL FOKINE (1880–1942)

Mikhail Fokine graduated from the Imperial St. Petersburg School as a second soloist in 1898, where his many-sided talent had been recognized from his first year as a student. Amongst his many teachers were Karsavin, Legat, Volkov, Johannson, Petipa, Gerdt, Ivanov and Cecchetti, from whom he gained his vast knowledge of both the principles and vocabulary of classical, romantic, *demi-caractère* and character dance. Throughout his school years he continued to occupy first place at the yearly examinations in dance, mime, music and drawing. In addition, he was extremely interested in reading everything he could obtain in Russian and foreign literature, and the histories of the theatre and art. He spent much of his free time in the museums, the Hermitage and other art galleries, where he copied the old and new masters, and made copious notes upon historical and stylistic details of movement, costume, furniture, scenery and the like. In this way he educated himself for his future career as choregrapher.

THE CLASS-ROOM AS A LABORATORY

In 1901 Fokine was appointed teacher of the senior girls and immediately turned his class-room into a laboratory where he could create, like Didelot (*see* page 48), that type of dancer he required for his particular choregraphic styles, which he began to practise in the form of exercises.

He demanded from his dancers, intelligent understanding and powers of interpretation with a sensitive feeling for the music, and although this was comparatively easy for his students, because these elements are the essence of Russian folk song and dance, he would explain all that he required. His dancers were thus able to understand how and why they were to create portraits for themselves, once he had guided them into his lines of dance.

Gorshkova, who worked in Fokine's first classes has written—

> To work with him was to work with an artist and was a great joy. He was an extremely gifted man with a rich imagination both musical and rhythmic. He loved serious music. All his movements were punctiliously linked to that music. Sometimes the movements of the arm, foot or head responded precisely to the call of the note and not merely the phrasing. Having accustomed oneself to his methods of work, it was very difficult to work with others. He strictly demanded the holding of a picture—the maintenance of a style. For lack of style he was ready to bite one's head off.

FOKINE'S FIRST MANIFESTO, 1904

Fokine's brilliant successes as a second soloist in many varied roles led to his promotion to the front rank in 1904, the year in which he first approached the Director of the Imperial Theatres with the libretto of a ballet he wished to stage. This work, *Daphnis and Chloe*, was rejected because the choregraphic ideas it contained were considered too revolutionary by the Director, Teliakovsky. Nevertheless these ideas were of such importance to Fokine's future development that they must be viewed in historical perspective. Some time before Isadora Duncan set foot in Russia, it will be found that Fokine's calls for the reform of the stereotyped, conventional formulas of Imperial ballet had already been voiced. But although Duncanism undoubtedly had some influence, it did not play a large part in Fokine's development. He believed: "That there could only be evolution and not revolution in art," and realized that without a firm technique and discipline, there "would only be anarchy. Every art must have its rules and whoever wishes to develop and further his ideas, must dare to dispense with the conventions which grow up round the basic principles of that art."

Fokine's ideas were stated in the preface to his libretto for *Daphnis and Chloe* and were further enlarged upon in conversations (with the late Edwin Evans and J. L.)—

> I believe that dance should interpret meaning and should not degenerate into mere gymnastics. Dance

should explain the spirit of the actors and their emotions, characters and lives as they live them on the stage, in the time allowed. More than that, Dance should be given sufficient details so that it expresses the whole epoch to which the subject of the plot belongs. For such interpretative dancing the music must be equally inspired, it will then underline the dance and its emotional content, create atmosphere and vital rhythm. In place of the old-time valses, polkas, *pizzicatos* and galops, a form of music must be created which expresses the same emotion as that which inspires the dancers. The ballet must no longer be made up of numbers, *entreés* and so on. It must show unity of conception and continuity of action. The action of the ballet must never be interrupted to allow the *danseuse* to respond to the applause. I do not wish to sacrifice ballet, which is a valuable artistic entity, to be the victim of the executante. . . . In the ballet every artist is important, every movement, every pose seen on the stage. Only thus will a genuine plastic symphony be obtained.

In place of the traditional dualism of mime and dance, the ballet must have complete unity, which is made up of a harmonious blending of the three elements, music, painting and plastic art.

Later Fokine added a great deal to these preliminary remarks in an article written about his work in which he ridiculed the Imperial ballet routine, particularly its conventional gestures (quoted by Sollertinsky in *The History of the Soviet Theatre* 1933)—

Ballet has renounced expressive gesture, therefore its dancers have become expressionless, acrobatic, mechanical and empty. In order that dance should regain its spiritual form and qualities, it is essential that the gestures should rise from it, but these must be built on the laws of natural expressiveness . . . I am asked: How can dance always be based on gestures? . . . Undoubtedly an *arabesque* has many meanings, but only when it appears as an idealized gesture. It is a very apparent gesture (in *Les Sylphides*), a yearning for height, for distance, an inclination of the whole body, a movement of the entire being. If there is not this feeling, if there is not this expression, if it is only "a raising of the leg," then the *arabesque* becomes intolerable nonsense.

Another mistake of ballet technique is this. It prepares the legs for the dance, where it should be the whole body that dances. Everything down to the last muscle must be expressive, be eloquent.

Fokine enlarged upon this last paragraph in order to propound his theories on the significance of the *ports de bras* as a vital means of communicating thoughts, ideas, emotions, moods and actions to the audience. He had been greatly impressed by the vivid *Speech in Dance* of the Siamese dancers ("The Ballet of the Hands"), who visited St. Petersburg early in 1905, where he saw it was impossible entirely to reject the conventional gesture, which was initially based on natural movement, but which had become stylized through long years of use on the stage. What Fokine felt he must do was to return to these natural expressive movements and ensure that his dancers performed them with genuine sincerity and feeling.

FOKINE'S THREE TYPES OF BALLET

THE CLASSICO-ROMANTIC BALLETS

Fokine made his debut as choregrapher in the same year that the Siamese dancers and Isadora Duncan visited St. Petersburg (1905) when he staged a mythological ballet, *Acis and Galatea*, for his students' graduation performance. In this he had wished the dancers to perform barefooted, but had to reject the idea on orders from the Director. (His first bare-footed dancers appeared in *Une Nuit d'Egypte*.) Amongst those dancing were the fourteen-year-old Lydia Lopokova (Amour), her brother Feodor (later an important Soviet choregrapher and pedagogue), the fifteen-year-old Vaslav Nijinsky, Oblakov and others, who later joined the Diaghilev company.

This work was immediately recognized by discerning critics as "a different work of art," both in quality and the content of the dance design, and its success strengthened Fokine's belief that only by concentrating upon choregraphic work would he bring about his desired reforms. This was not easy. The powerfully conservative elements within the Imperial Theatres and school looked upon his experiments with disapproving and suspicious eyes. They felt, that despite assurances to the contrary, he was out to destroy their carefully preserved traditions and discipline. He, with others, had been involved in the strike of theatre-workers during the 1905 Revolution.

Nevertheless, despite their hostility, the Directorate were forced to recognize his outstanding talent and from time to time grudgingly allowed him to produce a short work, either for the students, or for the Imperial stages, where he usually had to make do with costumes, scenery and props borrowed from other ballets. In addition, other influential persons saw that he was engaged to stage ballets and dances at balls and charity performances, and here again, he was seldom allowed specially composed music or designed costumes and décor. Yet it was possibly because Fokine originally had to produce ballets under such difficult circumstances that he developed into a choregrapher of distinct purpose, expressive movement and beautifully formed economical style. Lacking material aids he was forced to examine again and again the wealth of dance he had inherited from his famous teachers and the vividly expressive dancers, who were now entirely Russian, and many of them of his own teaching.

On 6th April, 1908, the students from Fokine's first graduation class were ready and he entirely restaged for them a ballet, *Chopiniana*, which he had first produced at a charity concert in memory of Chopin (10th November, 1907). The idea had been suggested by a suite of that composer's music orchestrated by Glazunov, and Fokine's original libretto was intended to show not only the composer's wide range of subject, but also something of his national feelings and the more poetic muse inspiring his compositions. But in re-editing the ballet for his students, Fokine eliminated the richly costumed Mazurka, Polonaise and Tarantella danced in national style, and concentrated on that part of his choregraphy through which he tried to personify Chopin's Muse as a romantic sylph-like figure (originally danced by Anna Pavlova). By so doing Fokine wished to demonstrate his new style of classical dance, which was expressive in line and content. But the sylph-like figure was also intended to conjure up more than the romantic figure of

Chopin's music by characterizing her as a figure from Romantic ballet. The Muse was intended to describe, in the tangible form of dance, something of the structure, melody and rhythm of the music itself, in somewhat the same way that Ivanov had done in his interpretation of Tchaikovsky's *Swan Lake* (*see* page 87).

The Structure of Chopiniana (Les Sylphides)

The choregraphy of *Chopiniana*, which was renamed *Les Sylphides* by Diaghilev when he included it in the repertoire of his first Russian ballet season in Paris (1909), was firmly based on classical principles. In it Fokine insisted that the dancers performed according to strict academic principles from the waist downwards, but from the waist upwards they had to be free to express themselves through arms, head and body within the emotional range of movement envisaged by the choregraphers of Romantic ballet, Taglioni and Perrot, and in absolute accord with the quality, phrasing and content of the music. Because Fokine had been gradually developing this style in his classroom, his dancers were ready to meet both the technical and musical problems he posed within each of the seven dances comprising the ballet.

Each dance has a slightly different content to conform to its music, nevertheless, the ballet finds unity in its leitmotive, the *arabesque*. It is that pose to, through, and from which every dancer must draw the lines they make, and despite the fact that the entire cast are involved as dancers only in the opening and closing items, the stage always appears to be filled with movement because the *arabesque* is the focal point of every picture painted by the dancers within the framework of their colleagues' encircling groupings. This gives the ballet its continuity and, it might be said, its development of action.

The content of each dance was summarized by Fokine in a conversation (with the late Edwin Evans and J. L.)—

Nocturne (op. 32, no. 2)

> This has a similar structure to Ivanov's Love duet in *Swan Lake* [*see* page 87], where the *corps de ballet* echo the movements of the soloists. But I try to bring out more clearly the relationship of my three soloists to the melody and that of the *corps de ballet* to the accompaniment. The latter mark the rhythmic beat whilst the principals are drawing their line of dance to the melody and harmonizing its rise and fall with the rise and fall of their movements. This rise and fall can be called "the breath of the dance." It is a very subtle movement and must harmonize exactly with the pulse of the music even though the entire ensemble hardly seem to dance.

Valse (op. 70, no. 1)

> I set my soloist four tasks. Firstly she has to mark the rhythmic beat of a valse. This means that in roughly every other bar she dances either some valse step, or steps with three changes of weight; or else marks the three beats by gradually lowering her hand (in the third phrase); or beats one foot on the other (at the end of the fourth phrase). This marking of the beat (or pulse) otherwise than by the feet is a particular

feature of some Russian folk dances which I utilized in order to make my classical dance seem more rhythmically sensitive.

Secondly, the dancer's movements follow the pattern of the melody. As the music soars up and down in an arpeggio and is then held on a high note during the first phrase, so the soloist soars upwards in a *grand jeté en avant*, momentarily holds herself in the air, falls into a valse step then, as the note is held, poses in an *arabesque*. Something similar happens in the second phrase where, instead of marking the beat with a valse step, she springs three times, each time lowering the leg very slightly to match the descending notes to which these *jetés* are danced. In the third phrase, the soloist not only marks the beats but also the descending notes with the lowering of her hand. During the fifth phrase she swings up and down with the lilt of the melody, turns in *attitude* as a high note is held, then she "embroiders" round her high note by making a circle round that same spot *sur les pointes* before crossing the stage to the opposite side with a long held *arabesque*.

Thirdly I allow the formal musical structure to dictate the choregraphic pattern. The first musical phrase of sixteen bars is repeated, so the second four short dance phrases are also a repeat of the first four movements. But because Glazunov made some slight changes in his orchestration of the repeat, I make slight changes in my choregraphy. For example, the *grand jeté en avant* of the first passage becomes a *grand jeté entrelacé*. The third, and first eight bars of the fourth musical phrase state new ideas, so does the dancer, but the last eight bars of the latter restate the third phrase and the dancer similarly repeats her long *arabesque*. But instead of dropping her front hand gradually to the descending notes, she presses both hands softly outwards, as if she were calling her fellow sylphs to the dance. The final phrase is a repeat of the last two bars during which the dancer turns and disappears from sight. This slight variation in the last two bars of a phrase I have noted throughout. The valse is made up of short four-bar phrases merging into each other, with an imperfect cadence at the end of each sixteen bars. The dancer is guided by these links in the musical continuity and usually repeats her *enchaînements* three times, but the fourth time she does not make a perfect repeat because she has to draw her line into a preparation for the next phrase and in the last *enchaînement* prepare the way for the next dancer.

Fourthly, I allow the musical structure to determine the floor pattern so that the circling of a valse is continually being made visible as the dancer circles the stage, or turns in her *grands jetés entrelacés, pirouettes* and other steps.

Fokine here suggested that during the third phrase "the dancer is stringing beads," because wherever she turned in her *grands jetés entrelacés* during her second *enchaînement*, she has to rise to her toes before moving forwards along the same diagonal line in her *arabesque* to the next pivotal centre.

The Girl's Mazurka (op. 33, no. 3)

In this soaring dance my intention is to convey the subtly characteristic feature of this Polish dance through the classical medium, but instead of marking the second beat of each bar with a strong accent on the heel, as in the native folk dance, I want my dancer to press upwards on her toes into an *arabesque* and hold this picture during some of her *enchaînements*. This is to emphasize her gossamer lightness as do the *grands jetés en avant* where she has to hold herself in the air like the dancer in the valse. But the timing of these leaps is different in order to distinguish valse from mazurka.

An interesting feature of the mazurka is the way in which the *corps de ballet* seem to trace the soloist's flight through the air after she has disappeared from sight and then call her back to repeat her flight before they enclose her dance within their outstretched arms.

The Man's Mazurka (op. 67, no. 3)

> I again want to mark the subtle accent of the native dance, but the movements of the *danseur* are based on some of the traditional steps, seen as it were, as ghosts of themselves. I give them that slightly downwards pressure on the second beat so that I can define the essential difference between the male and female classical dancers upon which I always insist. This does not mean that the man's movements are heavy, but that they have greater strength and characterization, even though the male figure has no basis in reality.

When Fokine was asked about the significance of the male figure, he replied—

> My ballet is a romantic reverie, an idea to summon before you the spirit of that era; perhaps he represents the masculine Muse who made Chopin's music possible. Perhaps he is the spirit of a poet from whose words the dances of the sylphs were born. Perhaps he is Love himself in a romantic, nostalgic mood. I do not know. I made it for a *danseur*, who can soar like a spirit, but who has the strength to dance with the wilis, and live, to dance again.

Prelude (op. 28, no. 7)

Fokine said about this most difficult dance—

> Please listen to the music, let it tell you what to do. Let it carry you in its arms.

That is exactly what he desired his dancer to do. She has to listen to the call of the note and when she has heard it, respond by movement, as if echoing its sound. That is—

> She appears to listen with her whole being to catch the melody and softly follows, wherever it may lead her. It is for this reason that she delicately suggests through her arm movements the conventional gestures of "listen" and "silence," just as other gestures flow through the *ports de bras* of the other dancers. These movements are only suggestions. My dancers must speak their innermost thoughts through the expressiveness of their entire being. If they frame something of a conventional gesture, it is because that gesture has become part of the speech of my classical dance style.

Valse (op. 64, no. 2)

In this *pas de deux* Fokine tried to bring out the musical qualities inherent in certain types of movement to parallel the sustained (*sostenuto*) and later more brilliant passages of Chopin's music. He did this by using slowly developing lifts and turns for the more sustained passages and by giving the girl soloist more precise and quicker *relevés* in the brilliant passages. As in the other dances the choregraphic patterns follow that of the musical structure and phrases.

Valse (op. 18, no. 1)

The ballet ends as it began with the ensemble dancing together. Sometimes the *corps de ballet* fill the stage with their valse-like steps, at others they mark "the breath of the dance" as a soloist answers the call of the notes; or else they freeze into some picture whilst a single dancer fills the framework of which they are a part. Finally everyone melts into that same picture with which the ballet began as if to stress that it is Fokine's reverie of "those spirits whose dance lives ever in the memory of those who love Chopin's music."

Some Other Classico-romantic Ballets

The expressive quality of Fokine's dance in his second version of *Chopiniana* owed much to his work on the revised and shortened version of *Le Pavilion d'Armide*, which he produced for the Marinsky (25th November, 1907). The libretto of this ballet was the work of the artist, Alexander Benois, and was based on Théophile Gautier's story, *Omphale*, about a Marquis who finds a lock of hair and falls in love with its owner. She is depicted on a Gobelin tapestry, which comes to life. This gave the choregrapher his first chance to make use of some of the knowledge he had assimilated during his student days.

Benois had long wanted to create a dramatic ballet through which he could express his love of the baroque and rococo periods. Also, like so many Russian balletomanes, Benois had fallen under the spell of Virginia Zucchi, the Italian *danseuse*, who had shown St. Petersburg audiences and dancers how much more important in the unfolding of the action of a tragic ballet was an artist whose every movement was of vital significance compared with one who relied on balletic conventions and technical virtuosity.

Zucchi, like Sallé (*see* page 31), Perrot (*see* page 64) and other famous dancers came from a company of strolling players and her methods of performance retained that spontaneity of expression which had distinguished the Commedia dell'Arte groups. Her appearances in the park, Livadia, despite their melodramatic nature and their cheap fit-up setting, made many Russian theatre-workers realize how devoid of dramatic action were most of the ballets in the St. Petersburg repertoire. Benois hoped to remedy this deficiency when, after deciding to devote his life to theatrical design, he discussed his ideas of a lavish baroque ballet with the composer Tcherepnine who created a score evocative of the period atmosphere and fantastic situations envisaged by the artist. Benois himself designed the scenery and costumes and, when the work was ultimately presented at the Marinsky, devised the complicated transformation by which the Gobelin tapestry gradually dissolved into the reality in which the Marquis met his beloved.

The finished work was an example of the way in which Fokine always disciplined his choregraphy and his dancers to the plot, even though not of his own choosing. Benois had intended *Le Pavilion d'Armide* to be a three-act ballet and it was so accepted by the Director, but during the artist's absence abroad, the latter had suggested to Fokine that the second act, "The Animated Gobelins", would serve as the central piece in the student's graduation performance. This, with Vaslav Nijinsky dancing as Armide's slave, was a success, and the Director decided to include the entire work in the 1908–9 repertoire, stipulating however that it must be shortened and form only part of a programme. Benois felt that this emasculation of his work would defeat his purpose in presenting a spectacle with dramatic action, evoking the necessary tragic and fantastic atmosphere, particularly as he felt the young choregrapher was too revolutionary in his ideas for dispensing with the conventional gestures, stylized dance and artificialities of behaviour which he knew were essential elements of his plot.

Fokine did not fail. His knowledge of historical dance, gesture and behaviour, and of the Gobelin tapestries, which inspired his groupings and poses, as well as his sensitive handling of the fantastic elements of the Benois plot and Tcherepnine score satisfied not only the critical Benois but also the audience and critics, and delighted all the dancers taking part.

Fokine's choregraphy was not a faithful reconstruction of the past. He realized that what had been legitimate in spectacles danced by amateur courtiers of the period envisaged by Benois, was impossible for professional dancers on a stage having its own conventions. Everything that might have been suitable in the intimate surroundings of a court theatre inside some château or palace, had to be broadened into movements visible to a large audience on the other side of the footlights. Similarly, what had been instinctive gestures and behaviour among the courtiers brought up to such niceties had to become part of the total movement of dancers trained to express themselves through the medium of classical dance and conventional gesture, from which Fokine himself was developing his own particular forms of *plastique.*

Fokine's *plastique* originated in his desire to eliminate the "traditional dualism of mime and/or dance" (*see* page 98) and by 1908 could be listed under two headings: (1) *mimed-dance* in which dance was the major partner, but was fully expressive of the character, and that character's moods and emotions, and (2) *danced-mime*, in which gesture might be said to play the major role in explaining the actions of the characters unfolding the plot, and was at the same time dancing movement, a part of the whole choregraphic line, which never ceased to flow throughout the ballet. In other words, there were no wholly static moments where the dancers acted without dancing, as in older works.

The plastic qualities of Fokine's classico-romantic dance and its dual nature became even clearer when he staged *Carnaval* (1910) for Diaghilev, after first presenting it at a charity performance. Although in it music and dance are as sensitively balanced as they are in *Les Sylphides*, the characters have greater actuality and dance out a more literary theme. They are drawn from the Commedia dell'Arte, but are seen through the eyes of a Romantic poet after the mist of time has dimmed their clear-cut portraits. Moreover they are dancers, not actors, and do not play extempore. They are disciplined by Fokine's choregraphic design, which, in its turn, is disciplined by the changing qualities of Schumann's score. In addition Fokine gave his choregraphic style greater significance by utilizing items drawn from the known facts about his characters. By this time Fokine had realized that once such facts had been placed on record and were available for study, the information gained was of the utmost value in bringing a dancing portrait fully to life. *Carnaval* also emphasized Fokine's belief that the male dancer has equal rights in the dance with the *ballerina*, if he sometimes does not excel, as he did in *Le Spectre de la Rose* (1911), where the soaring flight of Vaslav Nijinsky (the Spirit) was in absolute contrast to the almost *terre à terre* dance of Tamara Karsavina (the Young Girl) except in those moments when she too appeared to take flight, caught upwards by the ecstasy of her dream.

In these and all his later classico-romantic ballets (e.g. *Papillons*, *Les Elfes*, *Paganini*, etc.) Fokine demanded from his dancers as much understanding of classical technique as of the expressive content of his choregraphy. This developed out of the music which he himself usually chose because he felt that particular score expressed the theme he wished to communicate to an audience. In such ballets the décor and costumes were to him the necessary framework creating the atmosphere and background and, as far as possible, revealing the movement.

But Fokine did not confine himself to such ballets. His range of subject and styles of movement were wider than those of any earlier choregrapher. His other ballets can be divided roughly into two groups. The spectacular and the national. These should be considered before his place as the father of most twentieth-century ballet can be fully appreciated.

FOKINE AND THE SPECTACULAR BALLET

Fokine's deliberate selection and adaptation of steps and informative details to make movements appropriate for a specific character emphasized his desire to communicate narrative, descriptive and emotional meaning through dance. This attitude towards choregraphy was of great importance when staging those ballets which could be termed the spectacular and were usually inspired by a literary source having dramatic action. They deployed huge casts and excitingly varied *divertissements*. But they were very different from the old Petipa spectacles because Fokine, realizing the limitations imposed by the plot, exercised the firmest discipline over the mass of dance required and used his great knowledge to portray each character, or group of characters, and their actions in the most economical way possible so that every movement was subordinated to the exigencies of the action.

Une Nuit d'Egypte (1908, later *Cleopatra*) was the first of these spectacular works and was inspired by the pseudo-oriental melodramatic ballets presented by her management to display Zucchi's dramatic mime (*see* page 103). Fokine too had been impressed by her penchant for tragedy and felt his Russian colleagues could be equally expressive if they were given greater scope to act out their roles in dance movement. The ballet showed another facet of Fokine's erudition and ability to handle materials from diverse sources yet to discipline them in such a way that they were one with their subject—the fabulous court of the great Queen Cleopatra. Each group of slaves therein, Greeks, Jews, Syrians and Egyptians, had their own style of dance based on ancient pictorial and other evidence but each dance was only allowed sufficient time to establish the tiny part it played in the drama to be enacted, Cleopatra's seduction of one of her slaves, his subsequent death and his own beloved's despair. But the highly coloured melodramatic elements of the action only attained their full effect when *Cleopatra* was staged by Diaghilev (Paris, 1909) with firstly, superb décor and costumes by Bakst (in the Marinsky production Fokine had been allowed a few of Bakst's costumes, everything else was borrowed from *The Daughter of Pharaoh*, *Aida* and other productions) and secondly, after Benois with his unfailing instinct for the purely "theatrical" aspect of a ballet had suggested and obtained the two famous *coups du théâtre*. These were the gradual unveiling of Cleopatra after her entrance in a sarcophagus, which immediately drew attention to the fatal beauty of the Queen, and, in terms of a mad bacchanale, the weaving of the rosy silken tent in which Cleopatra enticed her infatuated slave for his single night of love.

Bakst and Benois also provided the rich décor and costumes, and superbly dramatic climax to Fokine's other early spectacle, *Scheherazade* (Paris, 4th June, 1910). In this ballet Fokine again broke away from classical dance as he had in *Cleopatra*, using instead his own adaptation of Eastern Russian and Caucasian dance, but using them with a far greater voluptuousness than in "The Polovtsian Dances" of *Prince Igor* (1909), his first venture into this barbarically expressive medium. The lyrically flowing *ports de bras* and sinuous body movements of the women of the harem contrasted with the almost primitive leaps and behaviour of the men slaves were in accord with the melodramatic content of the libretto, again with its magnificent *coup du théâtre* at the climax of the drama. The Queen's own lover, the Golden Slave, was killed and fell from the top of the staircase on to the silken cushions at her feet, another masterly idea of Benois.

Although Fokine's choregraphy in these early spectacles contained new styles of movements and their own dramatic expressiveness, the contributions made by Benois and Bakst were of greater importance to the history of ballet. These artists proved beyond any doubt that if a short dramatic ballet were to make its effect, then every element in that ballet must make an immediate impression on its audience, catching their attention and arousing their interest in the setting which forms the framework of the action. It was the choregrapher's task then not only to maintain their interest by creating appropriate movements for his dancers which would not only express the lives, moods and emotions of his characters as they lived them in the drama to be unfolded, but also to create choregraphic sequences of danced-mime and mimed-dance which would give logical continuity to the action and a proper development of the plot from the beginning to climax and end.

Neither *Scheherazade*, *Cleopatra* nor other spectacular Fokine ballets have fully stood the test of time despite their occasional revival. This may be due to inadequate preparation, both mental and physical, of the dancers involved. It may be due to a failure to recognize that what to one generation was an overwhelming experience of voluptuous dance and drama, light and colour, is to another generation, brought up on Technicolor films and extravagant musicals, only old-fashioned "ham" orientalism. Or perhaps, as with Vigano's dramatic melodramas (*see* page 51), and Petipa's classics (*see* page 74), it is due to a lack of proper score. *Cleopatra* was based on music by no less than five composers, and *Scheherazade* to a cut and adapted version of Rimsky-Korsakov's symphonic poem, which was descriptive of several tales in *The Arabian Nights*, and perhaps did not fit the libretto with complete conviction. The continued existence of Fokine's three great national ballets, "The Polovtsian Dances" of *Prince Igor*, *The Firebird* and *Petrushka* would seem to prove that only by allowing the composer to play an equal part with artist, librettist and choregrapher can a ballet be assured of some lasting existence.

FOKINE AND THE POLOVTSIAN DANCES FROM PRINCE IGOR

Disappointed of certain financial support Diaghilev was compelled to change his ideas for producing three complete Russian operas and three short ballets during his 1909 season which was to follow the phenomenal success of *Boris Godunov* in Paris of 1908. Instead he produced three ballets (*Les Sylphides*, *Le Pavilion d'Armide* and *Cleopatra*) and a series of *divertissements* called *Le Festin*, Rimsky-Korsakov's opera *Ivan the Terrible*, the second act of Glinka's *Russlan and Ludmilla* and the second act of Borodin's *Prince Igor*. He felt the latter might arouse the same enthusiasm that was engendered in St. Petersburg when it was first presented, but fearing that Ivanov's choregraphy was too formally ordered for the setting proposed by Roerich, an impressionistic setting of the Polovtsian Camp at night, he invited Fokine to devise new choregraphy.

The result was startling. The barbaric vitality and spontaneous expressiveness of Fokine's "Polovtsian Dances" took Paris by storm. Their success eclipsed even that of Chaliapin and other Moscow singers and chorus. The reason for this success lay not only in the completely uninhibited dancing of the cast, but also in the brilliant way in which Fokine orchestrated his choregraphy. He built it into a great contest of dance by contrasting one type of movement with another and allowing no dance a conclusion until the finale. The ballet thus appeared as a whole, and not a series of *divertissements*.

Fokine had studied some part of Caucasian and East Russian dance, and managed to transfer the three vital elements contained therein to the stage: its spontaneity, passion and proud freedom, disciplining this apparently unmanageable material so that it could be contained within the stage setting. He achieved this organization of primitive, traditional dance firstly by allowing each movement to grow directly from the musical context, secondly, by distinguishing clearly between the unwilling dance of the Persian slaves and the exhilarating spacious leaping of their captors and thirdly by defining clearly the supposedly different ages of his cast. By so doing he was able to create four types of dance-movement within a single style. This gave his ballet not only a great variety of characterization, but also orchestration in movement. This rose to a tremendous climax when all the dancers and singers came together for Borodin's resounding finale.

It was with these barbaric, primitive Warriors that Fokine restored the male dancers to their rightful place as an equal star with the *ballerina.* Nothing like their dancing had been seen in Western European ballet before. It bore no relationship to the virtuoso technicalities of the great eighteenth-century French masters. It stemmed from no academically nurtured classical school. As Benois says in his *Reminiscences*—

> Our wild Russian primitiveness, our simplicity and naïveté had proved to be more elaborate and more refined than all that was being created in Paris, that most cultured of cities.

THE FIREBIRD, PETRUSHKA, AND STRAVINSKY

The huge success of "The Polovtsian Dances" did not completely satisfy Diaghilev. It did not stretch his dancers' powers of dramatic interpretation to their fullest. This was the next task. For a long time Fokine had wished to create a purely Russian ballet and with the help of Serge Grigoriev (Diaghilev's famous *régisseur*), finally completed a libretto, *The Firebird.* It was based on several characters from favourite Russian fairy-tales and showed how the most beautiful Princess of all and her friends were rescued from the power of the evil Koschei by the simple Tsarevich. He had captured the immortal Firebird, but had given her freedom in return for a magic feather with which to summon her whenever he was in need.

The libretto was approved and Diaghilev first invited Tcherepnine and then Liadov to compose the music, but on their failure to complete the work, entrusted it to Igor Stravinsky then coming to the fore as a composer. There is no doubt that Stravinsky's music was the vital spark bringing *The Firebird* to life as a purely Russian ballet in the same sense as did his later score for *Petrushka* (1911). It was with these two works that Stravinsky also proved the need of every ballet based on a dramatic plot to be reinforced by music having absolute continuity and development of form and context in accord with the action, instead of being a score which linked the episodes by a series of leitmotives as initiated by Adam (*see* page 63). Each phrase of Stravinsky's music was part of the total conception of the action and was developed from particular elements inherent in the Russian folk music which forms its basis. Moreover Stravinsky, like other Russian composers, restored a vital energy and emotional context to dance on the stage by using traditional tunes and their underlying potent rhythms. This enabled both choregrapher and dancers to dance themselves and the action onwards with more realistic force.

The action of *The Firebird* develops from a conflict between good and evil immortals

(The Firebird and the Koschei) as well as between a mortal and an immortal (the Tsarevich and the Firebird). This conflict is only resolved when both mortal and immortal join forces to conquer evil. The conflict is marked by both dance and music.

Grigoriev writes of how Fokine worked with the composer, mapping out the movements and gestures, their rhythms, phrasings and action as Stravinsky sat playing, thus music and dance grew together. Fokine saw his mortals, the beautiful Princess and her friends as Boyar maidens at the court of some Tsar, dancing their dignified *Khorovods*, which were refined versions of peasant girl dances. He also saw the Tsarevich in somewhat similar terms. But the latter's crude behaviour (which distressed the sophisticated and orderly-minded Benois) stressed the prosaic nature of that favourite Russian character, the youngest son, usually considered the fool of the family until he wins all. The male servants of the Koschei were also drawn in terms of folk dance, made grotesque and heavy to stress their evil quality. The Firebird alone, as if to emphasize her immortality, danced classically *sur les pointes*, soaring, darting and leaping through the trees or posing momentarily like a painted, magical bird seen on some icon.

The conflict between good and evil, mortal and immortal, and the contrast between traditional and classical dance written into his choregraphy by Fokine gave Stravinsky a key to his music. He painted the mortals in diatonic folk tunes (e.g. the Tsarevich and Princess dance to a melody, "In the Garden," from Nijni-Novgorod, and the finale is a hymn "By the Gate") or to tunes having the same typical melodic features (e.g. "The Princesses play with the golden apples" was composed by Stravinsky, but it is sometimes thought to be traditional). From these melodies he drew certain motifs based on the intervals of the augmented and falling fourth (typical cadences of Russian folk music), and organized them into short series of ascending chromatic chords to form the themes for the Firebird. These same series of chords and others derived from them, sometimes played in a descending order, were used for the dances of the evil characters. Then, at the culminating points of the action (the conflict between the Tsarevich and the Firebird, his meeting with the Koschei, the Firebird's Lullaby and the Finale), Stravinsky fused both traditional and original musical phrases together. Thus score and choregraphy spoke the same language and were reinforced by décor and costumes derived from similar traditional sources by the artist, Golovin. (These were lost in 1922 and replaced by designs of a similar nature by Natalie Goncharova.) *The Firebird* thus lived within an atmosphere of fantastic realism created by choregrapher, composer and artist.

Petrushka has often been called the most perfect of all the Diaghilev ballets, perhaps because Benois, in his libretto, allowed the action to develop in such a way that fantasy could be seen to develop out of reality and culminate in the tragedy continually recurring in the history of the popular theatre. He wrote a Russian version of "He Who Gets Slapped," known elsewhere as the English Punch, the French Pierrot, the German Kasperlé and their Czech and other European counterparts. It was, therefore, of universal appeal because it told a human story in an imaginative fashion.

The creation of *Petrushka* occurred almost accidentally. After the success of *The Firebird* Stravinsky began to compose a ritual dance on symphonic lines which Diaghilev suggested might form a ballet (later known as *The Rite of Spring*). But when he inquired about its progress, he was faced with an entirely new work. Stravinsky had felt the need of experimenting further with the motifs created for *The Firebird* (*see* page 109) and the bitonal effects of the superimposed chords of C and F sharp major. He moulded from the latter a piece in which he imagined the piano being browbeaten by the orchestra and, remembering the favourite Russian puppet, Petrushka, called his composition "Petrushka's Cry." Inspired with the idea of describing the "poor, funny, sentimental creature constantly shaken with rebellious rage," he then visualized a poem of the mysterious life of Petrushka, half-puppet, half-human and composed a companion piece "Danse Russe."

Diaghilev was interested and wrote to Benois enthusiastically begging him to help Stravinsky create a ballet which they felt might incorporate a representation of the Shrovetide Carnival and a performance of *Petrushka.* Benois became excited. He had already tried to revive interest in these traditional puppets by staging some original performances at the St. Petersburg Arts Club. They had not been successful because the heads of real actors appearing above a curtain, co-ordinated with wooden legs dancing over the edge of the show-booth, looked more pitiful than funny. Hearing Stravinsky's music, he realized how the pathos of the puppet theatre could be expressed by dancers. They would appear as dolls, given life by a magician without losing their dolls' nature, and their triangular drama would be enacted at the St. Petersburg Shrovetide Fair. In this way Benois evolved the four scenes of his ballet, the first and last taking place amongst the nineteenth-century crowd at the Fair on the frozen Neva, and the others in the fantastic rooms of Petrushka and the Blackamoor in a show-booth, the apparently temporary structure of which allowed the action complete continuity.

Stravinsky brought this fascinating vision of reality and fantasy to life as he did in *The Firebird*, by interweaving two threads of musical idiom. For the former he used Russian folk tunes (e.g. the Nursemaids dance to "Down the Peterskoye" and "Oh my room, my little room," and the coachmen to "I was going up a hill") as well as popular songs and cries (e.g. one street dancer moves to a French music-hall ditty and the *Ballerina* to a valse from Joseph Lanner). But for the world of fantasy he created music based on the juxtaposition of bitonal intervals kept an augmented fourth apart and drawn from "Petrushka's Cry," which form and emphasized the tragic puppet's emotions when dancing in his room. These two different melodic strands were linked by the incessant throbbing noise of the Fair growing and diminishing as the action moved from reality to fantasy and back again. It was the persistent pulse of the drum beats symbolizing the Fairground which led the action to its tragic climax, Petrushka's death. Then they were silenced. But Petrushka lived on and suddenly appeared on the roof of the show-booth and made yet another strange, appealing, seemingly unfinished cry. This was another example of Benois' flair for the unusual *coup du théâtre*.

Fokine designed his choregraphy to harmonize with Stravinsky's score, shaping the movements of his characters so that the nursemaids, coachmen and grooms break into traditional dance at the sound of a familiar tune, and give way to the fantastic dolls as soon as they appear. These latter are fully characterized in unusual form (for their time, 1911). The *Ballerina* is a heartless jointed creature, possibly made of wax, using two expressions only, self-satisfaction and shocked surprise. The Moor, a primitive wooden figure, worships a coconut when he finds it is stronger than himself, and can only express his love for the *Ballerina* by trying to eat her. The Charlatan is the thread linking reality with fantasy, for it is his magic tune that quietens the crowds and brings his puppets to life, and this shows his power. But to see him chatting among the people and then his bewilderment when Petrushka makes his mysterious cry is to understand his human weakness. There are many other characters, the Merchant, gipsies, pedlars and the rest which Fokine defined by detailed movements based on his observation of the real people attending the Shrovetide Fair.

Fokine's masterpiece of choregraphy is however that for the puppet, Petrushka, created for Diaghilev's greatest dancer, Vaslav Nijinsky. Despite the fact that this puppet seems to be a two-dimensional figure pulled on strings with little depth or height to his dance, beneath the rags and sawdust beats a heart. His eyes speak volumes, his pathetic attempts to make his limbs express his love, joy, sorrow, and rage are those of a human being frustrated by his inability to communicate his thoughts to others. It was this problem of communicating untold emotions and ideas through dance-movement alone that had faced all earlier choregraphers. Fokine was the first fully to succeed in solving it in *Petrushka* and his other ballets.

It is for this reason that so much space has been given to Fokine in this book. He was the first choregrapher consciously to determine the dance style and infinite details of movement he needed to expose and express the action of each ballet. Through that style he created the atmosphere, established the characters and described their emotions, moods and actions. He was also the first to concentrate on the short ballet, a form forced upon him by the circumstances under which the Diaghilev company worked. Until his time, the long three- or four-act ballet had been the fashion. These could be likened to a novel in which the choregrapher could pad out the main theme with other events and incidents giving rise to *variations* and *divertissements* which might, or might not, throw some light upon the story. Fokine showed that the short ballet allows no such choregraphic freedom. In such a work it is only permissible to develop one line of action, staging only those incidents or events which throw some light on a single focal point. It is like a short story, and demands a disciplining of the essential details to disclose its meaning.

But this disciplining of choregraphic design is not so limiting as it may seem. Once Fokine broke away from Petipa's classical formulas he allowed the ballet to develop in many ways. He should be considered as the father of the twentieth-century ballet whenever a choregrapher uses a basis of academic, classical formulas for his dance design. Perhaps choregraphers in other mediums also owe something to his example, because from his rejection of classical dance, particularly *sur les pointes*, in *Narcisse* (1911) and other earlier Greek dances in ballets such as *Acis and Galatea* (1905), and "The Polovtsian Dances" from *Prince Igor*, and *Thamar*, and his creation of the strange two-dimensional, yet passionately expressive figure of Petrushka, he showed the great classical dancer of the Diaghilev company, Nijinsky, how to develop an entirely new choregraphic style. This style was to inspire such dancers as Mary Wigman, Rudolph von Laban, Kurt Jooss and other pioneers of that dance movement, now called Modern Dance.

FURTHER READING

BEAUMONT, C. W., (with SITWELL, S.), *Romantic Ballet* (London, Faber & Faber, 1937).
BORISOGLEVSKY, Y., *Materials for a History of Russian Ballet*, 2 vols. (in Russian) (Leningrad, 1938).
FOKINE, MIKHAIL, *Manifesto to "Daphnis and Chloe"* (1904).
FOKINE, MIKHAIL, *Conversations with Edwin Evans* 1923–4.
SLONIMSKY, YURI OSSIPOVITCH, *Masters of the Ballet* (Moscow, 1937).
SOLLERTINSKY, S., *The History of the Soviet Theatre* (in Russian) (Moscow, 1935).

CHAPTER 9

The Search for Expression: III
Diaghilev's Other Choregraphers

The content of the plot should determine the style of the dance.
(FOKINE)

DESPITE the fact that Fokine's unique choregraphic works were the main factor inspiring Diaghilev to show Russian ballet to Europe, the partnership could not be of long duration. Firstly this was due to the fact that Diaghilev was by nature an originator. Ever since his first Exhibition (*see* page 94) he had continued to show his flair for discovering works of art and talent, and directing these towards some definite goal. He could not do this with Fokine, who had planned his own choregraphic path before Diaghilev came on the scene. Secondly, as soon as Diaghilev placed his company on a permanent footing, he realized that, no matter how brilliant a choregrapher Fokine might be, he could not continue to provide all the works required for the new type of programme which had arisen through the creation of the short ballet. In one evening Diaghilev could show three different aspects of Fokine's genius, the classically romantic *Les Sylphides* or *Carnaval*, the spectacular *Cleopatra* or *Scheherazade*, or the nationally dramatic *The Firebird* or *Petrushka*. For Fokine to maintain the high standard of these early works was impossible, and Diaghilev, feeling no other progressively-minded choregraphers existed, decided to educate for himself those whom he could perhaps influence and in whose work he could play an active part in the actual dance design.

VASLAV NIJINSKY AND A NEW STYLE IN MOVEMENT (1890–1950)

Diaghilev's first choice fell on Nijinsky, whose ballet *L'Après-midi d'un Faune* (1912) was staged after he had gone through an educational process of visiting art galleries, museums, concerts, and meeting artists. It was an extraordinary work to come from the great classical dancer of the company. However, it seems that the inspiration for its suggestive primitiveness came from Diaghilev and Bakst. They had been on holiday in the Aegean Islands and were enthusiastic about the archaic works of art seen there. They felt they wanted to create from this strangely moving material something more primitive, more static and more pictorially effective than the lyrically flowing Greek-style dances, that Fokine had created for such works as *Narcisse* (1911) and was creating for the projected *Daphnis and Chloe* (1912) with its score specially composed by Ravel. (Nijinsky appeared in all these works.) In addition, Diaghilev had been impressed by the work of Jacques Dalcroze on the relationship between movement and music. He took Nijinsky to watch the Dalcroze students at Hellerau (*see* page 137) using the content of the music to discipline the patterns they made in movement without using anything but the simplest technical formulas, and without allowing their movements to be coloured by emotion or mood. The physical patterns made had to express the music itself without any literary connotation. Something of the Dalcroze patterning crept into Nijinsky's choregraphy.

Debussy had been inspired to compose his tone-poem *L'Après-midi d'un Faune* after reading Mallarmé's poem of the same title. Diaghilev chose this evocative music as the base for the proposed ballet as it created both the mood and atmosphere conjured up by Bakst in his sketches of the real Greece, which both producer and artist had experienced together, and which were to inspire the set and costumes.

Much has been written about the secrecy of the rehearsals for *L'Après-midi d'un Faune* and the difficulty of understanding what Nijinsky wanted from the dancers; the movements were so foreign to their technique. Both Diaghilev and Bakst saw Greek dance in the flat, as depicted on a frieze or a vase, therefore Nijinsky wanted them to move across the breadth of the stage with their unturned-out feet and legs working in perfectly straight lines forwards or backwards. But their bodies faced the audience and their arms only moved from straight to angular positions. The whole gave a two-dimensional effect. Another difficulty was to ally this strange configuration of geometrical movement with the music. It seems that Nijinsky had no musical knowledge and used the score merely as a background and this, to dancers used to working with Fokine and his sensitive appreciation of music, was extremely puzzling.

The ballet met with a mixed reception. Half its audience was outraged by the erotic movement of the Faun during the final picture, whilst the rest enthusiastically welcomed it as a novelty, the first in Diaghilev's career. Nevertheless Diaghilev was sure he had found a choregrapher and gave Nijinsky the task of creating *The Rite of Spring*, the ritual dance which Stravinsky had now completed (*see* page 110), and for which Nicholas Roerich had designed décor and costumes. The latter was one of the most Russian of artists, owing no allegiance to Western Europe, and both he and Stravinsky hoped to evoke the primitive spirit of ancient Russian belief by creating, through their music and décor, a true impression of rhythmic urge, vital energy and dramatic colour. The ballet was in three parts—

1. The adoration of the earth
2. The selection of the sacrificial victim
3. The sacrifice

It was the first time such a theme had been used for ballet and Diaghilev was sure it would succeed. But again the dancers told of the utter impossibility of understanding what Nijinsky required from them and Stravinsky has noted Nijinsky's ignorance of the fundamentals of musical technique.

Nijinsky's failure to communicate his ideas to others and create movements in accord with the music did not escape Diaghilev. He appealed to Jacques Dalcroze, who sent the young Marie Rambert, one of his students, to help both Nijinsky and the dancers work out the musical problems involved. She alone seems to have had no fear of disturbing the trend of Nijinsky's thought and endeavouring to interpret his ideas. But at that time (1912–13) her incomplete knowledge of an academic technique of movement must have prevented her clarifying the many details required in the shaping of dances for a long ballet.

The failure of *The Rite of Spring* (1913) was also due to other causes. Firstly the ballet was lacking in anything that Diaghilev's fashionable audience understood as being Russian ballet, and they were shocked by the primitive savagery of movements which were neither passionate nor beautiful, like "The Polovtsian Dances" and *Thamar.* Secondly, its first audience of Frenchmen failed to appreciate the dynamic rhythms of Stravinsky's music, which were its vital component driving the action onwards, instead of the more usual melodic leitmotives. Thirdly, there was nothing chic, daring or spectacular in the same way as Fokine's *Spectre de la Rose, Cleopatra* or *Scheherazade.*

The Rite of Spring raised the question whether a producer of ballet should suppose his audience has a knowledge of the subject under review. It must be admitted that after Fokine's final departure, Diaghilev usually believed his audience had some knowledge when he produced one of his modern works, because he never produced anything unless he himself were interested, and he lived and worked amongst a certain clientele, whose fashionable interests often gave him the inspiration for a new ballet. He produced *The Rite of Spring* because he was still immersed in the task of showing Russian art to the world and was convinced of the artistic value of the two young artists who created it. Stravinsky and Roerich had not yet assimilated the sophistication and culture of fashionable Parisians, for whom the ballet was originally intended and for this audience it was too stark, too primitive and too incoherent in its dance form.

Diaghilev's last task for Nijinsky, *Jeux* (1913) to music specially composed by Debussy, was also a failure. Karsavina makes it clear that again it was impossible to understand what Nijinsky required from his dancers, both by way of movement and musically. But it is important to note that this was the first time Diaghilev, whose idea it was, realized the necessity for sometimes introducing an immediately contemporary theme to the ballet stage. The dancers appeared in tennis costume to play an imaginary game. It was to somewhat similar ideas that Nijinsky's sister, Bronislava, returned in *Les Biches* and *Le Train bleu* when she became choregrapher for Diaghilev after the failure of his revival of the great Tchaikovsky-Petipa ballet *The Sleeping Beauty*.

However, although only one of Nijinsky's ballets had any success, his name as choregrapher, as well as a great dancer, must find a place in history. He showed in *L'Après-midi d'un Faune* that it was possible to create a new style of movement which could be pictorially effective, even though based on archaic forms of art. The failure of *The Rite of Spring* proved that without musical knowledge it is not possible to phrase and accent dance movement in such a way that its significance is communicated to an audience. Lastly, it was his lack of musical knowledge that brought Marie Rambert into the world of classical ballet and cast her for a vitally important role, the artistic adviser and director to most of the first major English choregraphers.

LEONIDE MASSINE AND THE DEEPENING OF CHARACTER (1895–)

If Fokine introduced new forms of ballet and dance, and established a better balance between the work of the soloists and the *corps de ballet* then Leonide Massine, Diaghilev's next choregrapher, enlarged upon those forms and created more characteristic, detailed and mannered movement which gave greater clarity to the action of any ballet, whether based on literature or on the musical content.

His work can be divided into two distinct phases. The first when he furthered the work of Fokine by developing national and *demi-caractère* dance. The second when, after the death of Diaghilev, Massine was invited to join the De Basil company to produce works specially for its younger members.

Massine had trained as a dancer as well as an actor in Moscow, and was working in the *corps de ballet* of the Bolshoi Theatre, when he was noticed by Diaghilev and invited to play the title role in *The Legend of Joseph* then being composed by Richard Strauss. Its production in Paris (1914) was not a success, nevertheless Massine made an immediate impression by his good looks and dramatic talent, a talent which was to shine out in ballet and films for the rest of his career. Diaghilev decided that this highly intelligent youth should become his next choregrapher, but being immersed in company affairs, entrusted the task of Massine's choregraphic education to Mikhail Larionov the Russian painter then living in Lausanne, as were other friends of Diaghilev such as Bakst, Stravinsky and Ansermet, the great conductor, all of whom helped to form Massine's tastes.

MASSINE AND TRADITIONAL DANCE MATERIAL

Massine's first attempts at choregraphy, like those of Fokine, were modest suites of dances or brief episodes, but they were unlike in style and quality. Possibly because he came from Moscow with its greater emphasis on characterization and the dramatic content of movement, and possibly because he was working among other Russian artists in exile through the fortunes of war, his first work was essentially nationalistic, because patriotic feelings were running high. *The Midnight Sun* (1915) was a suite of Russian Boyar and peasant dances to music from Rimsky-Korsakov's *Snow-maiden*. It had been suggested by Diaghilev himself, and Larionov had designed some colourfully fantastic traditional costumes, which shone before an enormous sun on a midnight blue back-cloth. The work disclosed Massine's understanding of any ballet based on traditional material and his ability not only to display the dynamic quality of the steps, but also to vary and increase their tension before releasing it at that moment when the joyous mood overtakes all the dancers, and they lose themselves in the dance. The dance thus gains momentum and expressiveness as each new group joins in. Massine used this important build-up to a climax and finale whenever he worked with traditional material (e.g. *The Three-cornered Hat*, *Capriccio espagnole*, and *Donald of the Burthens*).

The dynamic quality and rhythmic urge of the dances in *The Midnight Sun* may well have gained their particular effect from Massine's work on another project. Despite the failure of *The Rite of Spring* (*see* page 115), Diaghilev was still interested in the dramatic force of dance rhythm as expounded by Jacques Dalcroze and still more by Stravinsky in his ballets (*see* page 108). According to Seraphina Astafieva, Diaghilev felt that Fokine had not made enough of the sheer sound of the dancers' feet in *The Firebird* nor of the crowd in *Petrushka*, who moved for the most part as any crowd in ballet or opera, with little regard to the music. In order to give concrete form to his ideas of the dynamic and dramatic rhythms of dance, Diaghilev had discussed with his friends a ballet, *Liturgie*, whose sole accompaniment was to be the dancers' rhythmic stampings. It was abandoned, but not before Massine had realized the need for forming a pattern of sound in steps. It supplied the aural aid for the dancers to phrase and accent the steps for themselves and, by having to play an active part in making their own music, bring out the meaning of the movement with greater conviction. This pattern of sound in steps is an inherent element of traditional dance everywhere, thus when Massine came to its arrangement for the stage, he ensured that the rhythmic accuracy of each step was both seen and heard if only faintly.

But he did not concentrate only on the footwork exclusive to Russian dance. He understood that, whilst the correct performance of each step gives a true basis for such choregraphic design, it is also essential to follow the movement upwards through the body to head and finger-tips. It must be followed in such a way that with complete co-ordination of all parts of the body comes complete co-ordination with the pulse and melody of the music. This type of co-ordination was not considered by Saint Léon (*see* page 73), and other choregraphers using national dance. They were concerned with the physical performance of steps in time to the music without realizing that each country, whose dances they staged, had its own characteristic flow of melody. They were interested only in adding local colour and/or spectacle. By wedding the total movements of his dancers to both the rhythmic pulse and expressive melodies of his countrymen's music, Massine was able to present in *The Midnight Sun*, a sensitive picture of Russian dance in its many moods.

Admittedly Fokine attempted to interpret both the rhythmic pulse and melodic line in *Les Sylphides* (*see* page 100), but he was working with romantically styled classical dance which demanded no footfall be heard if the dancers are to convey the impression that they are lighter than air. Moreover in other ballets, such as *Carnaval*, where he also harmonized choregraphic design with musical content, Fokine was concerned to paint *demi-caractère* roles which, drawn from balletic fiction or fantasy (e.g. *L'Épreuve d'Amour*), did not need the strong earthy footwork essential for the coachmen and nurses in *Petrushka*.

Massine's abilities to bring out the specific qualities of traditional dance on the stage were made more obvious by his groupings. The relationship of the *corps de ballet* to soloists in *Les Sylphides* has been mentioned (*see* page 100), but with few exceptions Fokine's patterns and groupings for mass dance in his early ballets differed little from those of Petipa and Ivanov. All his dancers usually performed the same step at the same time in fairly conventional patterns or (as in the dance for the servants of the Koschei, *The Fire-bird*), each group had its own movement, but danced within the same pattern as the rest. Massine's patterns for the mass dances in *The Midnight Sun* took on a new form. They were unconventional and accommodated regular and irregular groupings as well as soloists or couples. Sometimes all performed the same step, at others each section, or even single dancers had their own movement to a particular phrase of the melody, whilst others danced, as it were, in counterpoint. Thus instead of giving the impression of an undis-ciplined crowd, which Benois had so deplored in the work of Gorsky (*see* page 91), Massine's crowd was both rhythmically and melodically co-ordinated with the musical context. It was this element which was to be outstanding in his interpretation of Brahms's Fourth Symphony (*Choreartium*) eighteen years later (*see* page 142).

MASSINE AND THE DETAILS OF CHARACTERIZATION

Massine's next step forwards was to define the particular traits of any one character in such detail that the performer had to conform absolutely to the movements laid down by the choregrapher. He or she could add little of their own to a role save an intelligent understanding of the problems raised, and the responsibility for making that role fit into the total design. Fokine had required something similar. But he was served by artists trained mostly by himself and knew in advance what such great interpreters as Tamara Karsavina, Vaslav Nijinsky and other St. Petersburg dancers would bring to a role, and how much, particularly the first-named, each would give of his own when faced with some new idea in the dance.

Massine had no such opportunities. He thus took a more objective view of his task and dictated every detail of movement, its expressive content and its relationship to the music. This new element in his work was noted in *Las Meninas* (1916) created after a holiday in Spain. The music chosen ("Pavane" by Fauré), was not particularly Spanish nor were the steps. Yet the steely dignity of the two ladies-in-waiting and their cavaliers, and the presence of the tragi-comic Dwarf conjured up the Velasquez paintings in the Prado Museum, Madrid, inspiring the ballet and giving it its dark mood.

In his next important ballet, Massine showed how he could differentiate between all the characters in an action even though they were confined within a closely prescribed style of classical dance. The idea of *The Good-humoured Ladies* (1917) belonged to Diaghilev, who had personally selected music by Scarlatti and a libretto derived from a Goldoni play, which had been based on a stock Commedia dell'Arte plot.

Diaghilev was living in Rome with a small group of friends and dancers whilst the rest of his company were making an American tour. In Rome the dancers were working with Maestro Cecchetti and the strong discipline of his academic classes as well as the distinctive personality of the Maestro himself, a superb mime of the old Italian school with its enormous reserve of gesture, exerted a new influence over Massine.

He began to examine the vocabulary of classical dance as taught by Cecchetti which differed considerably from that of his Moscow training with its generous flow and continually dissolving patterns. From this new material he evolved a highly mannered, precise style of *demi-caractère* dance, but it was more descriptive and realistic than that of Dauberval and Bournonville (*see* page 43). It painted the temperament, behaviour and idiosyncrasies as well as the age and class of each player. To create this style he selected those steps he felt most appropriate and added to them an exclusive set of *ports de bras* with specialized movements for hands, fingers and head. He then phrased his *enchaînements* by accent and tempo without resorting to conventional gesture, which might have seemed legitimate material for such a period ballet. Thus his *The Good-humoured Ladies* contained only dancing characters, even those of the Marquis and his Wife, wonderfully played by Maestro and Mme. Cecchetti.

It was in this ballet that Massine first outlined boldly those two characters to which he returned throughout his career, each time adding and broadening, or narrowing the implication of their movements, so that these became appropriate to the new situation, the period and style of dance required by the plot. The characters, Maruccia and Niccolo, were descendants of Columbine and Harlequin, the comic lovers and servants of the *Innamorato* of the Commedia dell'Arte. Fokine had romanticized them in *Carnaval*, but Massine recreated them as their own vulgar selves, with human foibles and failings. They made what might have been a dry stylized comedy of mistaken identities into a riot of fun. It was in their hand movements that Massine showed his command over gesture, a hallmark of all his choregraphy.

Maruccia was always busy, adding touches to the toilet of her mistress, handling dishes, manipulating letters, daintily ordering skirt, sleeves or hair as she flirted with her admirers, or shaking her fist if they took too much liberty. But her most expressive gesture was her raising of the shoulders as she suddenly clasped her fingers and lifted her hands, rocking to and fro in gales of laughter at the success of her own, or the failure of another's stratagem. Such gestures were never finicky because they were always in accord with the action. As Maruccia ran, turned, or otherwise stepped, usually *sur les pointes*, she revealed through dance alone her mischievous yet charmingly frivolous nature. When danced by Lydia Lopokova she was an adorable minx, whose descendants were to be the Cancan Dancer in *La Boutique fantasque* (1919), the Street dancer in *Le beau Danube* (1933); *Mam'zelle Angot* (1943) and others. In Niccolo, the waiter, Massine painted the strong, upturned hands and their swiftly expressive gestures of serving dishes, bottles and the like, or "cocking a snook" at some jape, as well as the strangely mobile body able to negotiate any obstacles no matter how fast the feet were dancing, and the obsequious yet never servile manner, which Leon Woizikovsky so brilliantly captured. Niccolo was the prototype of the male Cancan Dancer, the Barber in *Mam'zelle Angot*, all the waiters and perhaps the Peruvian in *Gaieté parisienne* (1938), and above all the Bar-tender of *Union-Pacific* (1934), the epitome of all waiters when danced by Massine.

Although Massine's next ballet *La Boutique fantasque* (1919) was little more than a series of *divertissements* strung round the idea of dolls coming to life, it had greater subtlety than older ballets on the same theme. Massine's dolls were not the usual stereotyped figures. They were well-observed types and of such realism that they could be recognized as belonging to certain nationalities, but seen through the eyes of a kindly caricaturist. The fantastic shop was also a meeting ground for two easily shocked, neat English old maids, two indulgent American parents and their inquisitive children, and a solid Russian provincial family before whom the dolls were paraded by the well-doing continental shopkeeper and his snotty-nosed boy. Yet despite their mechanical movement, even the dolls appeared as human beings because Massine was not afraid to add a common, even vulgar touch such as the cancan girl throwing her leg over her partner's head with a froth of deliberately raised petticoats, and the dancing boy-poodle using the small American boy as a lamp-post.

There are no stencils in *The Three-cornered Hat,* in which Massine was involved from the initial stages. It is one of the great masterpieces of the second Diaghilev period, created when Diaghilev was unable to refresh himself from Russian sources and therefore sought inspiration in the traditions and culture of those countries which welcomed his venture.

Like *Petrushka* and *The Firebird, The Three-cornered Hat* was the work of three artists, each outstanding in his own field, yet subordinating his own contribution to the needs of the dancers to communicate meaning through movement. The plot, based on an old story by Alarcón, had been written originally by Martínez Sierra for a mime play which Diaghilev had seen in Madrid. He was fascinated by the plot and by the incidental music composed by Manuel de Falla, and commissioned both artists to enlarge their work into a ballet. He then persuaded Pablo Picasso to supply décor and costumes. In reworking his libretto, however, Sierra retained the economy of action essential to any mime play and this gave no opportunity for the extravagances usual in ballets created by Spanish virtuoso dancers. For this reason *The Three-cornered Hat* possibly remains the best example of this genre yet staged by any exponent of the rich dance materials of Spain. Massine, coming to his task as a foreigner, was not intimidated by the spectacular nature of his material, nor had he any need to display his personal talent. Unlike the native dancers he did not neglect to weave each solo entrance into the total fabric of the ballet, a neglect of which they are usually guilty, so that his ballet had that continuity, development and climax which theirs lack, although each of their solos may have its own terrific climax.

MASSINE AND DESCRIPTIVE AND NARRATIVE DANCE

Massine's choregraphy for *The Three-cornered Hat* was a completely integrated design of national dance in which every detail of the descriptive and narrative passages was essential to the plot. The former painted the environment and characteristics of each player in the comedy and as well created the atmosphere. The latter formed the *plastique* sentences through which the dancers told their story. All the movements were the result of Massine's study of Spanish dance under the strangely inspired, yet untutored Felix, whose own dancing flowed passionately whenever the spirit moved him. To discipline such intractable materials was possibly Massine's most difficult task, but he was everywhere guided by the brilliant score of Manuel de Falla.

Like the members of the "Mighty Little Heap" (*see* page 71), this Spanish composer wished to give his native music more permanent form by creating works for professional performance which would be national in idiom. Sierra's libretto gave him a simple action which continually linked the descriptive and narrative passages necessary to outline and underline the plot, but was so economical of incident that De Falla was able to fuse the two distinct forms of Spanish music he was using as a base. The descriptive passages were derived from traditional peasant dances. These were comparatively regular in tempo, phrasing and pattern, and were, therefore, suitable material to form a stable background of melody and rhythm from which the main characters could emerge. For all such passages Massine utilized the traditional steps and qualities of dances like *jotas* and *seguidillas*, which were performed by the entire cast, with the Miller and his Wife standing out as leading characters because of some heightening or originality of movement.

De Falla's narrative passages were inspired by that more erotic form of Flamenco song and dance, where the performer improvises spontaneously on the situation, mood or emotion of the movement. They defined, as it were, the words spoken by the Miller and his Wife during the main action; when for example, the Miller encouraged his canary to sing, caricatured the Corregidor, or the couple drew water from the well.

The Three-cornered Hat again showed Massine's grasp of the place of the *corps de ballet* as a co-ordinate body in the whole action, although each member danced as an individual whenever they might react independently to some similar situation in real life: for example when the Miller danced his *Farucca*, or was taken prisoner, or threw the Corregidor out of his house after the latter had been in the river. These episodes gave the ballet its air of realism and, like the generally descriptive dances and the principal players' narrative passages, were performed throughout with strongly marked rhythmic patterns made by the dancers themselves in harmony with the music. Thus the ballet never once lost the dynamic energy and driving force that is the essence of Spanish dance.

The ballet would not have appeared so truly Spanish in quality if Pablo Picasso had not supplied the firm canvas on which to deploy dance and music. His décor and costumes were not replicas of traditional or authentic material, but were his own distillation of the shape, colour, style and feeling of his native landscape and costume, which he placed at the service of dance. Although his costumes were inspired by Goya they were timeless and, like the music and dance, suggested no period nor exact location. They gave only an impression of the real thing, it was the dancers who had to give life to the story. *The Three-cornered Hat* might be said to prove that only when all the artists collaborating in a national work can see deeply beneath the all too apparent surface details of their traditional materials will that ballet be able to convey to an audience the essence of a country's art and culture.

Massine also did this in *The Rite of Spring* when he entirely restaged the important Stravinsky–Roerich ballet at Diaghilev's request (1920), a request made because Diaghilev realized he now had a choregrapher able to bring out successfully not only the dynamic force and rhythm of dance itself, but also the meaning behind the primitive theme and the subtle nuances of Stravinsky's score. As in *The Three-cornered Hat*, the choregraphy of *The Rite of Spring* owed nothing to classical dance, save only Massine's manner of presenting the dances to the audience. Instead of keeping the dance as a self-contained unit requiring no spectators, as in real and primitive ritual, he allowed it to be seen and felt outside the enclosed circle, and no more so than in the superb dance of the Chosen Virgin, so wonderfully performed by Lydia Sokolova. This attitude towards primitive belief and traditional dance was perhaps Massine's next valuable contribution towards the development of ballet during his work for Diaghilev. He showed that when presenting such materials on the stage it was necessary—

1. To reveal through movement the rhythmic and melodic content of the music.
2. To recreate the dance in such a way that it looked outwards to an audience and created atmosphere, character, mood, emotion and action.
3. To disclose primitive beliefs in the value of dance as a means of communication, not only between men and gods, as in ancient tribal society, but also between dancers and audience in a sophisticated society.

By doing these things Massine brought the spectators into contact with the inner mysteries of movement and ritual.

The staging of *The Rite of Spring* at Diaghilev's request must have turned the young choregrapher's attention to the creation of ballets with deeply philosophical themes which were to become such a feature of his work after Diaghilev's death. It certainly opened up a wider field than had yet been explored by others. But Massine did not immediately take up the challenge of these new ideas. Almost simultaneously with *The Rite of Spring* he was designing *Pulcinella* (1920), which was based on another Commedia dell'Arte theme to some newly discovered music that Diaghilev believed to have been composed by Pergolesi and that was wittily orchestrated by Stravinsky, *Le Chant du Rossignol* (1920), a balletic adaptation of Stravinsky's opera and *Le Astuzie feminili* (1920) an *opera-ballet* by Cimarosa, which later became the *divertissement Cimarosiana* (1924). All these served to demonstrate how deeply Massine was exploring classical as well as folk dance as a means of communication.

INTERLUDE

Diaghilev once said: "Given the talent one can create a choregrapher in no time." This was certainly true of Massine, who made extraordinary progress during the five years 1915–20. It is perhaps not surprising that after this period of intense concentration, producing no less than eleven ballets under constant supervision, Massine felt he had a right to an independent way of life. Diaghilev dismissed him when he fell in love and married Vera Savina, a young English dancer.

Diaghilev was once more without a choregrapher and after ascertaining that Woizikovsky did not wish to undertake such work, selected Thaddeus Slavinsky, a young Polish dancer. He was entrusted with the choregraphy of *Chout* (1920), a ballet originating from a score by Serge Prokofiev; Diaghilev felt it would interest his audience because although modern in idiom, it described an old Russian folk tale about a clown. Moreover he hoped the renewal of his ties with modern Russian artists might prove fruitful.

Larionov was put in charge of both the choregraphy and the production and, as well as designing the colourful Cubist décor and costumes, seems to have devised the angularly acrobatic movements for the cast (according to Lydia Sokolova). But the ballet did not have the hoped-for success. Like *Parade* (1917), Diaghilev's first venture using modern ideas of pictorial art, the dancing in *Chout* was obscured by the kaleidoscopic juxtaposition of geometrical shapes scattered widespread over stage and dancers. *Parade* had made a greater impression, firstly because Pablo Picasso, its designer, had allowed some participants to move freely within their costumes and secondly because Massine's choregraphic design was sufficiently realistic in movement for the audience to recognize acrobats, conjuror, impersonator and stage horse as they paraded circus-like before them.

Despairing of finding an embryo choregrapher capable quickly of supplying the novelties he required to reinforce his repertoire, and realizing that the engagement of even so brilliant a group of singers and dancers as the Spanish *Cuadro Flamenco* was only a temporary solution to the problem of keeping his audience interested, Diaghilev decided to revive the glory of the Imperial Russian Ballet. After much preparation and the gathering of a star-studded cast he presented the great Tchaikovsky–Petipa masterpiece, *The Sleeping Beauty*, at the Alhambra Theatre, London, on 22nd November, 1921. There, within the superb sets and costumes designed by Leon Bakst, danced some of the greatest Russian dancers of their day as well as some whose work would ultimately place the name of England on the map of ballet history.

BRONISLAVA NIJINSKA, THE OLD AND THE NEW (1891–)

Bronislava Nijinska, like her brother Vaslav (*see* page 113) had been an original member of the Russian Ballet, engaged for the brilliance of her classical dancing and receptive mind. Diaghilev invited her to play an important part in the revival of *The Sleeping Beauty*, to design new dances for the excerpts from other Tchaikovsky ballets he was adding to the spectacle, and to reset, or polish the Petipa choregraphy revived by the *régisseur*, Nicolai Sergeyev, according to the Stepanov system he had brought from St. Petersburg (*see* page 90). Nijinska fulfilled her task brilliantly and when, after the financial failure of this wonderful undertaking, Diaghilev found ways of continuing his work, he chose her to supply the few new ballets he could afford.

Dame Ninette de Valois once said in a lecture on choregraphy that La Nijinska (as she later became known), represented the Woman's Suffrage movement in ballet, her most original contribution, *Les Noces*, being in absolute opposition to the classical precepts upon which the technique of the Diaghilev repertoire was based, until that moment when he began to seek only novelty, a moment when La Nijinska stepped into the role of choregrapher.

Nijinska had always been interested in Diaghilev's ideas of modernizing ballet production and in the possibilities of other types of movement. She had been the first to appreciate what had been required for the two-dimensional choregraphy of *L'Après-midi d'un Faune* (*see* page 114), it was therefore not surprising that when she was given full responsibility for *Le Renard* (1922) she experimented further with the choregraphic ideas of her brother. *Le Renard* was a burlesque ballet composed by Stravinsky, in which four dancers interpreted the action sung by four vocalists hidden in the orchestra pit. The idea was not new. Diaghilev had produced Rimsky-Korsakov's *Le Coq d'Or* somewhat similarly, with choregraphy by Fokine at the Paris *Opéra* (1914), nevertheless Nijinska's choregraphic portraits of fox and cock contained original movements as well as interesting groups in which she built her dancers into strangely geometrical shapes.

Diaghilev was satisfied with her handling of this difficult music and now entrusted her with Stravinsky's *Les Noces*. It was a further attempt to give stage life to primitive Russian ritual: a peasant wedding in four scenes representing—

1. The Benediction of the Bride
2. The Benediction of the Bridegroom
3. Departure of the Bride from her parents' home
4. The Wedding Feast

The score was very different from that of *The Rite of Spring* (*see* page 114). By this time (1923) Stravinsky was beginning to repudiate expression and emotion in music, and instead to exploit the qualities of the music itself by selecting only those instruments or voices for his orchestration whose particular sounds he felt fitted his purpose. Thus in *Les Noces* he wanted to convey the illiteracy and rusticity of the peasants, whose rites he was celebrating, by the highly organized sounds of three voices, four pianos, xylophone and percussion. He felt these would give his score the necessary degree of sparse sound and dissonance to depict people in an elementary state of development.

Diaghilev and his colleagues were now convinced that with the industrialization of Soviet Russia there had come a regimentation and drabness of life which they must reflect in *Les Noces*. Moreover they were interested in the experiments of functionalism and constructivism used by the Soviet stage producers, Tairov and Mayerhold, some part of which had begun to influence the Western European theatre. For this reason, Natalie Goncharova designed a starkly economical set before which the dancers moved in dull coloured, traditionally shaped costumes, that resembled industrial overalls. The movements designed by Nijinska were hardly dancing, but a continual forming and re-forming of architectural groups, sometimes of great beauty as dancer linked to dancer piled one upon the other, and then fell into some formal patterning before building yet another pyramidal design. She also used the various levels of the stage to give greater height and depth to her pictures, and bent and twisted her dancers' bodies in endless variations of angular movement so that arms, legs, heads and bodies seemed always to be working in opposition to each other as they fitted into yet another geometrical proposition.

These movements were allied to the music in somewhat the same way as were Nijinsky's steps in *L'Après-midi d'un Faune*. It was a purely formal relationship. The dancers moved soundlessly to their self-made rhythms, during the course of which they would meet certain points in the score at a given note or chord. At that point they completed a picture. This choregraphic method gave space and pattern to the movements but deprived them of that urgency of expression and dynamic rhythm native to Russian folk dance, thus *Les Noces* lacked the colour and life of the earlier Russian ballets such as *Petrushka*, but was representative of the theories on the form and content of primitive art held by certain contemporary artists and composers. For this reason, perhaps, *Les Noces* was a success with the fashionable Parisian audiences who were acquainted with those ideas when first it was presented, but in London, elsewhere, and later in Paris, it was dismissed largely as a joke. Nevertheless La Nijinska (and her brother) seemed to have been the first to insist on the right of dance to exist independently of the dictates of the composer of a ballet score, a point of view to be taken up later by her pupil Serge Lifar, and others.

Les Noces was an exercise in form and marks the point at which Diaghilev finally turned his back on the idea of giving stage life to anything from his Russian background and traditions. Instead he began to produce works inspired by the contemporary theories and practices of the artistically cosmopolitan circle gathered round his enterprise in Monte Carlo, where he had been able to negotiate a permanent home, and from November, 1922, until his death in 1929, the company spent six months of each year preparing new works and appearing in the operas and ballets at its Casino theatre. The contract had been made possible through the influence of Princess Edmonde de Polignac, a great patroness of the arts, and Diaghilev made use of many of the artists, composers and writers whose works she frequently commissioned or furthered by staging rehearsals for herself and her friends. She also helped by financing ballets, concerts and exhibitions, all of which were contemporary in idiom, content and style. Amongst the many contributors from these surroundings to the Diaghilev repertoire were the composers François Poulenc, Georges Auric, Darius Milhaud; the artists Juan Gris, Georges Braque, Utrillo; the versatile Jean Cocteau, whose first libretto for Diaghilev, *Le Dieu bleu*, was written in 1912, and Boris Kochno, Diaghilev's secretary and an ex-Cossack officer, who kept his eye constantly upon the interests current among fashionable circles and provided libretti for ballets that would amuse them.

Few of the ballets produced during the last six years of the Diaghilev era were of lasting value, yet some of them contained germs of ideas that were developed after his death.

Nijinska was the first to produce two purely contemporary works reflecting the topical interests of the fashionable Monte Carlo audience. In both *Les Biches* (1924) and *Le Train bleu* (1924) she showed these people themselves and the superficiality of their mode of living. Neither work had a plot. *Les Biches* (*The House-party*) involved a sophisticated Hostess, wealthy enough to employ Marie Laurencin, the fashionable artist, to decorate her house, herself and her friends. As a result her young male and female guests were able to indulge in their flirtations, athletic games and trifling intrigues in a charmingly pretty pastel set and costumes. *Le Train bleu* was imaginatively described by Diaghilev himself (in the London Coliseum programme)—

> The first point about *Le Train bleu* is that there is no blue train in it. This being the age of speed, it has already reached its destination and disembarked its passengers. These are seen on a beach which does not exist, in front of a casino which exists still less.

Despite the superficiality of both ballets, Nijinska made two choregraphic steps forwards by demonstrating how it was possible to enlarge the dancers' vocabulary of expressive movement.

In *Les Biches* she showed how purely classical steps and poses could be made to generalize upon certain modern types by incorporating movements borrowed directly from the fashionable "rag-time" ballroom dances.

In *Le Train bleu* she showed how one could generalize on other more "sporty" types by utilizing movements common to the golfers, swimmers and players of tennis and other beach games at any summer resort.

Finally, without apparently using the classical steps and poses she demonstrated how the classroom principles of that technique had to be applied to the presentation of such choregraphy if it were to be effective and show these realistic characters in balletic form.

It is not known whether Nijinska's new style of classical dance with its acrobatic and athletic tendencies met with Diaghilev's approval. From time to time he interfered with her work by insisting on ideas of his own. Perhaps he felt she had planned her own choregraphic path on the same academic principles as Fokine, which Diaghilev was now rejecting. Certainly she used them differently and created a more modern, freer idiom in order to paint pictures of her contemporaries and their environment. But even in those of her ballets requiring a period style, such as *Les Fâcheux* (1924, based on Molière's play) where Diaghilev persuaded her to arrange a dance *sur les pointes* for Anton Dolin, or in her later ballets for the Paris *Opéra*, *La Bien Aimée* (1928) and *La Valse* (1929), she paid far more attention to the geometrical patterning through pose and step, and gave her choregraphy greater classical exactitude and a more calculated expressive effect than Fokine would have countenanced for the romantic content of their themes.

Nijinska left Diaghilev in 1924, feeling that she could no longer brook his interference, nor work with Boris Kochno (*see* page 126), as she considered the latter too inexperienced to provide her with the serious libretti she felt necessary, even though Diaghilev himself believed his audience only wanted dancing and were bored with plots.

THE RETURN OF MASSINE

Diaghilev's conviction that his audience were bored arose because he was giving them so much to attact their ears and eyes and was himself uninterested in plot. Every contemporary group of artists was given an opportunity, through some of its members, to design the décor, just as contemporary composers were commissioned to write the scores. The plot did not matter because those concerned with each production were anxious to "get across" their particular ideas of art and music. The choregrapher had to run with the stream and try to create new movement, either to harmonize with or be independent of music and décor.

Although Nijinska's neo-classical dance with its sweep of movement and geometrical patterning was not immediately taken up by others Massine, who now returned to produce ballets intermittently until Diaghilev's death, followed up her ideas of more contemporary scenes. But these were of a more plebeian character and in *Les Matelots* (1925) his Sailors, the Girl and her Friend danced with the coarse movements of a European port and through them communicated the brief action (by Boris Kochno) to tell how one girl remained faithful to her boy despite the temptations offered by her friend. The characters seemed more real, despite their basis in classical dance, because of certain factual details which Massine incorporated into his choregraphic design. Amongst these were a card game played (without props) by the sailors sitting on the back of their chairs, and the entrance of a "busker" known to London theatre queues for his fascinating playing on spoons. These "common touches" reinforced the popular song type score of Georges Auric. The ballet also had its novelty. On either side of the stage were triangular *periaktoi* (*see* page 6), which revolved to mark a change of scene. These and the costumes designed by Pruna added to the fun and were forerunners of the mobile scenery to be used later by such choregraphers as Agnes de Mille and Jerome Robbins.

Le Pas d'Acier (1926) was an attempt to show contemporary life in Russia and was inspired by a score of Prokofiev's, which conjured up, in a strongly marked idiom, the assertive rhythm of factory noises. Without any change of scene, Massine had to show through movement alone the life of the peasants and that of the workers. The first tableau was little more than a well regimented series of *divertissements*, but the second was extremely interesting. The dancers became part of an enormous machine of which they themselves were the wheels, cogs and pistons driving it inexorably onwards, and from these forceful movements there were later to develop those used so significantly in the first movement of *Les Présages* (*see* page 141).

In *Mercure* (1926) and *Poses plastiques* (1926) and particularly in *Ode* (1928) Massine revealed an entirely new aspect of his talent. By this time Diaghilev and his colleagues had been joined by four dancers from Russia. These included Georges Balanchivaidze (later Balanchine), who discussed the experiments being made by Igor Goleizovsky in Russia. Grigoriev suggests that Balanchine had been influenced by this choregrapher who had come to St. Petersburg in 1920 with a programme which made a great impression. It included Goleizovsky's own version of *L'Après-midi d'un Faune* with a constructivist set, in which he made great use of the different planes built by the artist, Boris Erdman, and which became a strong feature of Balanchine's own work in *La Chatte* (*see* page 130). At that time Goleizovsky was working with a very fluid style of classical dance in which his dancers appeared to melt from one pose or group into another. This gave his ballets a static, but beautifully pictorial quality; firstly because he allowed only the scantiest of costumes, therefore every movement was seen and secondly because every movement had to arise out of the music and at the same time united with it.

Some of these ideas may have inspired Massine's *Mercure*, which was a similar series of beautifully, slightly athletic groupings sensitively allied to Eric Satie's score and danced in extremely simple costumes designed by Picasso. The idea may also have penetrated into *Ode* (1928), a ballet with far deeper content, but one which unfortunately the audience found incomprehensible, largely because the libretto, by Boris Kochno and based on a poem by Lermontov, involved philosophical argument. Yet the beautifully lyrical and expressive movements of the dancers, which harmonized with the strangely modern score of Nicholas Naboukov, gave the audience a foretaste of that broad-flowing free style of classical dance which Massine was to use later. These movements were devoid of his usual mannered, characteristic gestures. The dancers were given space to complete each movement and express the mood and organization of the music, despite the mass of ropes and dummy figures which cluttered the stage.

GEORGE BALANCHINE AND THE NEO-CLASSICAL BALLET (1904–)

George Balanchine who was the son of a well-known Georgian composer had had a sound musical training and had studied dance at the Imperial St. Petersburg school. When he joined Diaghilev (1924, *see* above) his choregraphic ideas had begun to crystallize under the influence of two important Soviet choregraphers, firstly Igor Goleizovsky (*see* above) who liked to interpret music not especially composed for dance, and create for each item chosen a particular style of movement to convey its form and qualities; secondly Feodor

Lopokov (*see* page 99), one of the most daring, creative and influential choregraphers of the 1920s. He introduced acrobatic lifts and feats into the stern Marinsky classics and was the first in St. Petersburg to interpret a symphony (Beethoven's Fourth, *The Greatness of the World*, 1923). His work was not so stylish and refined as that of Goleizovsky, because he was apt to work in contradiction to his music, sacrificing everything for the sake of daring new movement.

It was not until *La Chatte* (1927) that Balanchine was able to show his real talent as a classical choregrapher. Even though this ballet could be called a novelty, the originality of the choregraphic design could not be hidden by the unusual constructivist décor of Pevsner and Gabo. In fact the transparent mica and celluloid scenery and costumes backed by black American cloth curtains and stage-cloth, served to throw the dancing into high relief, and enhance the value of the movements and groupings as the dancers passed over and through the various planes in to which the set had been divided.

If *La Chatte* marked the point in Balanchine's career when he began to use the various planes of his set and the geometrical patterning of his dancers to give pictorial value to his choregraphy, then *Apollon musagète* (1928) marked the point when he entirely rejected the artificial conventions of classical dance and instead, began to simplify its principles and vocabulary in order to match it to the classical formulas in the score provided by Stravinsky, who also wrote the libretto. It was little more than a series of *divertissements* in two scenes—

1. The birth of Apollo
2. Apollo with the Muses

Nevertheless there was complete unity of dance style and a continuity of movement which, by linking each dance to the other gave a development of action because the dancing was staged throughout the length, breadth and height of the set. Nor was the ballet without expression, for within the dance of each Muse were found gestures symbolical of her art. *Apollon musagète* marked the beginning of a partnership between a musician and a choregrapher each sharing the same ideas: firstly, that their own art was complete in itself, but could when necessary complement the other; and secondly, that the classical arts of dance and music presuppose certain generalizations upon form and technique (*see* page 3) to the exclusion of the romantic idea that the individual with his moods, emotions and actions is the more important part of any work of art. However, Balanchine had not, at that time, rejected the need for expression in dance. Diaghilev's next task for him was to prove the contrary.

The Prodigal Son (1929) was Diaghilev's last ballet and was one of his greatest. He had attempted several times to stage ballets on a biblical or philosophical theme, but these usually failed either because his gay audiences were not interested or because some member of the group producing such a ballet failed to contribute his proper share. Diaghilev's

Posidelki: An old Russian Print
(Bakroushine State Theatre Museum)

Salammbo by Gorsky: Bolshoi Theatre
(Bakroushine State Theatre Museum)

PLATE XVII

Tamara Karsavina, the Great Ballerina of the Diaghilev Company, who brought to life so many of Fokine's Heroines

PLATE XVIII

The Firebird by Fokine, with Tamara Karsavina and Fokine

Spectre de la Rose by Fokine with Tamara Karsavina and Nijinsky

Petrushka by Fokine: the First Scene in the First Production

PLATE XIX

The Three-cornered Hat by Massine with Tamara Toumanova and Massine
(*Photo T. R. Vaughan*)

Les Noces by La Nijinksa
(*Photo Daily Mail*)

PLATE XX

Les Présages by Massine, First Movement

Symphonie Fantastique by Massine with Tamara Toumanova and Massine (*Photo Gordon Anthony*)

Les Présages by Massine with Irina Baronova and Anton Dolin (*Photo Gordon Anthony*)

PLATE XXI

The Green Table by Kurt Jooss, with Kurt Jooss and Otto Schuller
(*Photo Gordon Anthony*)

PLATE XXII

Anna Pavlova

Eugenia Kolossova, Didelot's Favourite Pupil

Two Great Russian Ballerinas who changed the History of Ballet

PLATE XXIII

Checkmate by Dame Ninette de Valois, with June Brae and Harold Turner
(*Photo Gordon Anthony*)

The Rake's Progress by Dame Ninette de Valois, with Walter Gore as the Rake, and the Sadler's Wells Ballet
(*Photo J. W. Debenham*)

PLATE XXIV

Les Patineurs by Sir Frederick Ashton, with Dame Margot Fonteyn, Pamela May, and June Brae
(*Photo J. W. Debenham*)

The Miracle in the Gorbals by Robert Helpmann, with Robert Helpmann, Pauline Clayden, and David Paltenghi
(*Photo E. Mandinian*)

Horoscope by Sir Frederick Ashton, with Dame Margot Fonteyn, Michael Somes, c.b.e., Pamela May, and the Sadler's Wells Ballet
(*Photo J. W. Debenham*)

PLATE XXV

Persephone by Sir Frederick Ashton with Svetlana Beriosova and the Royal Ballet
(Photo Anthony Crickmay)

PLATE XXVI

Symphonic Variations by Sir Frederick Ashton with Dame Margot Fonteyn, Anya Linden, Annette Page, David Blair, and Bryan Shaw
(Photos Anthony Crickmay)

PLATE XXVII

Symphonic Variations by Sir Frederick Ashton, with Dame Margot Fonteyn and Graham Usher
(*Photo Anthony Crickmay*)

PLATE XXVIII

Les Forains by Roland Petit, with Roland Petit
(*Photo Duncan Melvin*)

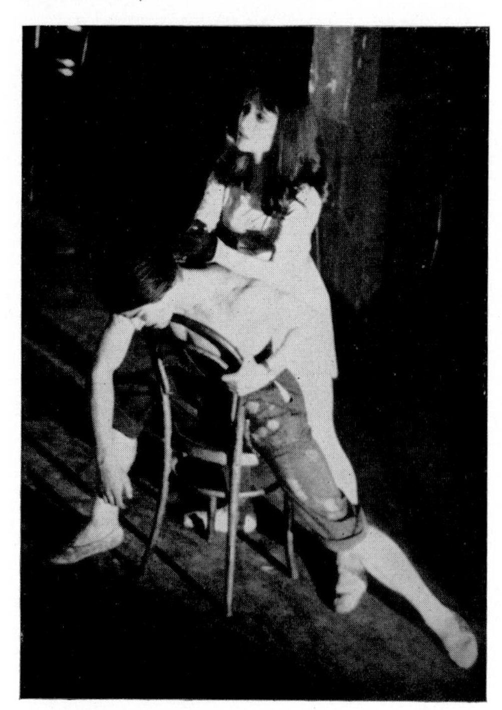

Le jeune Homme et la Mort by Roland Petit, with Natalie Phillipart and Jean Babilée
(*Photo Duncan Melvin*)

PLATE XXIX

L'Après-midi d'un Faune by Jerome Robbins, with Kay Mazzo and Jack Jones
(Photo Anthony Crickmay)

Études by Harald Lander, with Toni Lander, Erik Bruhn, Svend Erik Jensen, and the Royal Danish Ballet
(Photo Mydtskov)

Taras Bulba by Fenster: Bolshoi Ballet

PLATE XXXI

Romeo and Juliet by Lavrovsky: Kirov Ballet (1940), with Peoples' Artists Galina Ulanova and Constantine Sergeyev

PLATE XXXII

choice of artists for *The Prodigal Son* again revealed his understanding of the need to choose those sympathetic to a chosen theme. He was himself a religious man, like the artist Georges Rouault, who was for ever seeking a way of painting the tragedy of Christ and other biblical tales. Serge Prokofiev, the composer of the ballet, was deeply interested in ancient liturgy, and Balanchine, the choregrapher, had once thought of becoming a priest. All three men approached their task with deep thought and serious intent.

Their collaboration resulted in a profoundly moving ballet. It was possibly the first, since Massine's *The Rite of Spring* (1920, *see* page 122) in which plot and deep characterization through dance took pride of place. Such emotional content had been lacking in the gaily modernistic ballets which had intrigued Diaghilev's fashionable audiences, and although Balanchine brought an intellectual approach to his task, he had to bow to Diaghilev's insistence that his Russian dancers, members of the cast, should interpret their roles as they themselves felt proper. It was the fullness and sincerity of their expression which gave life to the strange movements that were sometimes interpolated into the unusually simple choregraphic design. The ballet showed that Balanchine could create a dance style, adaptable for each character in the drama and that, without using pure classical technique, he could draw upon its principles to heighten the effectiveness of some dramatic point in the action. But what was more important was his brilliant handling of the *corps de ballet.* He drew them into the action so that they not only played a vital part in building up the climax of a scene, but also so grouped them that the wonderfully rich yet sombre décor and costumes of Rouault were seen to be part of the drama, and not mere framework or background. Finally Balanchine created such *rapport* between the dance and Prokofiev's score that all its emotional surge, melody and rhythms were seen, heard and felt, and although the movements at times seemed perverse, it was these that gave the ballet its bitter quality and in the final scene, its infinite tenderness.

SERGE LIFAR (1905-)

The Prodigal Son was originally danced by Serge Lifar and with deep artistry. He had joined the Russian Ballet in 1923 as a pupil of Nijinska's and before dancing with the company was sent to study with Maestro Cecchetti. Later Diaghilev decided to educate him as a choregrapher, but his promised career did not take place under Diaghilev. He was given the task of restaging Stravinsky's *Le Renard* (1929) under the tutorship of Larionov (*see* page 125). The resultant extravaganza of acrobats and dancers was unsuccessful, perhaps because Diaghilev, a sick man, had lost interest in his ballet and did not interfere; perhaps because Lifar was surrounded by too many people out to shock or provide novelty.

Diaghilev died on 19th August, 1929. During the lifetime of his company he had produced no less than sixty-three ballets which were to change entirely the construction and content of ballet elsewhere. The changes initiated by Fokine and furthered by Diaghilev led to the intriguing *demi-caractère* and character ballets of Massine, where, in order to make the action speak through movement, the dancers had to submit to the absolute discipline of the choregrapher, and to perform highly characteristic, mannered gesture and at the same time to match them meticulously to the musical content. With the ballets of Nijinsky and his sister, they had to communicate meaning through movement entirely foreign to the academic technique by which they were trained and yet they were expected to give an impeccable performance of classical dance in *The Sleeping Beauty*. But the angularities of *L'Après-midi d'un Faune* and *Les Noces* found their way into some of Massine's work and made his dance more actual and pictorially effective. Moreover, it was the fusion of these two apparently incompatible styles, that gave rise on the one hand to the frivolous novelties of the later Diaghilev period as well as the more serious neo-classical ballets of Nijinska herself, and later still, when influenced by Goleizovsky and Lopokov, to the neo-classical ballets of Balanchine.

In addition, Diaghilev, in *The Firebird, Petrushka, The Three-cornered Hat* and others developed that type of national ballet which disclosed the temperament, character, emotions, moods, actions, in fact the spirit of a people. This form of ballet was to be created by Dame Ninette de Valois (*The Rake's Progress, see* page 159), John Cranko (*Pineapple Poll, see* page 176), Eugene Loring (*Billy the Kid, see* page 182) and other choregraphers during periods in the history of some company when ballets were needed to show that company had a right to a place in its own native theatre. These ballets were the collective enterprise of artists, each giving to the other to produce a work, exposing not only the traditions of their native dance forms, but of all the arts going to make a ballet.

However, in his search for the means through which to turn ballet into a major art form, Diaghilev frequently forgot that dance itself needed to have freedom through which to communicate dramatic and philosophical as well as light themes. With the dispersal of the Russian Ballet, Diaghilev's major choregraphers Fokine, Massine, Balanchine and the still untried Lifar were to return to the production of the serious ballet, each in their own way, with dancers not all of whom had that same firm discipline of classical dance upon which Diaghilev had always insisted.

FURTHER READING

BEAUMONT, C. W., *The Diaghilev Ballet in London* (London, Putnam, 1944).
BENOIS, ALEXANDRE, *Reminiscences of the Russian Ballet* (London, Putnam, 1941).
GRIGORIEV, S. L., *The Diaghilev Ballet* (London, Constable, 1953).
HASKELL, ARNOLD H., *Diaghilev* (London, Gollancz, 1935).
LIEVEN, PRINCE PETER, *The Birth of Ballets Russes* (London, Allen & Unwin, 1936).
LIFAR, SERGE, *Diaghilev* (London, Putnam, 1940).
LIFAR, SERGE, *Ballet, Traditional to Modern* (London, Putnam, 1938).

CHAPTER 10

The Search for Expression after Diaghilev

Each artist working in the ballet must subordinate his materials to the needs of the others, particularly to the dance.

(FOKINE)

THE balletic reforms initiated by Fokine and Diaghilev were taken up by others during their lifetime. Some of the most interesting of these were the ballets of the young Swedish choregrapher, Jean Borlin. He was a pupil of Fokine on whom he made a great impression and who encouraged his wish to design ballets. Borlin was lucky enough to find a rich patron, Rolf de Maré, who agreed that any company Borlin could form needed to have a cosmopolitan background and be contemporary in repertoire, although he also wished to present Swedish ballet in the same way that Diaghilev had presented some specifically Russian ballets. These were Borlin's *Nuit de Saint-Jean* (1920) based on Swedish traditional customs with balleticized folk dance, and the strangely moving *Foolish Virgins* (1920), based on an ancient Swedish tapestry in which Borlin created what can only be described as movements in Gothic shape, angular in detail yet arched and flowing in shape.

THE SWEDISH BALLET AND JEAN BORLIN (1894–1931)

The Swedish Ballet was born in Paris (1920) and quickly developed a repertoire of modern experimental works in which collaborated such controversial figures as the artists Léger and Piccabia, the librettists René Clair, Jean Cocteau and Paul Claudel and the composers Eric Satie, Darius Milhaud and Kurt Atterberg. Unfortunately most of Borlin's choregraphic design which gave expression to his dance was lost in the struggle for supremacy between artist, librettist and musician. There was much to admire because this promising young choregrapher was also dancing the leading roles brilliantly. But he was continually rehearsing his ballets and reforming the company, and this proved too much for his health. After five years of struggle (1920–5) the Swedish Ballet collapsed. But not all Borlin's work was lost. The scores of his *Création du Monde* (Milhaud) and *The Jar* (Casella) were taken by Dame Ninette de Valois, and something of the starkly angular technique, dark moods and tense emotions of his choregraphy were to become part of the materials of such Central European artists as Kurt Jooss (*see* page 138) and Birgit Cullberg (*see* page 185), neither of whom relied upon classical technique, as Borlin had done, but who both understood the strangely fatalistic temperament and tragedies disclosed in the ballets of this essentially Swedish artist.

THE PIONEERS OF THE MODERN BALLET

Rolf de Maré's interest in ballet did not end with the collapse of the Swedish Ballet, in 1931 he founded *Les Archives Internationales de la Danse* in its memory and that of Jean Borlin. It was at the 1932 competition of this body that the young German choregrapher, Kurt Jooss, won first prize with his tragic work, *The Green Table*. This ballet was quite unlike any yet mentioned in this book. Its technique, structure and presentation stemmed from very different sources, and although several important experiments had been made by others before Jooss, *The Green Table* was the first of the so-called "modern ballets" to be accepted by the larger ballet-going public. It was the one ballet to inspire other more classical choregraphers to probe further into the significance of movement, and to seek ways of producing more serious, contemporary themes.

The initiative for the revolt against the stereotyped conventions of classical dance was first taken by Isadora Duncan (1878–1927) (*see* page 97) when she danced more or less extempore to classical music and discarded tights, shoes and conventional costumes, preferring various types of Greek draperies. She was an extremely beautiful young woman with an intuitive gift for dance improvisation, and it was her spontaneity, expressiveness and feeling for the musical line in dance that had interested Fokine. But she did not concern herself with technicalities, although her brother, Raymond, eventually evolved a system of steps and poses from their joint study of ancient Greek friezes, vases and literature. These formed the basis of movements taught in the schools founded by Isadora and himself in several European towns.

MARGARET MORRIS, THE ENGLISH PIONEER (1891–)

One of the first to study with Raymond Duncan was an English dancer, Margaret Morris, who was dissatisfied with her academic training, although when she ultimately came to work out her own vocabulary of movement, she realized its value as a means to an end. She knew from her stage experiences with Ben Greet, the Shakespearean actor, that a firm technique and principles were required in any performance before an audience. Moreover, the Greek dance of Raymond Duncan was too limited for her. She wanted a vocabulary through which she could convey contemporary ideas as well as those of any period, because she was concerned with choregraphy as an art, involving as it did the collaboration of musician and artist, and as a means of creating an overall design of movement, expression and colour.

Margaret Morris formed her own school (1911) where students and children alike studied dance movement and improvisation through which she taught them to interpret the feeling and rhythm of the music. She did not follow Dalcroze, firstly because she disagreed with his use of different movements to denote note values, and secondly, because he had no basic technique in relation to body training. The students also studied acting, costume and scenic design as well as painting, and her own system of dance notation. From 1912 she began to produce regularly in her own small theatre. Her programmes consisted of ballets (e.g. Debussy's *Rond du Printemps*), song and poems interpreted by movement (the Scottish ballad *Edward* was a notable example), dance improvisations and compositions, amongst which was her own interpretation of Stravinsky's *Ragtime* which conjured up for many: "The syncopated rhythm of a lost generation" (the late Edwin Evans). Many important musicians contributed to these "club" evenings which were attended by leading figures in the contemporary worlds of art, music and the theatre.

These pioneer works of Margaret Morris were perhaps presented before their time for when her ballet *Ankhor*, inspired by Indian and Cambodian sculpture, was presented at the London Coliseum (1919) it was firmly rejected by an audience unused to dancers performing to percussion only and in strangely colourful costumes of cubist design. Yet all who found their way to her studio realized the value of her work, and many who came carried away ideas to be developed elsewhere. Amongst these visitors was Ruth Saint-Denis, whose beauty of movement strengthened Margaret Morris' conviction that creative dance should not stem from classic ballet technique.

RUTH SAINT-DENIS (1877–   ) AND TED SHAWN (1891–   )

Ruth Saint-Denis, the American pioneer of modern dance, had her first success with a Hindu-inspired ballet *Radha* (1906). She had not been interested in the Apollonian order of ancient Greek dance interpreted by her compatriot, Isadora Duncan. Requiring a more flexible, expressive medium, she had travelled to the Far East to study the aesthetic qualities, principles and inner content of Oriental dance. In 1915, she and her husband, Ted Shawn, founded their school, Denishawn, from which were to emerge some of the leading figures of the American schools of Modern Dance (e.g. Martha Graham and Doris Humphreys). At first their work was inspired by the dances of India, Japan and other Far Eastern countries, but gradually a much stronger, virile type of movement began to be developed, which eventually culminated in the production of an all-male group of dancers led by Ted

Shawn (1933). Their programme contained items of symbolical and dramatic interest as well as athletic prowess and geometrical patterning. In addition great emphasis was placed upon the virility of the men and the rhythmic content of the dance. This emphasis was largely due to the influence of other pioneering work undertaken by Mary Wigman, originally a pupil of Dalcroze (*see* below) and her teacher Rudolph von Laban working in Central Europe.

MARY WIGMAN (1886–) AND RUDOLPH VON LABAN (1879–1958)

The school of eurhythmics founded by the Swiss musician, Emil Jacques-Dalcroze, in Hellerau (Germany, 1910) was a valuable starting-point for several pioneers of modern dance. His system of musical training through movement concentrated attention on the content and principles of music alone, and required only the natural use of the body, plus a sense of linear design in order to shape and accent the patterns of any composition. This aspect of his work is still proving its worth in educating dancers musically in many countries. But some of his students, such as Marie Rambert and Mary Wigman, became far more interested in the movement side of their work. Each, in their own way, sought to develop a physical technique of dance through which to convey not only the purely musical content of any composition, but one which could also interpret any literary content that a ballet might have (Marie Rambert) as well as the musical connotations, or a technique that would stand as a medium of expression by itself, without any musical context whatsoever with the dancer making her own tempos, time-signatures, phrases, etc., as she went along with, or without some form of accompaniment (Mary Wigman).

Marie Rambert decided to achieve her medium by restudying classical dance with Maestro Cecchetti and later, Seraphine Astafieva, and allying that to her musical knowledge, because her work with the Diaghilev company (*see* page 115) had shown her the value of such a basis for the theatrical enterprise at which she was aiming (*see* page 152). Mary Wigman however rejected this traditional technique, and in 1913 joined the Central European School of Dance founded in Munich (1911) by Rudolph von Laban. This theorist had been greatly influenced by the studies into the causation and motivation of behaviour, movements, and similar topics undertaken by such psychologists as Freud and Jung.

Von Laban ultimately erected and elaborated upon a formidable theory and analysis of human movement as well as his own system of notation, from which later students of his ideas were to benefit. But he neglected throughout his lifetime to formulate any real technical principles of movement by which to put his theories into practice. This meant that any of his students, venturing into the theatrical world of dance, were free physically to interpret his ideas as they themselves thought fit.

Mary Wigman was one of the first of his students to emerge as a soloist with a very distinctive style of her own. Her dancing lacked any of the feminine grace and beauty which had endeared Isadora Duncan to her audience. It was extremely forceful, earthbound and frequently seemed to be tortured by the sheer labour of interpreting extempore some deeply philosophical idea, or through beating out the rhythms self-imposed by a dancer of great intellectual capacity, but of little feeling for humanity.

It was the intellectual approach to the theory of dance in all its phases taken by von Laban, that appealed to other German and those American dancers who rejected academic technique. Mary Wigman's performances showed how each of them could apply such theories to the practice of a personal style, and how to evolve a type of dance of their own which could be the means of conveying some message. The freedom von Laban thus gave to the individual for self-expression led, during the 1920s and early 1930s to a spate of solo recitalists and each performer provided some manifesto of his or her personal philosophy of dance. This ultimately led to the production of items which were only understood by those members of the audience personally acquainted with that dancer's theories.

KURT JOOSS (1901–)

Kurt Jooss was not such a soloist. From the beginning of his career he had been interested in the activities of the group. His musical studies had been influenced by the work of Dalcroze involving, as it did, the movement of groups from which the individual arose in order to interpret some theme and its relationship to the whole composition. His study of drama had also made him realize the need of collaboration between choregrapher, artists, musicians and experts in stagecraft, because he had seen the impetus given to contemporary theatrical production throughout Germany by such producers, designers and craftsmen as Max Reinhardt, Gordon Craig and Adolphe Appia. (The latter's theories and practical use of light, shadow and colour on the stage were always brilliantly realized in every Jooss ballet.)

Kurt Jooss joined the von Laban school in 1920 and soon set to work to give more practical form to his master's theories of self-expression. Their collaboration eventually resulted in the development of a series of exercises and dance-steps, which sprang outwards from the dancer's own body in all directions of space. This gave concrete design to every movement made and ensured continuity of line and pattern because each movement had of necessity to be joined to the next by the dancer's continued return to his or her own centre. Jooss also made a study of people's movements in everyday life, especially when the stress and strain of labour and/or emotion caused changes in the natural or normal uses of the body. He then inquired into the qualities of the movements to be made, and into the way in which the shape of those movements and their purpose had to be given proper phrasing and accent in order to make their effect.

Working in various German opera houses (from 1924) as choregrapher and leader of a group of dancers who were prepared to submit themselves to his ideas, Jooss became aware of the effect that the Allied victory of the 1914–18 War had had on his compatriots. He was sincerely convinced that the Treaty of Versailles would only lead to other wars and that it had already given birth to the Nazi movement in Germany itself. He felt he had to make a protest in the only way he knew and in 1932 (July) produced his great work *The Green Table*, which briefly showed: a conference of diplomats ending in the shot sparking off a new war; the parting of mothers and sons, husbands and wives, and lovers; the profiteers, prostitutes and the like making their money, whilst Death stalks the land until men lie dead everywhere, mourned by their womenfolk; then, once again—the conference table. It was a subject never before tackled by any choregrapher, and it was to exert an enormous influence over many future ballet-makers.

The Green Table ultimately won recognition throughout Western Europe and America because it was so pertinent to the political situation of the 1930s. Its pertinence was nowhere clearer than in the conditions under which Jooss himself worked. He and his dancers had become refugees from Germany when Hitler clamped down on all forward-looking enterprises, such as this, which dared to comment adversely on dictatorship, as Jooss was to do several times later in such ballets as *Chronica* and *Pandora.*

The interesting point of *The Green Table* was that its theme, Man and Woman against Fate, was the same to be used by Massine in *Les Présages* when it appeared nine months later (April, 1933, *see* page 141). But whereas Massine was to see his characters as symbolical representations of Man, Woman and Fate in a classical manner and created movements through which these figures could express the ideas and sentiments of Action, Love, Frivolity and overwhelming Power, Jooss took an altogether more realistic viewpoint. He saw the men and women of his drama as certain human types about whom he could generalize and he used for each a specific set of movements. These described the emotions, moods and reactions of easily recognized diplomats, soldiers, passers-by, mothers, wives, lovers, prostitutes, profiteers and the like in such a way, that the struggle of each player against the stylized figure of Death, appeared as a personal real-life tragedy in which all were involved.

There is no doubt that Jooss's introduction to the stage of these more real characters, stylized though their movements might be, showed many choregraphers and dancers how it was possible to introduce contemporary topics, situations and characters using naturalistic movement without losing sight of the fundamental theatrical principles and techniques. The choregraphers of today owe a tremendous debt to Jooss and those earlier pioneers, all of whom broke with academic conventions. Since 1923, others have followed new experimental lines. Some have developed a real human approach for when all is said and done, the men and women of Jooss's *The Green Table* and his other ballets in political vein, stood only as symbols for Everyman. They had no life save on the stage. Yet Jerome Robbins's Three Sailors in *Fancy Free* (1944, *see* page 184) and Agnes de Mille's Ranch

Hands and Girls in *Rodeo* (1942, *see* page 183) might easily be expected to walk out of the stage door, the former to go down to the docks, and the latter to ride off to their shacks. Other choregraphers have not been so extrovert as these Americans, and have sought to express their characters' most intimate, even unconscious thoughts and desires. Some of these ballets are very rewarding (e.g. Anthony Tudor's *Lilac Garden*, *see* page 171), because the exposure of such intimate ideas gives the dancing movements great subtlety of expression. Others have tried to explore the mind of some character and present the result as ballet. These experiments have rarely been successful because such a theme needs words to explain the complexities.

Jooss himself never indulged in such complexities. Although his libretti frequently had political, psychological or other implications, in essence the plot was simple and the audience could add, or ignore such undertones for themselves. None of his libretti involved a theme which could not be conveyed through movement, moreover they were never impeded by elaborate scenery and costumes. Jooss would rather heighten the drama, or ease tension, build up or resolve a climax by intensifying or flooding the scene with subtle lighting. He also used specially composed music which rarely stood in its own right. The musician had to follow and accompany the choregraphic design, so that the dancers, through their movements dominated the stage and conveyed the meaning of the drama.

MASSINE AND THE SYMPHONIC BALLET

I can only conclude that you dislike my balletic passages because they are ballet, not because they are bad. Perhaps you are right. Yet I cannot see why a symphony should not contain occasional dance tunes.

(TCHAIKOVSKY in a letter to the critic Laroche, who had complained that parts of the composer's Fourth Symphony were too balletic)

The work of Kurt Jooss undoubtedly helped to turn the attention of the more important classical choregraphers to the serious theme and to a reassessment of movement and Massine was one of the first to produce new ideas. During Diaghilev's lifetime and later he had worked both inside and outside the Russian Ballet, usually producing works with the same types of light comedy libretto as those with which he had first won the London Alhambra audiences (i.e. *La Boutique fantasque* and *The Three-cornered Hat*). Amongst these many typical Massine *demi-caractère* ballets were *Le beau Danube* (1933) and *Scuola di Ballo* (1933) and the later *Mam'zelle Angot* (1943) with their extraordinary diversity of characters and almost inevitable finale of boy winning girl, whilst the rest of the cast laughed at the fool they have made of some ridiculous character. After Diaghilev's death, however, Massine created some deeply serious ballets. These were the first symphonic ballets to be seen in the west and were produced for the exciting young dancers that Colonel de Basil, a new impresario, had found in the Parisian studios of *emigrée* Russian *ballerinas*.

These symphonic ballets stemmed from two sources, firstly the neo-classical ballets of Massine himself (*see* page 129) from which he drew the simpler technique, the straighter, more flowing lines and geometrical patterning of groups, to which he added certain more acrobatic elements. The second feature of his new style arose from his widening the range of Fokine's expressive movement. Fokine's movements could convey the purely musical content and romantic mood of the score as in *Les Sylphides* (*see* page 100), but Massine wanted a stronger form of mimed-dance, more generally descriptive of human beings and expressive of their actions and emotions which he felt were contained in the music he chose to interpret.

Massine's search for a more significantly expressive mimed-dance arising from music, occurred because by 1932, when he tried to work out his plans for De Basil, he found composers reluctant to contribute a serious score. He, therefore, turned his attention to important symphonies and interpreted these in terms of classical dance as had already been tried in Russia. His first efforts aroused great controversy, particularly amongst musicians, but it is worth recording some remarks of the great critic, Ernest Newman, who believed Massine's works, particularly *Choreartium*, were a valuable development of ballet—

> Strictly speaking no Art is translatable into another, not even poetry into music. The most we can get is convincing parallelisms between the two and the fact that some parallelisms are much more difficult than others, and have hitherto not been attempted is no reason for denying that a choregraphic genius like Massine has the right to attempt this . . . Massine has given us a transvaluation into choregraphic values of a hundred musical features of the Symphony, the ballet works itself out consistently as a design reproducing in the subtlest way the design of the music in the matter of subject, repetitions, balancings, treatment of episodes and so on. In the last resort, the more musical we are and the better we know our Brahms, the more pleasure we derive from *Choreartium*.
>
> (From the *Sunday Times*)

Ernest Newman's remarks could be applied also to Massine's first symphonic work *Les Présages* (1933), but here the choregrapher interpreted a theme taken from Tchaikovsky's letters to his patroness, Mme. von Meck, about his work as a musician. The composer was writing his Fourth Symphony and likened his efforts to those of a Man struggling with his Fate, a theme he hoped would be clear to those who could read his music. Massine exposed one aspect of Tchaikovsky's philosophical musings on this topic in each movement of the Fifth Symphony, introducing in each a character to symbolize its content, and thus clarify the total action which described—

How if Man would be master of his Fate, he must have—

1. Action
2. Love
3. Frivolity (Happiness in Tchaikovsky's letters)

How man with the aid of these attributes would triumph.

Massine could not produce these ideas in the same way as Beaujoyeulx who produced the Four Ladies of *Le Balet comique* (*see* page 17). Verbal imagery and elaborate props had long been banished from the ballet. Instead the soloists impersonating Action, Love and Frivolity were each given a clearly defined type of dance which described their being. This, to some extent, was echoed by the *corps de ballet*, who, as in the old Greek dramas, created the necessary atmosphere and mood, reacted to the intervention of Fate whenever he appeared at the climatic points in the unfolding of the action, and finally played a major role in driving this dread, bat-like figure from the stage. Every movement performed paralleled the musical themes, rhythms and cadences; the dancing in each section was coloured by the moods, emotions and actions Massine felt were engendered by the music, and by his need to convey the significance of his theme.

The first movement, "Action," was the most outstanding and brought an entirely new quality to classical dance. Its leader (Nina Verchinina) used *ports de bras* of great strength drawn, it seemed, from the occupational gestures of heavy labourers, yet so finely phrased and accented that they could only be performed by the best craftsmen. They had something of the mechanical action of *Le Pas d'Acier* (*see* page 128), but behind their inevitable drive could be seen, heard and felt the blood, toil, tears and sweat suffered by Man (David Lichine) as he continually struggled to rise again after another blow from Fate (Leon Woizikovsky). The second movement developed into a passionate *pas de deux* in which Man swept his Beloved (Irina Baronova) close into his embrace or raised her high in ecstasy, only to find her struck down and away from him again and again. Some of the lifts were acrobatic, but they always retained a classically lyrical quality which expressed the passion felt. The third movement (led by Tatiana Riabouchinska) was of the lightest quality, the dancers appeared to laugh as if the drama of life were forgotten. The last movement contained reprises of all that had gone before until Fate was driven from the stage, when the dance seemed to take on a new strength and optimism.

Massine's next work, *Choreartium*, was an interpretation of Brahms's Fourth Symphony in which he associated his soloists and *corps de ballet* either separately or together, with the various instruments or orchestral sections so that each musical theme had its counterpart in dance and dancers. In this way he achieved those convincing parallelisms mentioned above (*see* page 141), or as Edwin Evans once wrote: "He made the music visible in dancing pictures which moved ever onwards and thus held both ear and eye." Only the second movement of this abstract work might be said to have some literary content. It was perhaps the most moving of all Massine's dramatic works and one of the most beautiful examples of counterpoint in dance. The main theme was interpreted by a grief-stricken figure (Irina Baronova), who appeared to make a speech of protest, the *corps de ballet*, as a Greek chorus, accompanied her dance with sorrowful gestures, thus enhancing the tragedy of Brahms's theme and making it more vividly poignant.

Massine's further symphonic works reverted to the interpretation of some philosophical theme which had either been written by the composer himself, as with Berlioz's *Symphonie Fantastique*; or was one of his own choosing which he wedded to music, for example Beethoven's Seventh Symphony. To this he set—

1. A scene of the creation of the world
2. The story of Cain and Abel
3. (To the movement which has been called the apotheosis of dance) a scene of the Olympian gods and goddesses
4. A Greek bacchanale

With these latter ballets Massine might be said to have set the pattern for all so-called "symphonic" ballets presented since. They fall into two categories, the first are a plotless or purely abstract design in dance, which seeks only to be an interpretation of the content of some symphonic music, and is without characterization or dramatic action. Such ballets can be called classical, if the choregrapher uses that particular form of technique, e.g. Ashton's *Symphonic Variations* (1946) and Kenneth Macmillan's *Diversions* (1961). These so-called abstract ballets are now found everywhere and are usually interesting demonstrations of one particular country's, or company's school of dance.

The second form of symphonic ballet is based on a theme demanding characterization and dramatic action. It can be suggested by the composer himself (e.g. Berlioz's *Symphonie Fantastique*, Tchaikovsky's *Hamlet*); it may be suggested to the choregrapher through the content of the music (e.g. Anthony Tudor's *Dark Elegies* to Mahler's *Kindertotenlieder*) or is superimposed on to already existing music (e.g. Tudor's *Lilac Garden* to Chausson's *Poème*). But these types of symphonic ballet can only be so termed because they are danced to symphonic music. They are really *demi-caractère* or romantic ballets, because the choregrapher must break away from the purely classical medium and create movements through which the dancers can express character as well as mood, emotion, and the actions arising from the theme.

Massine's symphonic ballets also led to further reform in décor and costumes. His dancers were given greater freedom of emotional expression, which could not be contained within the abbreviated or longer ballet skirts of academic or romantic works. Such costumes presupposed a distinctive, but limited vocabulary of dance, as did the décor of such ballets, which suggested definite period and locality. The artists André Masson, who designed the décor for *Les Présages*, and Terechkovich and Lourie, who designed it for *Choreartium*, drew their inspiration from the Greek style draperies and created a fashion which ultimately became known in the ballet world as "symphonic costume." It revealed and enhanced every movement made because the soft draperies floated easily and became one with the dancer's line. The scenery merely suggested mood and atmosphere by a subtle use of colour, and by nebulous shapes painted on background and set. These all helped the audience to concentrate on the dance. It was a form of décor in which Sophie Federovich was later to excel when she helped such choregraphers as Frederick Ashton (*see* page 165) and Andrée Howard (*see* page 174).

Massine continued to produce works with deeply philosophical themes such as *Nobilissima Visione* with music by Hindemith (1938) and, as recently as April 1961, produced a form of mystery play as a choregraphic poem for television *Laudes Evangelii.* But neither work displayed any new facet of his genius, although both reiterated his imaginative use of characteristic movement and his sensitive feeling for the total content of the music.

GEORGE BALANCHINE AND THE NEO-CLASSICAL BALLET IN AMERICA

The sense of dramatic action which Balanchine showed in *The Prodigal Son* (*see* page 130) was never again so clearly manifested in his later ballets. Until he settled in America (1933) some of his works contained expressive undercurrents of emotion and mood. But the fascination of his *La Concurrence* (1932) and *Cotillon* (1932) lay in the personal interpretation of their roles given by the young dancers for whom Massine was later to produce his symphonic ballets (*see* page 140). This personal interpretation came about because these young people were Russian by birth (although *emigrés*) and had been trained by Russians whose every movement, even in the classroom, was expressive. Thus their students instinctively felt the *cantilena* of the music, and perhaps projected some deeper meaning through their dancing than that suggested by the lightly sketched libretti of Boris Kochno, and despite Balanchine's own dictum that—

> Nothing is left to the principals or the *corps de ballet* to do for themselves; I show them every tiny movement and the least mimetic action, and I count their every step.
>
> (*Dance Journal*, Aug.–Oct., 1931)

This suggestion is made because shortly after Balanchine settled in America he deplored the complexities of many modern ballets which could not be understood without reference to the printed programme. He also averred that classical dance was the self-sufficient medium for any ballet. His attitude was understandable, if it is realized that he had come to a country without any balletic traditions of its own. Although most of the great dancing stars had visited the U.S.A. and some had opened their own schools (e.g. Mordkin, Kosloff, Fokine) no particular national style or ballet had emerged. Nor had it been Balanchine's intention to found a national school when invited to America by Lincoln Kerstein and Edward Warburg to start such a venture. But the results of his teaching and theories, expounded at the American School of Ballet, have now become apparent in every American dancer and ballet using classical technique.

All Balanchine's classical ballets bear his very distinctive visual hallmarks shown in his way of patterning certain technicalities and his choregraphic design is always subservient to certain musical principles. These ballets are abstract in content and have a single purpose, to display the classical dance qualities of the participants as they reveal the purely musical context of the composition Balanchine chooses to interpret. His choregraphic methods are quite unlike those of Fokine and Massine. He seems to regard his task as an intellectual exercise and with the eye of an expert in the science of geometrical equation and design, and the ear of an expert in sound, he deploys his dancers according to certain given formulas which he himself has devised and by which he disciplines himself.

BALANCHINE'S VISUAL HALLMARKS

Balanchine's visual formulas aim at a simplicity of dance-step and pattern with the design revolving round a central point which is the centre of the stage. Here dance the soloist, couple, trio, quartet or those who lead the various dance phrases. All others, if on the stage, direct their movements towards that centre so that the eyes of the audience are always focused on those dancers immediately in their central field of vision. All other dancers beyond that field usually echo the movements performed centrally, because Balanchine believes that the eye should not be distracted away from the main theme by any attempts to orchestrate dance as Fokine did in his classico-romantic ballets and Massine did in *Choreartium*. It is only when Balanchine wishes to discuss or introduce a new idea engendered by the music, that he places a different phrasing of movement in some secondary part of his design. He does this in such a way that the eyes of the audience will immediately change focus and relate this idea and its importance to the total design.

BALANCHINE'S MUSICAL HALLMARKS

The lack of orchestration and counterpoint in Balanchine's ballets arises from his personal definition of those terms. The only counterpoint he "sees in dance are the movements of arms, head and feet, which are contrapuntal to the static or vertical position of the body." He does not believe counterpoint can be achieved by contrasting the movements of two dancers or two groups as this type of choregraphic design results in disunity (*see Dance Index*, Vol. IV, nos. 2 and 3). Balanchine thus limits his movements to those through which he can give interesting shape to the line of the dancers' bodies by the angles and curves made by their legs and arms. But these shapes, angles and curves are never fussy or over-complicated. They are absolutely straightforward and clear in form. They have developed into what Lincoln Kerstein envisaged as a style springing from the American environment, "from the basket-ball courts, track and swimming meets, and junior proms" (*Blast on Ballet*, 1938). It is a style which displays the athletic physique and prowess of the American dancers to the greatest advantage because it has been pruned of all superfluities and outworn conventions. It is energetic rather than lyrical, yet it is feminine in essence. Balanchine finds few places for the male dancer, who might contrast too heavily with his carefully designed plans for the *danseuses*.

All Balanchine's movements are engendered by and parallel the musical content. But just as he has, so to speak, stripped his classical dance to the bare bones of physical movement so he has stripped his music. He hears and sees it in terms of note values, time signatures, cadences, chords, runs and other elements forming the musical structure. To each bar, or phrase he sets a particular step or series of steps, whose timing, accent and quality he believes parallel the notes written. Thus repetitions in the music are matched by repetitions in dance and so on. In other words, he tries to equate dance movements with what is written in the scores, and no matter whether the composition is by Bach, Mozart, Bizet, Stravinsky, or a modern American composer, provided the score is written according to the principles of classical composition, Balanchine applies the same formulas and frequently arrives at the same *enchaînements* in all his abstract works (e.g. runs in the score are usually matched by dancers running; quick *marcato* passages, by dancers stabbing their toes into the ground in the movements known as *posés*.)

Such choregraphic methods are controversial as not all members of the audience, nor dancers, nor musicians hear and see music in such terms. Natalie Roslavleva (the Soviet critic) writing about Balanchine's *Theme and Variations* (Tchaikovsky, and danced by Ballet Theatre in Moscow, 1961), stated that the performers danced to the notes but not to the music.

Nevertheless Balanchine's place in the history of choregraphic development in America is of great importance. Although his type of abstract ballet may lead nowhere, his streamlining of academic technique and theories on stage pattern, design and the relationship between music and dance taught young American dancers to re-examine this basic material for themselves. They ultimately discovered that it was not a dry-as-dust museum piece, but a living entity when, as a new generation of dancers, they began to practise it for themselves.

SERGE LIFAR AND THE REFORM OF FRENCH BALLET

Serge Lifar, Diaghilev's last embryo choregrapher, came into his own when he became leader of the Paris *Opéra* ballet. Posterity alone will decide whether he should not be considered as the most important figure in twentieth-century French ballet. He seems to occupy a somewhat similar place in France to that of Balanchine in America, not as an innovator of ballet as a spectacle, but as a *Professeur de Danse*. His work as choregrapher was considerable, but it was during his period as *Professeur* (1932–58) that his teaching and scholarship woke the ancient edifice from its lethargy and not only produced some great dancers such as Yvette Chauviré, Renée Jeanmaire, Jean Babilée and Roland Petit, but inspired the last-named to revolt and create modern works which were essentially French in content, style and flavour.

When Lifar became *premier danseur* at the *Opéra* (1930), its repertoire reflected the tastes of the late nineteenth century. Very few of the Fokine-Diaghilev reforms had found their way into the classrooms or into the ballets produced by masters adhering to the ideas of Saint-Léon and Petipa. The *premières étoiles* were all-important, therefore, even ballets by Balanchine and Nijinska had little chance of success if they did not meet with the approval of these ladies. Another weakening factor of the *Opéra* ballet was that women still occasionally appeared *en travesti*, and the few men were usually relegated to the positions of porters or walkers-on. Lifar changed this conception of ballet by setting to work in three ways—

1. By restoring the male dancer to his rightful place as co-lead or even sole hero in the ballet.
2. By constructing a new repertoire to further this aim.
3. By reforming the teaching in the school.

Lifar's difficulties lay in the fact that he had to work on all three tasks simultaneously and was himself leading dancer, choregrapher and teacher; thus he created ballets to display his particular talents, which were considerable. He was an excellent classical dancer of a modern style. His studies with Nijinska and Cecchetti had given him a firm technique based on the Russo-French and Italian schools, a knowledge amplified by his dancing specially created roles in the neo-classical ballets of Balanchine (e.g. *La Chatte* and *Apollon musagète*), Massine and others. It is not surprising, therefore, that when he commenced choregraphic work he felt the need to express himself through the medium in which he excelled. Moreover he was working for that body in which classical ballet had originated and he wished to restore its prestige. Thus the libretti of most of Lifar's ballets, especially those in which he starred, were usually based on a heroic subject from Greek or Roman myth, legend or history (e.g. *Prométhée*, 1930, *Icare*, 1935, *Alexandre le Grand*, 1937, *Phèdre*, 1950). He also created several abstract ballets in which he exploited that style of classical dance he had formulated from the vocabulary of his teachers and those choregraphers for whom he had danced.

At first little alteration could be perceived in the actual dancing at the *Opéra* when Lifar's ballets were presented. The *danseuses* retained their very feminine, somewhat formal expression, *ports de bras* and steps. The *danseurs* lacked the strength and, perhaps, the courage to emulate the sheer physical energy and enthusiastic dancing of Lifar himself, they had been in the background for too long. The discrepancies between the dancing of the star and his cast did not escape the notice of the management. In 1932 they made Lifar *Professeur de Danse*.

The opportunities offered by such a position were many and Lifar made the most of them. He carefully studied classical dance both historically and practically and allowed the knowledge thus gained to colour his choregraphy and teaching. In a very short time dancers began to appear who understood what he required from them because, unlike most choregraphers, Lifar committed himself to print and in his various books laid down the precepts by which he disciplined both his dancers and his choregraphy.

However excellent these precepts might be, Lifar was the first to admit that although he rarely contradicted his technical writings, his choregraphy was often at variance with those writings dealing with his work as *choréauthor*, a self-appointed title, defining his work as originator and producer of the entire synthesis of arts known as "a ballet."

LIFAR'S CLASSIC DANCE

In defining that form of dance he termed "classic," Lifar sought to determine the quality, line and composition of dance movements performed by dancers according to the academic steps laid down by the great teachers. They are generalizations of dance movements performed by many people in different walks of life and phases of development, they are broad in outline, pictorial in effect and clear in execution. They lose their quality if coloured by emotion or characteristic detail. They are seen at their best when utilized in ballets whose libretti deal with themes of dramatic interest and implication, as understood in the ancient Greek and Roman theatres (*see* page 2), or in abstract ballets of which they are the only medium of expression. The choregraphic design of most of Lifar's ballets was spacious in gesture and architectural in form. The lines drawn by the dancers were all-important because the patterns, and particularly the slow massing of groups, were deployed over the various levels into which his sets were usually divided. This slow massing of groups into some pose was effective in drawing the eyes of the audience to the relationship between the various dancers as they gradually froze into a complete picture, bounded only by the proscenium arch and footlights.

Lifar's method of thus grouping and setting his dancers into pictures might be said to have let light into the design of French ballet and given it back that calm, calculated expressiveness it had had in the past, and which it had lost in the works of choregraphers elsewhere anxious to interpret either the *cantilena* and emotional content, or the purely musical context of their score. The statuesque posturing in Lifar's ballets would not have been so apparent if he had not taken up so strong a position *vis-à-vis* his music.

LIFAR AND MUSIC

On assuming the role of choregrapher, Lifar made it clear that he considered himself a "Petipa" (*see* page 77) and bowed to no one in asserting his right to call himself the originator of the dancing, that is the principal and only part of the spectacle that mattered.

He coined the term *choréauthor*, a title which cleared up any ambiguities arising from the terms *ballet-master* or *choregrapher*, which in this book have been used to describe those artists responsible for giving life to any story, theme or essay by means of dance, mime, danced-mime or mimed-dance.

Lifar's reasons for the change were justifiable. He had noted how Diaghilev's choregraphers left him when they began to resent the impresario's dominant position as producer and initiator of so many fruitful artistic collaborations. Lifar had also experienced the way in which composers and designers could play so prominent a role in a ballet that dance scarcely existed in its own right.

He had become convinced that dance, most of all classical dance, should not and could not be an illustration of music. It must make its own rhythms; and although it could do without music, he did not believe this was often possible, because music could heighten the expressiveness of movement by playing upon the emotions and sympathies of both dancers and audience.

Unfortunately Lifar did not define what he personally meant by rhythm. He was alive to the problems that were raised by the weakness of academic dance rhythms, and realized that Fokine and Massine in their classico-romantic and *demi-caractère* ballets had allowed their composers to inspire and to supplement their groupings of steps and poses to give them sense.

In *Icare* (1935) Lifar created his own movement groupings of timing, intensity and flow of line, and reinforced the rhythmic patterns made by percussion, thus following the example of several pioneers (e.g. Margaret Morris and Mary Wigman). But his work was not so effective as theirs.

His experiment aroused controversy as many of his audience failed to appreciate the rhythms made through academic dance, which is by nature soundless. The accompanying percussion only emphasized this weakness because it was too strong and incisive in character to accompany movements which were meant to be seen, and not heard. Such an accompaniment suggested a more informal type of dance, with strong well-accented sounds from the footwork made by the dancer himself to emphasize his reactions to the events overtaking him.

Lifar did not experiment further with percussion only, but continued to dictate to his composers the rhythms of his choregraphic design, or else imposed his own rhythmic phrasing on specially chosen music, which he treated as being subservient to his dance, and not an equal partner.

His methods certainly drew attention to the predominant element in all his ballets, the slow dramatic qualities of classical dance movement, particularly when performed by men. It was this revival of masculinity that was so important to French ballet, as Roland Petit was to prove after the 1939–45 War.

ANNA PAVLOVA AND THE AUDIENCE (1881–1931)

No history of ballet can be complete if it does not mention the name of Anna Pavlova. Although she contributed nothing to the development of choregraphic design (*see* page 57), her services to the art of dance are immeasurable. It was she who showed world-wide audiences the infinite capacities of a great artist to express, through dance, joy and sorrow, life and death, and all the moods and emotions of some of the most beautiful and simple things of nature. Her interpretation of *The Dying Swan*, *The Californian Poppy* and *Christmas* were only three of her exquisite miniatures which enthralled thousands of people of all races and in all places. Her dancing in these and such well-tried favourites as *Giselle*, *La Fille mal gardée* and *The Fairy Doll* taught them what was meant by expression, line, musicality and artistry in dance. None who saw her will ever forget the lessons she taught them every time she stepped on to the stage to recreate one of her many delicate, yet deeply etched portraits of a living being, with feelings and passions like any of her audience. She gave of herself ungrudgingly all the time.

But what is, perhaps, as important as her winning of audiences for ballet is the inspiration she gave to those embryo dancers in her audience, to make them seek to emulate her example and become the dancers of yesterday and today. Their names are legion. Many came from the Commonwealth, but many more from England where she finally made her home (1912).

Perhaps English ballet owes more than it realizes to Anna Pavlova. Her popularity with English audiences paved the way for other dancers to offer themselves to the London and provincial theatres. Moreover, the fact that she would accept English-trained dancers into her company brought other teachers and dancers to London, such as Seraphina Astafieva, Tamara Karsavina, Lydia Kyasht, Legat, Morosoff, Novikov and Cecchetti. It was from their schools that the first English dancers came to join Diaghilev and later to become the nucleus of the first English ballet companies.

FURTHER READING

BEAUMONT, C. W., *Complete Book of Ballets* (London, Putnam, 1939).
BEAUMONT, C. W., *Supplement to the Complete Book of Ballets* (London, Putnam, 1942).
EVANS, EDWIN and LAWSON, JOAN, *The Dancing Times*, articles and criticisms in.
LIFAR, SERGE, *Diaghilev* (London, Putnam, 1940).
LIFAR, SERGE, *Ballet Traditional to Modern* (London, Putnam, 1938).

CHAPTER 11

English Ballet

Let his Attitudes be suitable to the Subject, so as to express the Thoughts and Conception of the Mind by the Motions of the Eyes, Hands and the whole Body.

(John Weaver)

The success of John Weaver's *The Loves of Mars and Venus* and later *ballets d'action* (*see* page 29) did not lead to the founding of an English school of ballet. There are two possible reasons: *firstly* the harlequinades or pantomimes, which had developed from the masques and burlesques of Weaver's work became too popular; *secondly*, there was plenty of ballet. After the Restoration, and particularly from 1717 onwards, when Marie Sallé made her first appearance (*see* page 31), London was entertained by such dancers as Mesdames Rose, Théodore, Taglioni, Grahn, Elssler, Grisi, Cerrito, Genée, Kyasht, Pavlova and Messieurs Dupré, Vestris, Didelot, Perrot, Mordkin and finally the Diaghilev company. But after Diaghilev's death English ballet came into its own. In the brief space of thirty years it has become as famous as other longer-lived companies in Paris, Leningrad, Copenhagen, Milan and Moscow.

The date upon which English ballet was born is unknown. It could be when Phyllis Bedells took over the leading role from the Russian, Lydia Kyasht, at the Empire Theatre in 1914, or when the "Haines English Ballet" set out from Manchester (1915). Another date is 1920 when P. J. S. Richardson, O.B.E., and Édouard Espinosa laid the foundation of what was later the Royal Academy of Dancing whose aim was to raise the technical standards and qualifications of both teachers and dancers. Seen in retrospect, Diaghilev's production of *The Sleeping Beauty* (1921) might also mark the birth of English ballet, instead of being another milestone in the history of ballet in England, because it proved that some English dancers were capable of meeting that impresario's demands for technique and artistry. But it was not until 1930 that a distinctive form of English balletic art began to emerge from two London schools, who sometimes joined forces to present evenings of ballet under the auspices of the Camargo Society. This body was founded by P. J. S. Richardson, Edwin Evans (the music critic) and Arnold L. Haskell (later Director of the Royal Ballet School), to further the art of ballet and the careers of English dancers when, after Diaghilev's death, there seemed to be no outlet for their services save in pantomime, revue, the music halls or other musical shows.

The present success of English ballet is however primarily due to the work of Dame Marie Rambert and Dame Ninette de Valois, neither of whom were English born, the former being Polish, the latter Irish, but both of whom established their own companies in England and helped to originate most of the valuable traditions to which all present English ballets owe their being.

DAME MARIE RAMBERT (1888–)

Dame Marie Rambert occupies a unique position in the history of ballet, not as a dancer, nor a choregrapher, but as a pioneer in the teaching of choregraphic form and design, whose inspired guidance of several English choregraphers was so effective that even their earliest ballets were seen to be most sensitive amalgams of the various arts which make up the whole, and ideally suited to the youth and enthusiasm of their performers and their audiences.

Her training for such work was far from orthodox. Her early dance lessons in Poland might be said to have been nullified when she came under the influence of Isadora Duncan but at least they gave her a sense of theatrical discipline. Later she studied with Dalcroze (1910–13) for whom she taught and designed ballets in his Dresden school, that were more organized and polished in form than those of his other students. On being sent to help Nijinsky stage *The Rite of Spring*, she again became interested in classical dance and, after studying with Cecchetti and Astafieva, opened her school in London (1920) from whence gradually emerged an interesting group of young dancers, who made one of their first appearances in *A Tragedy of Fashion* in a revue, *Riverside Nights* (1926), at the Lyric Theatre, Hammersmith. This was the first ballet by Frederick Ashton, who was later to become the leading English choregrapher.

The Marie Rambert dancers gave two seasons at the same theatre in 1930 with such success that Dame Marie decided to found the Ballet Club, which worked at the Mercury Theatre (owned by her husband, Ashley Dukes). Here her own dancers performed together with guests, some of whom were famous (e.g. Alicia Markova) and some who were to become famous (e.g. Margot Fonteyn). At first the venture was purely experimental but the interest it aroused in ballet lovers and the dancing profession soon allowed the Club to stage regular Sunday performances. It was the regularity of creative work in a theatre that gave these young dancers and choregraphers valuable experience, a stage upon which to experiment and prove themselves worthy of stepping into the arena of world ballet, when the time came during and after the 1939–45 War.

The most important part of Dame Marie's work at the Ballet Club and later for Ballet Rambert was her guidance of young choregraphers. Among these were Frederick Ashton, Anthony Tudor, Andrée Howard, Walter Gore and others. This work can be briefly summarized under four headings.

MUSICAL KNOWLEDGE

Dame Marie's ability to impart her musical knowledge and feeling for the content of all types of music, meant that no dancer or choregrapher working for her could fail to understand the implications of each score chosen for interpretation. Without imposing too rigid a formula, or dictating the principles upon which to wed dance and music, as Balanchine and Lifar had done, she ensured that the choregraphic design was properly phrased and enhanced by accent and the changing qualities of the movement, no matter in which style the movement was couched. This helped both dancers and choregraphers to express through dance, the atmosphere, mood and movement inherent in the score.

SENSE OF THE THEATRE

Dame Marie's work with Diaghilev had made her realize the need fully to develop each element in a ballet. She understood the limitations of the tiny Mercury Theatre stage, and, to some extent, the inexperience of her dancers. She never allowed any excess of choregraphic design, affectation of movement or over-exuberance of emotional dance to cloak the action, if a story were told. This meant that her choregraphers had to learn very early the need of being economical in their use of dance when creating the structure of their plot.

The limitations of both the Mercury Theatre and its financial backing helped Dame Marie to stress the need always to find the appropriate movement to give expression and reveal the content of the plot, without the aid of elaborate costume and scenery. These latter, however briefly sketched in the ballets presented, had to reveal the movement as well as be appropriate to the period and location of the action. She insisted too that stage lighting played its part in enhancing and helping to create the necessary illusion of mood, atmosphere and time of day or night.

EXPERIMENTAL WORK

Perhaps the most vital element in Dame Marie's work as Director of the Ballet Club and later of Ballet Rambert was her fearlessness. From the very beginning of her career as producer, she was never afraid of experiment. A choregrapher could always try some new idea, either by way of subject (e.g. Andrée Howard's *Lady into Fox*), by dance material (e.g.

Anthony Tudor's *Dark Elegies*), or by unusual costumes and set (e.g. Sophie Fedorovitch's black and white designs for Ashton's *Les Masques*). Dame Marie's belief in experiment has more recently proved valuable in the first ballets of Norman Morrice (e.g. *Two Brothers*, etc.) where the young choregrapher succeeded in presenting a contemporary plot with a firm contemporary style of movement, which he is continuing to develop.

DAME MARIE RAMBERT AND HER DANCERS

In the same way that she has exposed and fostered the talent of those choregraphers stemming from her school, Dame Marie brought out the talent of particular dancers. This tended to make her company, in its early stages, a group of interesting individuals. It was this individuality that was so important to the English dancers when they began to step into the leading roles of the English ballet companies, in which foreigners were to play only a minor role as guest stars for a short period.

THE ROYAL BALLET AND ITS CHIEF CHOREGRAPHERS

History shows that choregraphers can be divided roughly into two types. To the first belong such artists as Didelot, Fokine and Massine who create ballets because they love the art itself and believe certain subjects give them the necessary outlet through which to make innovations and develop the art more fully as a medium of expression. Such choregraphers usually begin by establishing their new ideas in the classroom. Then, when they create a ballet, they plot all the fine details of movement, its characterization, relationship to music and other elements, and insist that each dancer maintain exactly the design laid down. To the second category belong such choregraphers as Taglioni, Saint-Léon and Lifar, who see the potentialities of certain artists and build ballets to suit their particular abilities and personalities.

Both types of choregrapher are of the utmost value. The former will develop the potentialities of their dancers by broadening their experience of physical movement and by the mental exercise of expressing themselves only through the medium laid down. The latter give their artists confidence by building upon and finding new ways of presenting the movements best suited to the personality and qualities of a particular individual. Thus the former will create a company disciplined to conform to the idea of ballet as a whole. The latter will develop the individual talents within that company and bring them to the leading roles.

Since 1935, the Royal Ballet (as it is now known) has had two main choregraphers, Dame Ninette de Valois and Sir Frederick Ashton, the former belonging to the first and the latter to the second category mentioned above. The result of their joint effort is clearly evident, as Soviet critics were quick to note during the company's very successful visit to Leningrad and Moscow—

> Every ballet presented and every dancer therein are witness to the sound basis of their classical school. Every performer works as part of a collective, so that even the most prominent of artists in its midst are seen in their proper perspective, as leaders in a ballet by right of the part they play in the action.
>
> (*Soviet Culture*, 1961)

DAME NINETTE DE VALOIS AND THE NARRATIVE BALLET (1898–)

> It is the ballet and not the individual that matters.
>
> (DAME NINETTE DE VALOIS in a lecture to teachers, 1949)

Dame Ninette de Valois is the twentieth-century John Weaver (*see* page 27). Unlike him, however, she has succeeded in founding *firstly*, a native ballet, known as The Royal Ballet with its roots firmly based in the traditions of the English theatre and *secondly*, in establishing an English school of classical dance, that has been evolved from the teaching of French, Italian and Russian masters. But she has added elements inherent in the physique, character, temperament and capacity for movement of the English dancers. These have gradually manifested themselves as both she and Frederick Ashton have gained a deeper insight into the particular qualities and abilities of the dancers with whom they work, into the traditions and techniques of the various English arts helping to form the basis and background for their ballets, and into the appetites of their audience. The creation of this audience is one of Dame Ninette's most interesting achievements for no other choregrapher mentioned herein has had to set out to win and hold an audience, and make it larger until the moment when the Royal Ballet became, in all but name, one of the first two State theatrical enterprises in England; the other was the Old Vic Theatre company.

This winning of an audience, where none existed before, came about because Dame Ninette has always seized upon every opportunity to present dance in every kind of theatre. Starting in a troupe of girl dancers touring the provinces, dancing as a soloist in pantomime, opera, revue and in the Diaghilev Ballet, she also staged her own solo act in that most exacting of theatres, the music hall. Here she learnt the hardest lesson of all: how to make an immediate impression and win the attention of an audience, hold it during the six minutes allowed and take the applause so that the next turn on the bill got a warmer welcome. Dame Ninette has never forgotten that lesson. One of the important hallmarks of her ballets is the way in which her choregraphic design immediately establishes location, atmosphere, mood, period and character by a few swift but sure strokes of movement as the curtain rises.

It was not until she had experienced all forms of theatre open to dancers, that Dame

Ninette founded her own Academy of Choregraphic Art (1926). Its story and the story of *The Sadler's Wells Ballet* (now Royal Ballet) has been told by Mary Clarke. Therein is described how, from a small nucleus of students, Dame Ninette has developed an organization embracing a Junior and Senior School, a ballet company numerous enough to be divided into two sections of varying size, one part resident for the most time at the Royal Opera House, London, and the other touring the provinces or abroad. In addition Dame Ninette also helps to organize or advise other national companies. Among these activities her work as choregrapher is overlooked. But Dame Ninette's ballets are a vital part of the English choregraphic traditions.

DAME NINETTE AND ENGLISH TRADITIONS

Dame Ninette's first concern as teacher is to obtain the correct style and quality of movement for the task in hand. Anyone privileged to watch her taking a class quickly realizes how carefully each step is set within an *enchaînement* and phrased and accented so that the dance passage demonstrates the particular purpose of the exercise. Similarly her main concerns as choregrapher are *firstly* to create the proper style, quality and form of movement which will characterize and paint the being, action, behaviour and emotion of each player as he narrates her tragedy or comedy, *secondly* to ensure that all movements are co-ordinated with the music and bring about the appropriate moments of tension and relaxation as the plot unfolds, thereby maintaining the necessary mood and atmosphere, *thirdly* to set her dancers firmly within the framework of her set so that they appear to be living and reacting to the events and stimuli round themselves, and do not, therefore, appeal, as individuals, to the audience.

At the beginning of her career as ballet-mistress at the Old Vic and later when producing ballets at the Sadler's Wells Theatre, Dame Ninette was interested in establishing a school and repertoire which would appeal to and, to some extent, foster a love of classical dance in her almost ignorant audience "on the wrong side of the river." At the same time she was fully conscious that if her undertaking were to become truly national in spirit, she must seek inspiration from those sources in which lay the strength of English art, namely the narrative powers of the greatest English dramatists, novelists and poets who are deeply interested in character and action, unlike the French who prefer to discuss behaviour. Many English artists and musicians have also shown a strong leaning towards the dramatic, literary and lyrical, and attempt both to characterize and dramatize the motives and actions of their subject, within the limitations of their own medium. William Blake did this when he illustrated *The Book of Job*, and depicted its characters in action and emotion and at the same time conveyed his own belief in and reverence for the Bible; and so did William Hogarth, who registered his protest at the abuses of his time in *The Rake's Progress*, and Thomas Rowlandson, who mercilessly caricatured the world of fashion and the theatre, and whose drawings formed a base for *The Prospect before Us*. Such graphic artists inspired Dame Ninette to create ballets which revealed their strongly national, narrative traits and demanded a more characteristic and expressive medium than that offered by classical dance.

DAME NINETTE AND PLASTIQUE

Dame Ninette believes classical dance is the essential base for the repertoire of the Royal Ballet, but she has never denied the validity of other dance mediums, if the subject demands them. She herself understood the limitation of academic technique when she designed movements for the Chorus in the Greek Plays produced by Terence Gray (Arts Theatre, Cambridge, 1926–31), and the *Plays for Dancers* by W. B. Yeats (Abbey Theatre, Dublin, 1928–34). From her experience of working in Fokine's ballets, Dame Ninette worked out her own system of *plastique*, exercises based on the same natural laws of opposition and balance as academic dance, but completely eliminating the turn-out so that the limbs worked in natural relationship to the body. Such movements were designed to make students understand how to adapt their bodies to different choregraphic designs and through them to explore space by moving in horizontal, perpendicular and other lines and planes. They learnt how to make or define quality of a movement by passing from strength to weakness, lightness to heaviness and so on. Each exercise was firmly wedded to music, which could change and thus change the quality or speed of the movement.

Although such exercises explored space, that space was limited by the pattern through which the dancer moved, and which often offered some geometrical proposition of lines, angles and/or curves. The discipline this gave helped her students to understand the demands made by different choregraphers. But its real value was seen in those of Dame Ninette's ballets that were inspired by the artists William Blake, William Hogarth, Édouard Manet and Thomas Rowlandson. Her firm grasp of the principles of design through movement allowed her to bring to life successfully the content and characters of *The Book of Job*, *The Rake's Progress*, *Bar aux Folies bergères* (created for Ballet Rambert) and *The Prospect before Us*. Each artist had depicted the set, placing and action of the characters and suggested the atmosphere and mood of the whole. Dame Ninette drew her lines of dance from one picture to the next and, by the expressiveness of her choregraphic design within the limits of frame and content, convinced the audience that the characters painted had come to life to tell their story.

Nowhere was Dame Ninette's use of *plastique* so effective as in *Job*, the great *Masque for Dancing* devised by Doctor Geoffrey Keynes (the authority on William Blake) and the composer, Ralph Vaughan Williams, O.M. It had been rejected by Diaghilev as "too solemn and English." Yet its very English factors made it so different from his ballets and acceptable to its first English audiences. It was the "most satisfying achievement of the English theatre season" of 1931 (Ashley Dukes in *Theatre Arts Monthly*). That it was produced at all was due to Constant Lambert, the vital musician who laid the foundation of the Royal Ballet's excellent musical background. He believed in the potentialities of *Job* and persuaded the Camargo Society to offer it to Dame Ninette for production at their fourth performance (5th July, 1936). It was an exciting challenge to the choregrapher.

Job was built on the heroic scale of an English masque and, because of its biblical origin, possessed something of the ritual essence of the older miracle plays. The libretto contained both narrative and descriptive passages (*see* page 121), the former to define the active struggle between Good and Evil, the Godhead and Satan, and Satan and Job, the latter to create the atmosphere and display the results of that struggle. To establish rhythms suitable for dancing, Vaughan Williams used some well-known dance forms. But his virile "Pavane," "Sarabande," "Gaillard," and other dances would have overwhelmed those gentle court footings and any classical dance *sur les pointes* which the composer deemed impossible mediums to paint Blake's mystical subject. The music had the grandeur of much English church music which gave the masque its feeling of spacious reverence and air of ritual. At the same time the composer utilized much that is inherent in English folk music, and this gave the necessary vigour and character to those narrative passages where the action defined Satan's challenge and struggles with Job.

Yet despite its traditional background, Vaughan Williams's music belongs to no period. It was and is timeless, like Blake's illustrations to *The Book of Job* from which Gwendolen Raverat drew her designs for set and costumes. It was the great merit of Dame Ninette's choregraphic design that it captured this timelessness. Her *plastique* was no fashionable, temporary idiom. It had its roots in simple dance movements, but so framed that they clearly painted all the characters and defined their actions and reactions to each situation arising from Satan's struggle with Job. Moreover they clearly marked the difference between the two opposing forces; those of Good were softly lyrical and rounded in form, those of Evil strongly angular and assertive. It was the first time that movement within prescribed lines and space had been used to heighten the emotional content of a dramatic masque. It was the first English ballet in which the narrative quality of dance was seen to be the most vital element of the production.

Two other ballets by Dame Ninette also owed much of their narrative strength to her use of *plastique*, *Orpheus and Eurydice* (1941) and *Don Quixote* (1950). In the latter she created a host of characters from a simple leitmotive of movement arising from the briefly descriptive dance of the village slut, Aldonza. It was crude, awkward, even vulgar as Aldonza "cocked a snook" at the gaunt old knight. But as he gazed into her eyes, she drew a lock of hair across her face and began to turn, and as she did so her movements became more beautiful, more truly classical. Then from amongst the dim figures that circled round her, there emerged the Dulcinea of the Don's dream. From this point all the figures surrounding the Don in reality took their colouring from Aldonza's dance, but those surrounding him in his imagination took their movements from Dulcinea and some of the most beautiful were the truly classical *pas de deux* when the Don told his tale of *The Age of Gold.*

It was this link between the movements of the two sets of characters that gave *Don Quixote* the continuity it would otherwise have lacked because the score, by Roberto Gerhard, was too episodic to allow proper development of action. Similarly by so quickly melting the moments of reality into fantasy and back again through movement Dame Ninette was able to bring her characters into close contact with each other and with Edward Burra's imaginative sets. Thus the narrative was more clearly understood.

DAME NINETTE AND NARRATIVE DANCE

The strong feeling for narrative dance as well as the musical features which Dame Ninette displayed in *Job* were carried further in *The Rake's Progress* (20th May, 1935) and *Checkmate* (15th June, 1937) whose scores she inspired by outlining the action before the composers began work. The former required music of a definite period quality because Hogarth's paintings were not classical generalizations (*see* page 156), but were of particular persons at a particular place and time. To supply this Gavin Gordon, the composer, borrowed from the street songs and ballads of Hogarth's London and provided a score redolent of English sentiment and picturesque incident, in which the narrative and descriptive passages were so closely knit that the Rake progressed from wealth and sanity to destitution and madness at an ever-increasing speed. This pace arose from Dame Ninette's handling of her libretto, which was a masterly example of her directness of purpose. She selected only those incidents in Hogarth's paintings which would allow her to show the causes of the Rake's downfall in sufficient variety to warrant his final madness. Each musical passage had to drive the action onwards yet allow each character time to establish itself and play his or her part in the tragedy. By thus controlling her music and dance material and by carefully balancing intense periods of action with relaxed periods of description, Dame Ninette was able to narrate her story and paint her characters at almost one and the same time. This was most obvious in the first and last scenes, where she suggested only some of the interests on which the Rake squandered his heritage and only some of the tragic inmates in Bedlam, the mad-house.

In balancing her periods of tension and relaxation, Dame Ninette went further than any of Diaghilev's choregraphers in developing his idea that the dancers themselves must be seen and heard to play a vital part in making the rhythms if a drama be given a sense of reality. Fokine and Massine had shown how this could be done when working with folk-dance material in which the sound of the footwork is usually essential (*see* page 117). But Dame Ninette was working with *demi-caractère* dance and *plastique* in order to give her choregraphy greater narrative qualities. To create the impression that the dancers were motivating the music she regulated the tempos and what can be termed the pressure of the movements. There are many examples: in the first scene the Tailor, Hornblower, Jockey, Fencing and Dancing-masters dance in turn to the same tune at the same tempo while the Rake picks up first one and then another's movement with an undecided form of footwork which is perfected during the dancing lesson. But as soon as he arrives in the Brothel, the tempo of his movements fluctuates as each new incident finds him becoming still more "unbuttoned" in his behaviour. In the third scene (the Gambling Den), Dame Ninette emphasized the speed at which the Rake is deteriorating by loudening the sound of her characters' footwork and hand movements to reinforce the urgent tone of the music. The composer created a persistent, recurrent phrase which the card players punctuate by stamping their feet, slapping their thighs, and noisily taking snuff to mark their impatience. Then, when the Rake arrives, the game begins, and they emphasize the tune's persistence and heighten the tension already roused by slightly increasing the tempo as each round of cards is more loudly slapped on to the table, and the dice shaken a little longer until the final throw when, in the sudden silence and stillness, the Rake is seen to be mad.

This same increase in the speed and pressure of movement to bring about the final denouement was outstandingly effective in *Checkmate*, where the Red King was both seen and heard to be deliberately trapped within the staves of Black Pieces, until the momentary silence when he was finally immobilized and the musical cadence when the Black Queen removed his crown and killed him.

The score of *Checkmate* offered greater problems than that of *The Rake's Progress*. Although Dame Ninette had outlined her plot to the composer, Sir Arthur Bliss, he seemed to require longer than the choregrapher to establish character and develop action. Thus some narrative passages lost their dramatic urgency because prolonged by introductory descriptive phrases. Nevertheless the choregraphic design was fully deployed within the limits and particular moves of the game, which gave Dame Ninette time to etch in the action of Red losing all. The choregraphy, based on classical dance, avoided conventionalities, its narrative and emotional content was conveyed by strongly expressive movement evolved from two sources. The steps of the chessmen were largely determined by the space in which they moved. The Pawns danced fussily from square to square, the Knight leapt and turned diagonally and the Black Queen, by virtue of her leading role, performed steps of all types.

But it was not only the spatial quality of the steps which determined the characteristics of the players. Dame Ninette realizes the effect that age, emotion and events can have on the body. She has always used this knowledge to give greater realism and expression to her dance. It was apparent in *The Rake's Progress*, where the Rake was seen to deteriorate mentally and physically and the Young Girl to become more resolute as the plot unfolded. Such physical changes in movement strengthen the narrative quality of dance, as Perrot proved in *Giselle* (*see* page 166). There was no deterioration but a subtle distinction was made in the movements of *Checkmate*. Dame Ninette was narrating a classic struggle between Life and Death with Love intervening, and the players were variously symbolized in movement.

Although the Red Knight was strong in battle he was gentle in his loyalty to his King and Queen. Therein lay the weak streak of his character, which was shown vividly when the moment came to kill the Black Queen who had won his love. The Red Queen symbolized the tender love a woman has for a man in all his weakness, but the Black Queen was seen to be ruthless in her love to possess and dominate, particularly when dancing under the shadow of Death. This highly stylized figure stalking the stage again drew attention to Dame Ninette's concern with subjects narrated by great English writers and which arose from their Protestant background—namely the struggle between Life and Death or Love and Death.

Despite her preoccupation with dramatic narrative, clearly stated in terms of good and evil, Dame Ninette has also concerned herself with comedy, as in *The Prospect before Us*, which some complained was too broadly based and vulgar to be effective in ballet. These critics forgot the traditions of English theatrical humour and its sometimes bawdy fun; it was, therefore, quite legitimate to draw on such sources and create a ballet, particularly as its theme was based on a true story of the London theatres and contained an imaginative reproduction of an eighteenth-century ballet at the King's Theatre, once drawn by Rowlandson.

An interesting element of *The Prospect before Us* was the score. In itself the music by the English composer, William Boyce, was charmingly entertaining for performer and audience in an eighteenth-century drawing room. But with that infallible sense of timing, which he alone of the Royal Ballet conductors has possessed, Constant Lambert has brilliantly orchestrated and brought out its life and its gaiety in such a way that it gained character and was thus able to underline the wit and the humour with which Dame Ninette invested her tale of the great artist Noverre and his colleagues and managers (*see* page 37).

Both *The Rake's Progress* and *The Prospect before Us* are evidence of the need to soak oneself in the appropriate materials before setting out to create a ballet utilizing realistic sources. Like Fokine before her, Dame Ninette had to discipline her choregraphy by referring to the known facts about her subjects, particularly when her characters had lived so vividly, that artists and writers could record their activities. Yet no matter whether the players in her tragedies or comedies are drawn from fact or fiction, everything about them is drawn in terms of characteristic dance, which is pertinent to one character in that one ballet. The dancers, therefore, like the English character actors, have to extend themselves fully into the role laid down and give it life.

DAME NINETTE AND THE MALE DANCER

The important role Dame Ninette's narrative ballets have played in founding an English choregraphic tradition, also bears witness to the vital part she has played in establishing the right of the English male dancer to a prominent place in the ballet. Until recently no other English choregrapher has so fully exploited the male dancer. No one, outside Russia, has understood like Didelot (*see* page 45) the difference that must be made in the choregraphic design if the male dancer is to be anything more than a porter. Until she created the role of Satan in *Job* for Anton Dolin in 1931, the powers of that outstanding dancer had never been so fully extended in any ballet created for him. His interpretation of this earthbound, fallen Angel, with his arrogant pride and virile sense of evil-doing not only proved him to be a great character artist, but set an example to all his compatriots. The creation of *The Rake's Progress*, with Walter Gore as the Rake, deepened the impression that the English *danseur* would excel in character roles when closely held within the choregraphic discipline. But the dancing of Harold Turner as the Red Knight in *Checkmate* and Robert Helpmann in *The Haunted Ballroom* showed that Dame Ninette was fully aware of the need to develop also the purely academic dance of her boys, if she were ultimately to produce the great classical ballets which, she insisted, would serve as the basis for the Royal Ballet repertoire. Perhaps the most convincing evidence of her success in bringing the English male dancer to the fore, in a country where his presence had hitherto been ignored, was during the Royal Ballet's visit to the U.S.S.R. Both critics and audiences noted their excellence and variety, ranging from the characterization and eccentricity of such artists as Grant, Holden and Edwards to the classical manliness of Shaw, Blair and Usher.

SIR FREDERICK ASHTON AND THE POETRY OF DANCE (1906–)

Dance and only dance is what finally matters.
(Fokine)

The outstanding feature of all Frederick Ashton's ballets is the dancing quality of his choregraphic design, no matter in which style they are couched. Few other choregraphers have worked with such varied subjects, ranging from the severely classical *Symphonic Variations* and *Scènes de Ballet* to the sophisticated burlesque of *Façade*, the simple *Capriol Suite* to the richly humorous *La Fille mal gardée*, and from the delicate *Nocturne* to the spectacularly evocative *Persephone*. In all these and many other ballets he shows his mastery and original use of the classical vocabulary. Ashton is a great classicist and it is his originality in the handling of this medium that has proved to be the most valuable asset of English ballet. Without it, it is questionable whether the Royal Ballet and its dancers would have reached the predominant position they now occupy. He is that rare choregrapher who captures the elusive ideas he feels, hears and sees in music and poetry, and gives them tangible form through the movements of those dancers upon whose individual qualities he seizes. His ballets are conceived only in terms of dance, his sole means of expression, except in those rare cases where the period and location of his plot demand more conventional means (e.g. *La Fille mal gardée*).

These important qualities have been evident since his earliest works, *Capriol Suite* and *Pomona* (1930). When Ashton staged his first ballets in *Riverside Nights* and for the Ballet Club (*see* page 152), he was faced with three problems. The first problem was to produce ballets for audiences little interested in their artistic content, but enjoying sophisticated humour; and an audience fully interested and anxious to build an English ballet, but knowing little how to help and having as their only guide the Diaghilev repertoire and Dame Marie Rambert's careful handling of her choregraphers' work; the second was to create ballets for dancers, whose technique, like his own, was at a formative stage, and the third, to stage everything as economically as possible. Ashton had one solution to these problems, to study dance and produce ballets in which simple *enchaînements* were made more interesting because the steps and poses were linked and used in new ways and were expressive of his ideas and themes.

ASHTON AND CLASSICAL DANCE

Ashton's use of the classical vocabulary has always been different from that of Nijinska, Massine and Balanchine in their neo-classical, symphonic and *demi-caractère* ballets. Like Fokine with the *arabesque* in *Les Sylphides* (*see* page 98), he seeks the expression within the movement itself and, by simple adjustments in the line made by the dancer and by a careful imposition of subtle detail throughout the movement made by the whole body, he changes the usual conception of academic dance as practised in the classroom and makes his dancers give it expression when they reach the stage.

It is in his exploitation of the *arabesque* that Ashton has perhaps taught his dancers and audience why dance is the sole means of expression for ballet. This pose in his works rarely follows its technical definition. Nor does he see it only as a pose to be held as the culminating point of an *enchaînement* as in a purely classical dance (e.g. *Scènes de Ballet*). He often exploits it as a travelling step, carrying his *danseuse* widely over the stage (e.g. *Symphonic Variations*) or allowing her to float in her partner's arms (e.g. *Ondine*) or to describe her emotions as the plot develops. There is the tragic *arabesque* of the Poor Girl in *Nocturne* as she plunged across the square in deep sorrow, the joyous one of *La Fille mal gardée* as Lise throws her pink ribbon into the air, and the deeply felt loving *arabesque* as *Cinderella* falls into her Prince's arms.

Ashton often gives his choregraphic design significant meaning by accentuating a detail in some part of the dance. This particular facet was noted in the "Pavane" of *Capriol Suite* (1930), where the lovely use of the *ports de bras* lent a tender lyricism to what might have been a stilted Promenade. It expressed the emotions of lovers who dare not speak their thoughts aloud. Later the exquisite arm and hand movements of the Bride in *The Wise Virgins* (1940) brought life to the simple purity of a dedicated maiden. Ashton developed these subtle gestures much further for his *ballerina*, Margot Fonteyn, in *Daphnis and Chloe* (1951) and *Tiresias* (1951), until they became as flexible as those of an Indian dancer in *La Péri* (1956). In these ballets and *Madame Crysanthème* (1955), the influence of Eastern dance on Ashton was seen, as the Siamese *Ballet of the Hands* had influenced Fokine (*see* page 98). But whereas Fokine was inspired by the general flow of these movements to give greater depth of meaning to the particular style of dance he created for his character and *demi-caractère* ballets, Ashton used this flow, together with some finer details, to make his classical dance more pictorially effective and expressive.

It is in his uses of the *pointes* that Ashton breaks away from orthodox formulas more frequently than other choregraphers, and he rarely uses them for spectacular effect. It is noticeable in the dances for *Ondine* (1958), where his naiad gives the impression that she is for ever floating through water, so lightly do the tips of her toes touch the ground before she takes every step. In *Sylvia* (1952) he achieved quite the opposite effect, his nymphs appeared more Amazon-like because of the forceful steps they performed *sur les pointes*.

Yet despite his preoccupation with the classical idiom, Ashton did not create his first essay in pure dance until his return to the Royal Ballet after his war service (1946). His *Symphonic Variations* then stated what has become the English school of classical dance. It is difficult to define, as it has many subtle qualities. It may be said to represent the arts of a nation which reflect the simplicity and form of natural things, and are stated with the lyricism of poetry by an artist who has something to give to everyone without overstating his theme or pointing to the difficulties of his technique.

Symphonic Variations is danced by six dancers, dancing as equals. Their technique is based on classical traditions, but their school is so young that they and their choregrapher have come fresh to the task of displaying so formal an art on the stage. There are no rigidly styled variations, *pas de deux* or ensembles. The dancers' movements flow continuously onwards from step into pose and on again, and from one dancer to the next so that the pictorial value of their dance is only appreciated when the onlooker, like the dancers, can follow the continuity of the whole pattern. Yet this continuous movement does not give the impression of hurried effort, because every step has an ordered, balanced form in which symmetry and calm spaciousness allow the dancers time to develop each step and pose to its most finished state. Each movement is seen in its proper relationship to the total picture, which in its turn is set within the simplest of back-cloths and wings, and in the simplest costumes by Sophie Fedorovitch. Each movement has its relationship to César Franck's music. But this is not a formal relationship as in Balanchine's work (*see* page 145), nor an emotional interpretation as in some of Massine's symphonic works (*see* page 141). It is a relationship which expresses Ashton's belief in the power of dance to convey the dancers' joy in the patterns and movements they can make with their whole being, and thus bring a warm, pulsating flow of life to the ancient conventions of the ballet theatre.

With the exception of his classical ballets, it is impossible to place Ashton's works into rigid categories, and it is the varying qualities of these classics which explain this difficulty. Each of them displays a different quality and style of academic dance. *Symphonic Variations* (1946) is the epitome of the English school. *Scènes de Ballet* (1948) is better described as following the formulas laid down by Petipa, but containing certain modern innovations inherent in Stravinsky's music, which is classical in form and content, but modern in harmony and orchestration. The choregraphy for *Homage to the Queen* (1953) took its qualities from the Four Elements, which were pictured in Malcolm Arnold's music. Thus Earth was confined to the ground with swift *terre à terre* steps, but Water flowed in an *adagio* with beautiful *ports de bras*, or soared like the jets of a fountain. Fire darted and all but expired, only to flare up again. But Air, Queen of all, scarcely touched the ground as she and her spirits drifted to and fro. *Birthday Offering* (1956), staged on the occasion of the Royal Ballet's twenty-fifth birthday, was a perfect example of Ashton's sensitive handling of the individual *danseuses*. His seven *ballerinas* were each given a solo summing up, as it were, her own qualities. The ballet also showed that Ashton was now concentrating on the work of the *danseurs*.

This was not to say he had not used his *danseurs* adequately before. But few of their dances were so interesting as those of the *danseuses*, except in *Les Patineurs* (1937), where he made some use of that eccentric streak running through the history of English stage dance, a streak that he finally exploited to the full in *La Fille mal gardée* (1960).

ASHTON AND ENGLISH TRADITIONS

The eccentric streak of English stage dance derives from the subtle comedy and broad humour to be found in certain morris and sword dances where the man-woman, hobby-horse or other character disturbs the solemn ritual by some clowning as he enters the magic ring; or where some clog dancer breaks rhythm to perform an unexpected trick-step and startles his audience into laughter. Ashton first showed his understanding of the place of this eccentricity in English ballet in *Capriol Suite*, where his peasant boys indulged in several quaint capers, and in *Façade* where he brilliantly took off the loose-limbed soft-shoe dance of the musical comedy hero in "Popular Song."

Further touches of this peculiarly English tradition appeared intermittently in such ballets as *Wedding Bouquet* (1937), *Les Sirènes* (1946) and even in such serious works as

The Quest (1943). In *Cinderella* (1943), Ashton's first three-act ballet, he introduced two favourite pantomime figures, the Ugly Sisters played by himself and Robert Helpmann. But despite their audacious playing of the well-known Dames, their presence was not supported by Prokofiev's score. It failed to underline and time such well-known scenes as dressing for the ball, dancing with inappropriate partners and trying on the shoe, which were part of English traditional pantomimic play.

Strangely enough Ashton's most English ballet to date is *La Fille mal gardée* (*see* page 42). In anglicizing this French work he first establishes his comic characters as essentially English pantomime favourites. The animal impersonators become cock and hens, the broad comedian becomes the Dame, Mother Simone, and the eccentric comedian, the simpleton Alain. But he establishes them all as dancers, using for the first some highly original farmyard scratchings; for the second a typical clog dance with interesting rhythmic patterns; and for the third, his own brand of highly eccentric dance, in which he has always poked fun at "ballet dancing." Ashton then borrows from the simpler morris, maypole and sword dances to give atmosphere and background to the *corps de ballet* work. He plucks from the maypole the pink ribbons by which his hero and heroine plight their troth in a cat's cradle. This fanciful play with the ribbons provides the ballet with its sentimental leitmotive and it is the judicious balancing of sentiment and humour which makes the work so English in content.

ASHTON AND THE THREE-ACT BALLET

It was undoubtedly Ashton's varied choregraphic genius which re-established the three-act ballet in Western Europe. When the Royal Ballet reopened at the Royal Opera House (London) after the war (20th February, 1946) it presented *The Sleeping Beauty*, as it was felt this would offer a spectacle rich in dance, which such a large theatre demanded. Because the venture was not expected to be so successful as it finally turned out to be, only this work was performed. But when the contract was renewed, programmes of three short ballets were added. As not all the dancers were yet sufficiently experienced to project such subtly dramatic works as *Nocturne* and *The Rake's Progress* in this large theatre; when the company's future was finally decided and the Opera House became their permanent home, new productions of *Swan Lake*, *Giselle* and *Coppélia* were staged.

The interest shown in these longer ballets persuaded Dame Ninette and Frederick Ashton that the time was ripe to produce new works on similar lines. Ashton's first choice was *Cinderella* (1948) with music by Prokofiev. This gave him a ready-made score and a well-known subject into which he could introduce something of the English pantomime traditions (*see* above). But it was not fully successful, firstly because Prokofiev's score had been written with the collaboration of the Soviet ballet-master, Zakharov, and was built on the same pattern as the Tchaikovsky, *The Sleeping Beauty*, with its set pieces, and perhaps did not always inspire Ashton. Secondly, Ashton and his designer Malclès seemed afraid of using purely theatrical devices, such as machinery to effect the necessary transformation scenes and other illusions.

Ashton's next choice was *Sylvia* (1952) with its well-known score by Delibes and variety of dance. Here his designers, Robin and Christopher Ironside, not only conjured up the necessary period atmosphere, but also used several well-tried stage tricks to create illusion and add to the spectacle. The machinery was however only used when it added to the fantasy of the dance. For example, when the walls of Orion's cave fell away and the nymph, Sylvia, was free to spin away to her Aminta. But the ballet occasionally flagged because too many of the *divertissements* did not stem directly from the plot.

Three years later Ashton produced *Romeo and Juliet* for the Royal Danish Ballet in Copenhagen (1955) and here he had a score which gave him that continuity of action, a hallmark of all his ballets. The music had been worked out by Prokofiev in close collaboration with the Soviet choregrapher Leonide Lavrovsky, the designer Peter Williams and several Soviet theatre experts, all of whom were determined to retain the spirit of Shakespeare's tragedy to the full and transmit its poetry through danced-mime and mimed-dance (*see* page 188). On its presentation at the Kirov Theatre, Leningrad (11th January, 1940) Soviet critics recognized that, for them, it was a new type of ballet which was a further development of Fokine's work. Through it ran complete continuity of action without unnecessary episodes or *divertissements* to distract attention from the main theme of the star-crossed lovers. It was a beautifully balanced production and both facets of the tale were shown in almost equal proportion. Passages of violent action depicting the quarrels between Montague and Capulet were swept aside by scenes of lyrical, tragic beauty showing the lovers' meetings, and these in their turn were lightened by tiny humorous episodes. Although Ashton had not seen Lavrovsky's work the score acted as a sure guide to his choregraphy and inspired him to create some of his most lovely dances, particularly the lovers' duet in the Balcony scene, which became the high spot of the ballet. *Romeo and Juliet* was undoubtedly so successful because Ashton was working with an experienced company, whose gift for acting through dance was first developed by Bournonville (*see* page 59). It is a quality which colours all their work and, no matter who the choregrapher or what the subject, the dancers dance their role. Ashton was also working in Copenhagen with a stage staff experienced in the art of creating illusion and spectacle and well able to quicken the tempo of any production by their swift, silent manœuvring of scenery whilst the dance continues. Thus in *Romeo and Juliet* scene melted into scene and the dancers moved from one situation to another without leaving the stage and without stopping the line of their dance. Ashton's ballet matched Lavrovsky's masterpiece in its faithfulness to the swiftly unfolding drama of Shakespeare.

Such an experience undoubtedly helped Ashton when he staged *Ondine* (27th October,

1958). For the first time he was in complete control not only of the choregraphic design but also of the entire resources of the stage, which worked, so it seemed, only when commanded by the dancers and when vital to the action. For example the marvellous play of light upon the fountain, whose movement was made by the pyramid of dancers, and the extraordinary effect of the rolling of the boat, which was achieved not by mechanical contrivance alone, but by the slow controlled swaying to and fro of the dancers and their balancing themselves against the swell. But the greatest illusion of all was achieved by the dances Ashton created for Dame Margot Fonteyn, who always appeared to be floating on and through water. It was her exquisite interpretation of the role that made the ballet an enormous success, for the music by the young German composer, Hans Werner Henze, was not fully successful. Despite its leitmotives and continuity of action, it was sometimes too modern in tone and undefined in rhythms to support so romantic a theme as that which Lila de Nobile had captured in her scenery and costume design.

Ondine is a perfect example of how an Ashton ballet attains its success because of the brilliant way he handles the qualities of his original cast. This is at once a strength and a weakness, for a ballet of his frequently loses something of its freshness when taken on by newcomers who are not so sensitively fitted into their roles.

ASHTON AND HIS DANCERS

Ashton joined the Royal Ballet at a crucial point in their history (1935) when Alicia Markova and Anton Dolin left to form their own company. No one was ready to step into such roles as *Giselle*, which had been staged to show the lyrical gifts of this first English *ballerina*; moreover economic circumstances demanded that focus be made on dance and dancers. Had Ashton failed at this moment, it is doubtful whether the company would have developed so rapidly, as Dame Ninette could not simultaneously organize, teach and create, and maintain the high standard she set herself. Ashton did not fail and gradually built up a repertoire which exploited the company's youthful talent for lyricism and characterization.

He sought inspiration from both music and poetry, and, with the help of Constant Lambert, developed the potentialities of his dancers in comedy, tragedy and suites of dances based on some particular theme (e.g. *Les Patineurs*, 1937, *Les Rendezvous*, 1933). From time to time a work of intense dramatic content would emerge such as *Apparitions* (1936), which had the same theme as Massine's *Symphonie Fantastique*, although appearing some five months before it. In *Horoscope* (1938) with its interesting score by Constant Lambert and starkly simple costumes by Sophie Fedorovitch, Ashton exploited the gradually emerging talent of Dame Margot Fonteyn and Michael Somes, C.B.E., as well as the *corps de ballet*. Hitherto he had not been able to use large numbers, as the company was too small, and had preferred to use his cast as individuals or, if numbers were available, along fairly orthodox lines as Petipa had done to create atmosphere and background. But in *Horoscope* he visualized the struggle of the followers of Leo with those of Gemini in a series of wonderfully designed choric groupings in which the strong virile movements of the former were violently contrasted with the timid sensitive steps of the latter.

A somewhat similarly violent contrasting of movement between the conflicting forces in the action was shown in *Dante Sonata* (1940), a strongly impressionistic work inspired by Liszt's tone-poem "Après une Lecture de Dante." It was the only ballet in which Ashton used a plastic modern idiom; the dancers appeared in the slightest of draperies and danced through an almost empty set, which Sophie Fedorovitch had based on ideas from Flaxman's illustrations to Dante's *Inferno*. The impact this work made was possibly stronger than it might have been as its production coincided with the "waiting" period of the 1939–45 War, which seemed to stress its theme of souls in purgatory.

At other times Ashton would stage ballets of the greatest subtlety, which only hinted at tragedy and created a tense feeling for the mood and atmosphere surrounding some tiny incident, as for example in *Nocturne* (1936). This work had great poignancy and conjured up a meeting between a poor girl and rich man during some Parisian ball, which was overlooked by an almost impassive onlooker, a role played by Ashton himself to perfection. No one else was able to show such sympathy and humanity. But whatever the theme or story that he handled, a pastoral *Daphnis and Chloe* (1951), or a darkly romantic *Rinaldo and Armida* (1955), Ashton has never ceased to develop new angles to the traditional formulas of classical, and to introduce new-old steps as his dancers have progressed technically.

Through this continuous reworking of the old steps Ashton's dancers have become very sensitive instruments, able to respond to the demands of both old and new choregraphers. Few Royal Ballet dancers owe so much to his exploitation of their gifts as Dame Margot Fonteyn and Michael Somes, C.B.E. For them he has created his finest dances through which their audience have learnt to appreciate their artistry. By working on such roles as Sylvia, Chloe, Tiresias, Ondine and countless others, Dame Margot has learnt to use sensitively every part of her body, so that when ultimately interpreting the great *ballerina* roles of Giselle, Odette-Odile and Aurora she has brought all that knowledge to her task and charges these more formal choregraphic portraits with a living expression of emotion and action. Similarly Michael Somes has learnt how to respond to and sensitively collaborate with her every movement, as well as to dance as an equal partner in the drama.

Recently Ashton has exploited the lively, more earthly talents and superb technical facility of Nadia Nerina in *La Fille mal gardée*, and displayed her ability to express freely her love and enjoyment in dance itself, something that is frequently lost when a dancer takes over the leading roles as a *ballerina*. Moreover Ashton provided her with a partner, David Blair, equal in technical status, energy and sense of fun. In the same way that he developed Dame Margot's artistry, Ashton has slowly drawn out the unusual qualities of Alexander Grant both as a character dancer and an eccentric, capable of being strangely moving as the Sea-god in *Ondine*, and wildly funny yet pathetic as the simpleton, Alain, in *La Fille mal gardée*. But Ashton has still something more to say. On 12th December, 1961, he presented *Persephone*, the melodrama by André Gide and Stravinsky, originally commissioned by Ida Rubinstein, a wealthy pupil of Fokine. Perhaps he has produced that work at which De Baïf was aiming when he tried: "to unite music with dance, song and measure as in the ancient days of Greece', (*see* page 13) because in Svetlana Beriosova Ashton found a rare artist able to declaim a poem and dance as expressively and musically as her colleagues. The starkly simple choregraphic design is stripped of all affectations and is both an illustration and interpretation of the content and mood of Gide's poem. The dancer-speaker is thus able to move easily from speech to dance and never to lose the rhythm of the music, which both accompanies and activates the movements and song of the participants in the ritual of death and resurrection. It remains to be seen whether Ashton will develop this new-old form of spectacle still further, a spectacle wherein speech, song and dance are joined, as in the older English masque.

OTHER ENGLISH CHOREGRAPHERS

During the thirty years since England discovered its own art of ballet it has encouraged more choregraphers of talent than any other country during the initial period of development. Some have contributed to both the Royal and the Rambert companies; several have produced works abroad. These choregraphers can be divided into two groups, those from the Ballet Club and those from Sadler's Wells. The first to emerge were Anthony Tudor, Andrée Howard and Walter Gore, whose ballets might be said to reflect the tastes of Ballet Club audiences, who were more sophisticated than those at Sadler's Wells. Their works can be divided into three categories: the first, essays in dance suggested by the music and centred round some theme; the second, sophisticated comedies or burlesques that occasionally indulged in jokes understood only by their own audience; and the third, dramatic works based on a literary source, or an original theme devised either by the choregrapher himself, or by those closely connected with the Rambert venture, either dancers or audience. There is not space to discuss fully the work of these English choregraphers, particularly as it is not yet clear if they are to develop further.

ANTHONY TUDOR AND THE PSYCHOLOGICAL BALLET (1909–)

Anthony Tudor, like Ashton, came late to his training as a dancer with Marie Rambert, but quickly showed choregraphic talent, producing works based largely on classical themes and technique which he formed into interesting designs. But not all of these were happily wed to their music. He seemed anxious to stress his personal style which differed from that of his colleagues, Ashton and Andrée Howard, both of whom showed greater sensitivity towards their music. But in 1936, after Ashton had joined Dame Ninette (*see* page 168), Tudor presented an important work, *Jardin aux Lilas*, which established his particular contribution to ballet.

Jardin aux Lilas was one of the first so-called psychological ballets in which human relationships were seen when about to break down under the stress of social convention, somewhat in the manner of a Proust novel. It was a similar theme to some presented by Kurt Jooss and other modern dancers, who followed the theories of Freud and studied movement arising from the instinctive, or conscious and unconscious desires of various personalities. Anthony Tudor's choregraphy was of greater subtlety and tenderness than that of Jooss because of his objective handling of his characters and the classical idiom into which he introduced many delicate, colloquial gestures in keeping with the sentiment inherent in Chausson's *Poème* to which the ballet was danced. The couple, about to be parted through the girl's marriage to another, were seldom allowed close contact, so that what might have developed into the usual *pas de deux*, was continually interrupted or frustrated by the intervention of other dancers, or by the couple's own realization of the hopelessness of their situation and inability to be explicit in their desire for each other.

But there was more in the couple's movements than their lack of contact. Despite their flowing romantic style, they were tense and constricted not only by the proximity of the other dancers, but also by their own inhibitions and failure to communicate. *Jardin aux Lilas* was the first ballet in the classical idiom to express clearly such deep personal relationships and showed how far a choregrapher could probe into the emotions and actions governing human behaviour to give life and greater intimacy to a ballet.

Tudor's next work, *Dark Elegies* (1937), was an interpretation of Mahler's *Kindertotenlieder*. It was not a literal interpretation of these lyrical yet morbid songs. Couched in a plastic idiom, in which emphasis was placed on the constriction of the body by the tightly enclosing hands and arms, Tudor created a sad dance ritual which gained effect by the sympathetic and intimate relationship he established between the mourners. But although Mahler's songs have variety of tone and tempo, Tudor's design had an almost monotonous continuity because solos and ensembles merged and no performer stepped outside the inward looking circle to appeal to outsiders. The dancers expressed no other emotion but a sorrow which was moving but not fully explained. In this way the feeling of frustration expressed was maintained. Some, to whom the word sung meant a great deal, felt *Dark Elegies* was no more than an essay in eurhythmics. To others it seemed to open a new chapter in ballet. It certainly showed the value of choric movement, and the need to integrate soloist and *corps de ballet* when creating ballets where mood must be established before theme.

Tudor's most important psychological ballet was created on his arrival in America after leaving the London Ballet, which he had formed in 1938. *Pillar of Fire* was performed by the New York City Ballet in 1942, and made an immediate impression because of the superb playing of its cast led by Nora Kaye who demonstrated, for the first time, those remarkable powers of acting she has never ceased to practise. *Pillar of Fire* posed a somewhat similar problem to that of *Jardin aux Lilas*, a heroine's inability to communicate with the man she loved because of her own neurotic temperament and inhibitions brought about by the social conventions and environment surrounding her. But Hagar's story was not a delicate, sentimental romance like *Jardin aux Lilas*. Tudor made a realistic approach to an unpleasant subject. The Edwardian setting, costumes and the choregraphic design created an atmosphere and background which stressed the impropriety of Hagar's behaviour in the eyes of her older sister and various passers-by with their tightly-laced spinsterish ways. Tudor also emphasized the conventional and unconventional behaviour of his characters by strongly differentiating the qualities of the movements performed by the Lovers in Innocence and those in Experience, who lived in the shady house opposite. Their wanton lust was abhorred by the respectable, but eyed with frightened curiosity and perhaps envy by the nerve-tortured Hagar.

Such subjects were often produced by modern dance groups, but so cloaked with symbolism and incoherent movement that they frequently bewildered their audience. *Pillar of Fire* was more satisfying because it told its story in explicit dance terms. Moreover Tudor had the courage to give his ballet an optimistic ending. After the sordid scene of Hagar's seduction by the unpleasant Boy from the House Opposite, the Friend, for whom she had longed, at last relaxed and walked with her into the forest. This finale was in keeping with the score, Schönberg's *Verklärte Nacht*, a strange choice for so dramatic and clear-cut a work.

Tudor's choice of music, particularly since he left the Rambert Ballet, is, however, always curious. He seems only to select such music as will create atmosphere and mood, and to use it as a background and time-keeper only. Thus, whenever he finds a score with a well-sustained mood, such as Chausson's *Poème* and Schönberg's *Verklärte Nacht*, he is successful. But if he selects music which has some literary content, or is not consistently descriptive of mood, his works lack continuity and strength. This is true of a number of ballets where the choregrapher takes music with a definite theme and imposes another on to it.

ANDRÉE HOWARD AND THE BALLET OF MOOD (1910–)

The most important ballets created by Andrée Howard fall under two headings, those with strong narrative qualities based on some literary work which exactly moulds her very explicit dance by verbal description; and those which sensitively evoke a sad, disquieting mood through the delicate nuances of emotional movement arising from the deeper implications of her theme. Both types arise from her reactions to the romantic theme as discussed by Edwardian writers, and because she approaches her work with feminine intuition she obtains her results through her ability to convey the subtleties of human behaviour, rather than her ability to refashion classical dance, on which her ballets are based.

Andrée Howard showed a flair for narrative through explicit gesture in her earliest works. Unlike her colleagues at the Ballet Club, she produced ballets containing colloquial gestures, that were at once descriptive and either narrative or emotional in quality, rather than flowing movements. They could be strongly emphatic and coupled to deliberate foot-work, which stressed their rhetorical significance, or delicately suggestive and only served to hint at some sad story.

These colloquial gestures were of the greatest interest in *Lady into Fox*, David Garnett's novel representing an Edwardian view of the conflict between the worlds of reality and fantasy (*see* page 55). Andrée Howard developed the action as a long *pas de deux* interrupted and encircled by the suspicious neighbours, who gradually disrupted the tender relationship between the husband and his beautiful wife. But beneath the conforming behaviour of Mrs. Tebrick, the fox was always visible.

This ballet was a forerunner of *Les Demoiselles de la Nuit* (1948) and *Le Loup* (1953) of Roland Petit. But whereas *Lady into Fox* gave reality to a strange story by its closely integrated human and animal gestures, Petit's works lived in a world of fantasy within an impressionistic background.

Andrée Howard's most graphic narration occurred in *A Mirror for Witches* (1953), based on a novel by Esther Forbes, when the Stepmother gave her evidence at the trial of the witch-child in such forceful language, that she communicated through colloquial gestures alone, all the hate and fear felt by a narrow-minded community towards the child of nature in their midst.

There could be no greater difference between two ballets than between *A Mirror for Witches* and *La Fête étrange*, Andrée Howard's most beautiful ballet. Originally produced for the London Ballet (1940), it was then reproduced for a larger cast by the Royal Ballet, whereby emphasizing her gift of conveying the most subtle ideas through nuances of mood within the movements. Like Ashton's *Nocturne*, *La Fête étrange* takes a tiny episode and turns it into a tragedy of youthful love without any histrionic touches to disturb the strangely sad, nostalgic mood evoked by Fauré's music (selected by Roland Crichton, who supplied the theme), and Sophie Fedorovitch's exquisite set and costumes. These lend distance and that dreamlike air of reality seen through the eyes of a true romanticist. The ballet revealed again Andrée Howard's sensitive feelings for the music she chooses to support her dance, when her theme suggests and does not illustrate graphically her story.

It also stresses, as did every ballet décor that was designed by Sophie Fedorovitch, that only when the artist-designer evokes the same mood as musician and choregrapher and gives to the dancers space in which they have freedom to express their roles, can a ballet have true colour and life, no matter how delicate or how strongly passionate the theme may be.

WALTER GORE AND DRAMATIC EMPHASIS (1910–)

Until 1939 Walter Gore was mainly concerned as a dancer of dramatic talent and musicality in creating some of the major roles in English ballets (*see* page 162). He also produced dances in plays and seemed concerned, when he produced two of his earliest choregraphic works, with the literal translation of words into dance. These dramatic interpretations of poems by Robert Browning, *Confessional* and *Porphyria's Lover*, were produced for the Oxford Ballet Club (1941) and revealed Gore's strong feelings for the rhythmic pulse, cadences and significance of words. The poems were spoken off-stage, their rhythmic cadences created the rhythm of the movements and the words coloured the content of the dance.

This partnership of words and movement was not new, but was employed in a different way from that of the verse-speaking choirs of the 1930s. The dancer (Sally Gilmour) was both seen and heard to express through her dancing the tragic melodies of the verses, because the emotional passion and strength of her movements emphasized their phrasing and accent, and the sound of her footfall served to increase tension as the climax gradually grew and ended in death.

The strong rhythmic movements created by a single dancer in tune with the vocal and verbal content of a poem, eventually led Gore to reinforce the more dramatic moments of other ballets with the sounds made by the dancers themselves. It was particularly notable in *Antonia* (1949) and *The Night and Silence* (1957). Both ballets had themes of jealousy arising from a lover's suspicions of his love, the former being a grim episode in the life of the painter, Raphael, which ended as he killed his mistress; the latter told of a tragic misunderstanding between two lovers, but ended in reconciliation.

The music (by Delius and Bach respectively) only created and reflected something of the changing moods of the action. Neither score illustrated the passionate narrative that was explicitly outlined by the dancers. But Gore supplied the rhythmic urge his dramatic scenes required by making his lovers supply this for themselves. Thus they faced and moved round each other, and as the man's passionate anger rose and as the woman became more and more fearful so the tempo and sounds of their feet reinforced their tragic quarrels and finally seemed to drown the music, which had hitherto been the link forging their love. Gore has not yet used this valuable element in any ballet employing numbers of dancers.

ROBERT HELPMANN AND THE THEATRE (1909–)

The debt the Royal Ballet owes to Robert Helpmann, that brilliant dancer and actor, has yet to be properly assessed. He was the mainstay of the company throughout the war years, giving generously of himself to every role, whether as Prince, Clown, Witch or the like. There seemed nothing he could not tackle, primarily because he was a man of the theatre, and this, above all his other talents, was something that the company needed once the foundation stones had been truly laid. He did not create ballets until the company's lack of male dancers and the uncertainty of their presence (due to the call-up), made it necessary to produce works in which students, or even the ladies of the company could be disguised. Perhaps also at this time it was necessary to believe in the Englishness of the Royal Ballet's enterprise in carrying on throughout these grim years that Helpmann's first choice fell on an interpretation of Milton's *Comus* (14th January, 1942). It owed its success to the beauty of the verses spoken by Helpmann in the title role and to the lyrical dances he arranged for Margot Fonteyn as the Innocent Lady.

Four months later (19th May, 1942) Helpmann produced his highly dramatic interpretation of *Hamlet*, inspired by the Prince's words "For in that Sleep of death, what dreams may come." In it he caused to be enacted every incident of Shakespeare's play as they flashed through the mind of the dying Hamlet, an illusion he created by commencing and ending his ballet with the Bearers picking up and carrying away the Prince's body. The illusion was reinforced by Leslie Hurry's décor. It contained many symbolical details drawing the eyes of the audience, as it were, into the mind of Hamlet and enabling them to focus each episode as the players, in turn, took the stage and the limelight. The work was set to Tchaikovsky's fantasy-overture, "Hamlet" which gave a breath-taking speed to the tragedy. But by working at such speed and with such economy of gesture, Helpmann all but deprived his work of dance, and produced something in the nature of a mimo-drama. It was a valuable experience for the dancers involved because it increased their understanding of dramatic gesture and stagecraft.

Miracle in the Gorbals was Helpmann's most important ballet, and posed the question: "What if Christ came again?" This modern morality was written by the stage director, Michael Bentall, and was set in the Gorbals, Glasgow. The décor and costumes of Edward Burra brilliantly evoked the atmosphere and background of tenements, dockyards and pubs to which The Stranger came to revive the Suicide and change the lives of those who lived in such squalor. The score, by Sir Arthur Bliss, supported the poignant sentiment of the action and emphasized its reality. Not only did it give life to the sounds of the dockyard and the sentimental ditties dear to the hearts of the Scots but, more important, it gave the choregrapher those characteristic rhythmic qualities of primitive dance and religious fervour on which to develop his mimed-dance.

It was exceptional choregraphy because its quality and expression changed as the action unfolded, thus demonstrating how dance will always adapt itself to the circumstances in which it is practised. At first the characters were influenced by their confined surroundings and by the fashionable dances of the time. Jazz-like movements were mixed with coarse colloquial or occupational gestures, children's games from poor streets and mere loitering at street corners. Later, when The Stranger had raised her from the dead, the Suicide began slowly to dance some simple Scottish steps which became ecstatic as the crowd, at first doubtful, then joyous as the miracle worked, gradually joined in. The joyous dance then became the spontaneous, syncopated frenzy of a revivalist meeting, and when everyone dispersed they seem to have been given a new and freer life. But as suspicions mounted against The Stranger, so the earlier movements again became obvious and grew until they developed into those of the murderous razor-slashing gang, who finally killed The Stranger.

Miracle in the Gorbals was the first ballet in which such a strongly dramatic, and philosophical theme with a contemporary setting had been undertaken by any classical company. That it should have appeared in England during wartime, was evidence of the changes Helpmann was furthering in the expressive dancing of the Royal Ballet, and of the interest leading theatrical and other artists were taking in the art of ballet as a whole. Helpmann was also making wartime audiences aware of the serious contributions the art of ballet could make to the theatre.

JOHN CRANKO AND ENGLISH INSTITUTIONS (1927–)

John Cranko was the first South African choregrapher to produce for the Royal Ballet and his contributions to their repertoire are evidence of the great fertility of his ideas. They range from the lyrical and simply told story of *Beauty and the Beast* (1949) to the hilarious Edwardian *Bonne-bouche* (1952), which resembled a lush, bound volume of *Punch*; and from the controversial *Antigone* (1959) to a British masterpiece, *Pineapple Poll* (1951). It is the fertility of his ideas that frequently leads Cranko to produce ballets which are so full of imaginative touches and original choregraphy, that the main action is lost in secondary episodes; or else his characters dance in so many different styles that the eye is distracted by dance and loses the meaning of the story. Sometimes his story can suggest a different conclusion to each member of the audience. Nevertheless in those works where he has exercised self-discipline, Cranko has much to give.

He is very conscious of the personal relationships between his dancers as they appear in the story, between them and the framework of his set, and of the need to convey meaning through narrative gesture. He is also aware of the need for careful timing, particularly in comedy and it is this particular factor in his choregraphy which may prove to be his most valuable contribution to the development of realism in ballet because he has the gift of showing how near laughter is to tears. He can bring pathos into comedy and, by so doing, change comedy into near tragedy as he does in *The Lady and the Fool* (1954). Despite the wildly funny antics of his two Clowns disputing over a red rose, Cranko never allows them to forget they are two human beings, whose deep friendship has not and never will be broken. What they have suffered and enjoyed together are the realities of their life, and it is the way Cranko forges this link between them, by utilizing the merest glance or touch of a hand, that shows his understanding of their relationship and problems.

Cranko's greatest success so far, from the audience's point of view, is undoubtedly *Pineapple Poll* (1951). It was produced when the copyright of Sullivan's music for the famous Savoy Operas lapsed and its great merit is that he retained all the wit, humour and "sniping" at the traditional British Institutions, which were the main features of Gilbert and Sullivan, when working together. This undoubtedly happened because Cranko took his libretto from "The Bum-boat Woman's Story," a Gilbert ballad and the superb score arranged by Charles MacKerras from Sullivan's music.

The rumbustious style of choregraphy Cranko used for *Pineapple Poll* can be described as variations on a Hornpipe. Into it he stowed colloquial gestures from sailors' slang, back-chat, movements describing nautical behaviour on and off shore, and the charming gossip and "vapours" of the ladies. Yet even in this happy frolic there appear from time to time those sensitive gestures by which Cranko establishes the sympathetic relationship between his characters and by so doing, brings to his best ballets a human touch. This means that no matter from whence his themes derive, fantasy, philosophy, comedy or tragedy, his dancers bring a sense of reality to the stage by the way they play a human character. They are not mere dancers performing to order.

KENNETH MACMILLAN AND THE MODERN THEME (1930–)

It was with *The Burrow* (1958) that Kenneth MacMillan followed the lead of Helpmann in translating an important theme of social content into ballet. His originality of movement and macabre fantasy had been evident from the first of his works, *Somnambulism* (1953), produced at a showing of experimental ballets by aspirant choregraphers from the Royal Ballet. From then until *The Burrow* he tended to rely more on formal patterns and a dissection of movement, rather than expressive dance and gesture. This dry analytical treatment of classical steps was invaluable in the works of Stravinsky to which they were set (e.g. *Danses Concertantes*, 1956, and *Agon*, 1958), as it matched the composer's emotionless classicism. But if a story were communicated, the strangely two-dimensional movements only stressed the young choregrapher's desire to be different because they avoided the passionate lines of dance which would have fully communicated character, action and emotion.

The Burrow however showed MacMillan's deep interest in humanity. It was based on the tragic *Diary of Anne Frank*, a young girl who died in the Belsen concentration camp. It painted the tensions, comradeship and passionate desire for life of those imprisoned and hidden, yet always waiting discovery. It had no beginning, no climax and end—the prisoners listened for the dread knock of the Gestapo. But when the door was flung open, only a shaft of sunlight entered. This inconclusiveness at the climax of an action had been noted before in MacMillan's work and here may have been due to his choice of music, by the Swiss composer, Frank Martin, which was not written for so strong and moving a theme. Nevertheless this inconclusiveness served to emphasize the hopelessness of these tormented souls, whom MacMillan characterized with definite strokes of angular, yet classical movement, and clearly differentiated between youth and age, love and hate, fanaticism and resignation, and most movingly of all, hope and despair. Within the limits of his design, MacMillan also expressed the deep personal relationships which grow when human beings are subjected to close confinement and living in circumstances beyond their own control. To convey such ideas through classical dance was proof of how far this medium had developed from the delicate French court dance.

The Invitation (1961) also deals with human relationship, and although overloaded with symbolism by way of props and *divertissements*, it demonstrates that English classical ballet can be as outspoken in sexual matters as those of any other country or style. Yet despite its unpleasant subject, the rape of both Boy and Girl by an older, experienced couple, MacMillan demonstrated his sympathy with Youth and its problems by creating movements of the same tenderness and beauty in his duets between Boy and Girl, as Ivanov and Ashton had done in their romantic ballets. But MacMillan's dance is modern and conveys subtly the youth and innocence of children, about to be adult, and as well it is more suggestive of the passions rising as they grow to maturity, the Boy to enjoy life more fully, and the Girl never again to dare to love, so great has been the shock she has suffered in an older man's hands.

It may well be that Kenneth MacMillan will be the English choregrapher to demonstrate the necessity of showing youth and age, innocence and experience in more optimistic ballets. By bringing more mature artists into the limelight, he strengthens the actuality of the theme played out on the stage. For unless a company can embrace dancers of all ages and employ them usefully, it cannot be said to reflect reality and the social problems which ballet finds necessary to do from time to time, if it is to win the applause of the large audience.

FURTHER READING

EVANS, EDWIN and LAWSON, JOAN, *The Dancing Times*, articles and criticisms in.
LAWSON, JOAN, *Mime* (London, Pitman, 1957).

CHAPTER 12

The Real World in Ballet

The Dancer by his Gestures, Motions and Actions, without speaking, made himself perfectly understood by the Spectator, in whom he rais'd the Passions of Anger, Pity, Love, Hate and the Like.
(JOHN WEAVER)

ALTHOUGH the 1939–45 War prevented that interchange of artists and ideas that had led to so much development after the death of Diaghilev, the fact that each country necessarily became a self-contained unit, helped England, France and America to find inspiration within their own borders, and create what are national ballets, in addition to other works stemming from the reforms of Diaghilev and Jooss. The interesting aspect of French and American national ballets is their choregraphers' determination to bring real-life drama and characters on to the stage. But whereas the Americans frequently broke with classical ballet, the French remained within that medium and created impressions of the urgent tragedies of real life because of their more traditional training and background.

THE FRENCH BALLETS OF ROLAND PETIT (1921–)

Les Ballets des Champs-Elysées was the first company to visit London after the war (9th April, 1946) when the works of Roland Petit made an immediate impression by the realism of their setting, dance, medium and action. This erstwhile student of the Paris *Opéra* was more interested in transforming the classical medium into contemporary material than producing a classical ballet, although occasionally using an ancient theme (e.g. *Les Amours de Jupiter* (1946)). On leaving the *Opéra* he joined Irene Lidova (a French critic) and Boris Kochno to form a group, later known as Les Ballets des Champs-Elysées. The presence of Diaghilev's secretary, whose penchant for collating the materials of contemporary ballets has been noted (*see* page 126), at once brought other important and progressively-minded artists to help create a new type of French ballet. Amongst these were such writers as Cocteau and Anouilh, the designers Bérard, Clavé and Wakhevitch, and the musicians Darmasse and Saguet.

Kochno contributed the libretto of *Les Forains* (1945), a brief episode in the lives of circus folk, which first caught the eyes of London audiences with its insight into the pathetically sordid life of these travellers as well as its tinsel glamour. This glimpse into the reality of backstage life showed Petit's mastery in presenting through dance alone, the behaviour of characters in a given situation so that their movements laid bare their temperament, thoughts and personal reactions to the scene in which they found themselves. The movements were not characteristic, like Massine's, but grew out of their own feelings and personal involvement in the action. Petit also added touches of that fantasy which all theatre folk possess and this helped to reconcile the reality of the action and the behaviour of the characters with the purely technical problems of telling a realistic story through the medium of classical dance. Similar strong touches of fantasy later emphasized the poetic lyricism of such ballets as *Les Demoiselles de la Nuit* (1948) and *Le Loup* (1953).

There was however little fantasy in Petit's *Le Rendezvous* (1945), a grim episode of a young man's solitude and death in the heartless Parisian underworld. Much of the realism in this work was conjured up by the photomontage décor of Brassai, which emphasized the actualities of the situation and the banal score by Kosma, against which the man struggled to find a solution to his loneliness.

Le jeune Homme et la Mort (1946) was a justification of Petit's attempts to turn classical into a contemporary medium capable of dealing with every dramatic situation. It answered those modern dancers who decried its artificialities because here they were seen to be broken down by the emotions raised within the two characters, neither of whom observed the niceties of technique, manner or style of the old-fashioned choregraphic design. The stark drama was suggested by Jean Cocteau and told of a Young Man whose Girl, cruel and cold, spurns him until he threatens suicide. At last interested, she arranges a noose on a beam in his squalid attic and leaves him to kill himself. As he dies the attic walls fall away, revealing the Parisian roof-tops and lights, over which the Girl, disguised as Death, leads him into oblivion.

The work aroused great controversy, firstly because of Petit's choice of the great C Minor Passacaglia by Bach to accompany so crude and violent a theme. But the impersonality of the music, relentlessly carrying the listener onwards to its climax, suggested the wholly impervious attitude of the Girl, who, in the Apotheosis, was unchanging Death. And although it barely suggested the tortured mind of the Young Man, because the musical climax coincided with death and transformation, the incompatibility of ideas between theme and music was both seen and heard to be resolved.

The second point of controversy was Petit's choregraphy. It was violent, angular and acrobatic, so much so that many felt it negated everything on which classical dance depends: grace, harmony of line and calm. Others felt that by destroying the purely academic viewpoint, Petit showed how the idiom was capable of development, if one examined the qualities of each movement, and ignored entirely the conventions within which it had been bound for so long. He proved the truth of this when creating *Carmen* (1949), although it had not the same air of actuality as *Le jeune Homme et la Mort.* This happened because Bizet's score did not give Petit the freedom he needed. In fact, *Carmen* upset many because parts of the score were torn from their context and this helped to convince them that dancers only required music as a time-keeper and not as an equal partner in the production.

The artist-designers in Petit's early ballets were always equal partners and showed how large a part décor and costumes play in any ballet. From the mere suggestion of a tent made by a few draperies (*Les Forains*), or a row of washing (*Le Bal des Blanchisseuses*) to the squalid realism of an attic (*Le jeune Homme et la Mort*), Petit's artists disciplined themselves to suggest, or solidly represent, the necessary venue and atmosphere of reality in drama or comedy.

Unfortunately Petit himself was not so disciplined, nor so served in his later works. The many productions staged between 1944 and 1953 demonstrated a variety of styles and ideas. But gradually those works increased in which décor, montage, props and other appendages became more interesting than the chic *divertissements* and witty solos. Finally dance seemed to be sacrificed either to the kaleidoscopic cutting and close-ups of a film (*see* page 182), or to the build-up of a Parisian revue which, in 1961, is where Petit showed yet another side of his creative abilities.

AMERICAN BALLET (1914-)

The realism of the first American ballets presented by Catherine Littlefield, and after the war by Ballet Theatre, was quite different from the French. Roland Petit usually dealt with the squalor of poverty in tragic circumstances and ended in death, or with more artificially comic episodes reminiscent of music hall. The American choregraphers were oblivious of class, status, or race, and dealt with life as experienced by themselves or their grandparents. They presented completely extrovert works of laughter or deeply introverted themes of narrow-minded sects. They usually relied on a dance medium which paid some lip-service to classical dance, or something of the many styles used by their compatriots at home or in musicals and films.

Catherine Littlefield's *Barn Dance* (1937) was no more than its title suggests. It captured its London audience by the sheer exuberance and rhythmic vitality of the dancers. These qualities were more evident when Ballet Theatre presented *Fancy Free* (London, 1946) and *Rodeo* (London, 1949). Such works were reconstructions in dance of American folklore.

Barn Dance and *Rodeo* pictured life in the outback with its bucolic humour, hearty health and sheer fun; *Fancy Free* gave an urban view of life and owed its popularity to its topicality. Even after the cease-fire, Londoners were still subject to the fortunes of war which brought similar American sailors to the city pubs, and the portrayal of three of them in their New York bar, impressing their own girl friends with the magnitude of their exploits during the last engagement, was a slice of life no other ballet-master had yet attempted. At that time the ballet came close to what Londoners felt was the real thing, brought to the theatre by a mere matter of translating a lively anecdote into dance.

The translation of slices of life into dance was not the only contribution of American choregraphers to the art of ballet. Another important aspect of their work, and one which has not yet been used fully, was their employment of film techniques which gave some works a swift, flowing continuity and broke the unities of time, place and action, which had held choregraphers within bounds for so long.

THE PIONEER, EUGENE LORING (1914–)

Billy the Kid (19th October, 1938) created by Eugene Loring, was the first American ballet to tell a story of pioneering days, of Red Indians and of Robbers. It was also the first to use the film techniques of flashbacks, fades and cuts whereby the audience were carried backwards and forwards in time as the various incidents of the outlaw's life flashed across the stage to represent "a fragmentary, if symbolic incident in the expansion of our vast frontier" (LINCOLN KERSTEIN in *Blast on Ballet*). This attempt to introduce symbolism excused some of the "corny" episodes, where flash ladies and gun-pulling gave way to glycerine tears and repentance. Nevertheless the production showed the value of sets which could be easily moved by the dancers and, in conjunction with variously focused spotlights, isolate sections of the stage, allowing each episode to follow straight upon the other and bring continuity to the action, as in a film. The speed resulting from this cutting brought excitement to the climax, and was followed with great effect by Agnes de Mille in *Fall River Legend* (1948) and other choregraphers, notably Roland Petit after he had been to America (*see* page 181).

Eugene Loring made another valuable contribution to American choregraphy in *Billy the Kid*. This was his styling of occupational gestures introduced to give authenticity to the characterization of pioneers driving their wagons through wild forests, herding and riding horses and performing the various work of those who fight both nature and life in order to survive.

No other ballet had used such gestures so clearly as a means of communication. That Loring also used *les pointes* might be explained by Kerstein's belief that classical dance must be the base of all ballet (*see* page 145) and was fitting material to help point the symbolism of some episodes.

AGNES DE MILLE (1909–   )

Agnes de Mille followed Loring's pioneer work of introducing occupational gestures from American life when she staged *Rodeo* (1942) a simple story of boy gets girl at the Saturday-night dance. But her ballet had greater originality of expression which stemmed from her experiences in England. Having studied classical dance in America she came to London to work under Dame Marie Rambert when Tudor, Andrée Howard and others were developing greater expressiveness of design by the use of colloquial gestures (*see* page 173). These subtly explained feelings could not be spoken (*see* page 171). With Agnes de Mille these colloquial gestures became the coarser speech of the Ranch with its knowing nods and winks, or bashful acknowledgements of broad compliments paid by not-so-shy boys.

Rodeo also had the rhythmic urge of true folk dance, because the dancers themselves were both seen and heard to create the sounds and tempo of their music. It was particularly interesting in *Interlude*, where the Boys and Girls danced a "running set" to nothing more than the sounds of their own hand-clapping and stamping. *Billy the Kid* lacked this rhythmic urge, despite the wonderfully theatrical score composed by Aaron Copland, who also provided *Rodeo*.

Fall River Legend (1948) is Agnes de Mille's masterpiece and is a successful attempt to portray another side of American life. It is a grim tragedy without gaiety or humour. It developed no new angle in choregraphic design nor solved any problems arising from the film techniques now being widely used; but it was a consolidation of the principles first used by Loring and furthered by a deeper study of movement, which Tudor had introduced to America in his *Pillar of Fire* (*see* page 172), and by the pioneers of modern American dance led by Martha Graham, whose influence during the war years had become increasingly important among those who were setting out seriously to create American ballet for themselves.

Like so many ballets dealing with lives frustrated by the conventions of Victorian and Edwardian society, *Fall River Legend* depicted a self-tortured, nerve-wracked spinster, vainly trying to communicate to others. Lizzie Borden's frustration however seemed greater because of the space in which the drama was enacted. It should have given her the freedom she so badly needed to express herself. But the space was dominated by a single house, revolved by the dancers, so that no matter in which way Lizzie turned, the house and the hated stepmother always appeared to accuse her, even during her most innocent activities. Moreover Morton Gould's score, like the choregraphy, underlined every episode in much the same way that a pianist would emphasize the old film dramas, by playing appropriately descriptive music to draw attention to the sentiment, drama, rush of events and the like. The result may have been naïve and stark, but it had reality and proved American choregraphers were finding their own ways of developing dramatic ballets with characters and plots from their own background.

JEROME ROBBINS, CLASSICIST OR MODERN (1918–)

That Jerome Robbins, the most modern of Americans working for large audiences in popular shows, should create a masterpiece from classical dance is surprising. That his *L'Après-midi d'un Faune* should be inspired by the same Debussy music which Nijinsky, the great classical dancer, used for the most modern, controversial and unacademic work of its time, is even stranger. But that *L'Après-midi d'un Faune* should also be one of the most real of Robbins's works is the most surprising of all. From *Fancy Free* to *N.Y. Export, Jazz* (1958), and in musicals such as *West Side Story*, Robbins has succeeded in showing on the stage, one or another aspect of American life as it is. He has frequently laughed at or with classical dance (e.g. *Interplay*, 1945, and *The Concert*, 1956), or distorted its line to make nightmare clinical studies of humanity which occasionally verge on the pretentious (e.g. *The Cage*, 1951).

Here in *L'Après-midi d'un Faune*, a faun-like boy and girl dance out an episode that might occur in any dancing studio, to any dancer anywhere on a sunny afternoon and in the cool light of a mirrored studio.

Lazily setting to work after a brief rest, the Boy begins to perfect the newly learnt steps. Bending, stretching and correcting, he gazes into the mirror, which is the fourth wall of his space and is imaginatively situated between himself and the audience. He becomes aware of the Girl, who has also come to perfect her dance. Gazing at their own reflections, they fall into a *pas de deux*. Their movements flow, are held, corrected or changed as they join, fall apart and come together again. They become one in the dance as their gestures grow stronger, more tender, sometimes searching as they wonder at the patterns they make together. Then after an embrace which might close any *pas de deux*, they become aware of each other as real people—a boy and girl falling in love. Or has the Girl become aware of her power over the Boy, of growing up, of her colour? (In London, 1962, the *pas de deux* was danced by the Negro Jack Jones and Kay Mazzo). These and many other questions are suggested but left unanswered except by each member of the audience, in his or her own way. Does this inconclusiveness matter? Perhaps in its very inconclusiveness lies the great magic of this exquisite masterpiece.

Denis Johnston once said: "The Players give your play life—the audience bring it sense." But the audience can only bring it sense if the author makes his intentions clear to the players, and if the players bring their roles to life and communicate meaning.

Jerome Robbins' contribution to ballet has been to enlarge the means of communication and so involve his dancers in the actions of real life, that in their dance they do communicate meaning.

THE ROYAL DANISH AND ROYAL SWEDISH BALLETS

The traditions of acting out the character in dance established by Bournonville (*see* page 59) is that element in which the Royal Danish Ballet still excels. Its repertoire today largely consists of internationally important works by Fokine, Ashton, Petit, Balanchine and others. To such ballets the dancers bring their artistry, stagecraft and technical facility, and frequently give a more closely integrated performance than that staged by the companies originally producing such works. These dancers are willing to sink their own identities into the role played with the result that the life they live in each ballet becomes a reality for their audience. But they have still found no native choregrapher to follow Bournonville.

It seemed at one point that Harald Lander would provide original ballets stemming from Danish traditions. His *Qarrtsiluni* (1952) evoked a ritual of those ancient Eskimos, who wait longingly for the sun to burst through the silence of the long winter and as its rays pour over the horizon, break into an ecstasy of dance. Lander's choregraphy was starkly primitive and, in the manner of a deeply felt ritual repetitive and slow, until the final frenzy of joyous movement. The score by Riisager provided its vital rhythmic urge and the dancers captured the drama of living through the excitement of the dawn of spring.

Lander's *Études* (1948) was in absolute contrast to this primitive outburst, and was an essay in classical dance. It was moulded from the Bournonville technique to which Lander added elements from his studies of important modern Russian choregraphers, so that the gentleness and grace of the girls, and the brilliant elevation and beats of the men, became athletic, stronger and straighter in line. It was exhilarating, as the dancers had to prove themselves only as dancers, and give themselves freely to the task. Unfortunately Lander had to leave Copenhagen before furthering this new style in a narrative ballet. But his work on *Études* prepared the dancers for the modern choregraphy of Balanchine and the others.

The Royal Swedish Ballet was founded in 1773, but has not yet produced any notable choregrapher of its own. Its history is closely tied to that of Western European ballet-masters and stars of the nineteenth century. Since the development of the Central European School of Dance however, several Swedish choregraphers have produced ballets utilizing its theories, particularly those of Kurt Jooss (*see* page 138). It is to one of his dancers, Birgit Cullberg, that the company now owes two original works. Her *Miss Julie* (1950) was originally produced for another company and owed its success to the libretto devised by Allen Fredericia from Strindberg's play, and the interpretation of the leading role by the Swedish dancer-actress Elsa Marianne von Rosen. It is a literal translation of the play into dance in which the strong narrative qualities of modern movement are reinforced by elements from the classical idiom. This merging of conflicting styles has resulted in a design of strong, almost vicious force, which fully delineates the main characters. The work is a *tour de force* which has not yet been developed further in ballets of equal dramatic content.

Moon Reindeer (1957) was created by Birgit Cullberg for Royal Danish Ballet and was inspired, like Lander's *Qarrtsiluni*, by ancient traditions: a legend of a girl from Lapland who became a reindeer. The score was also composed by Riisager and had the necessary rhythmic vitality. The ballet's most notable feature is not so much the expressiveness of the movements, which characterize the girl-reindeer and her companions, but the extraordinarily spacious effect of such a tale being danced out on an almost empty stage. Lighting alone seems to paint the scene and lend that air of fantasy to the snowy waste pictured. Birgit Cullberg again shows here that she is another choregrapher to have seen the value of amalgamating the theories of the modern dancer with the principles of classical ballet. Perhaps when she has more fully studied the latter she will produce works with the same realistic content as those of the Americans who have delved deeply into the motivation of movement and have produced works of greater actuality.

SOVIET BALLET

The developments taking place in Soviet Ballet since the 1917 Revolution have been quite different from those of the West. Although the reforms initiated by Fokine made headway in Leningrad and served to give a greater flow of line and expressive musicality to the movements of the dancers, it was the dramatic qualities of acting through dance introduced by Gorsky, first in Moscow and then in Leningrad, that had a greater influence over the work of the choregraphers. His insistence upon the need for the entire action to be unfolded by means of dramatic movement (*see* page 91), coupled with the authorities' need to provide their vast audiences with ballets which could be understood and appreciated, led to the production of works based on such well-known themes as Pushkin's *The Prisoner in the Caucasus* (1938) and *The Fountains of Bakhshisarai* (1934) and Gogol's *Taras Bulba* (1940); or on themes in which the political aims of the new régime or revolutionary topics and social conflicts were portrayed. Among these were *The Red Poppy* (1937, now *The Red Flower*) dealing with the adventures of some Soviet Sailors in China, *The Golden Age* (1931) which contrasted Soviet achievements with those of the Fascists, and *The Flames of Paris* (1932), a story of the French Revolution.

These and many other ballets with an epic theme quickly ousted the early revolutionary works using constructivist and other modern ideas of stage production, which had been driven from the stage before Diaghilev staged his first ballets on these lines (*see* page 125).

The concern of Soviet choregraphers to present their vast audiences with ballets of social and dramatic content, at first led them to produce works in which the purely dancing elements tended to be forgotten, so much attention had to be focused on the need to communicate the social implications of the theme. The methods and theories of Stanislavsky had been assimilated by the dancers of the Soviet companies, and it was not difficult to convey through their vivid interpretations both the characters and action of the drama. But the audiences' demand for dance soon led such important choregraphers as Lopokov, Zakharov, Vainoonen and Chaboukiani to select themes of important social content that would also give opportunities for staging abundant dance *divertissements*. Thus in construction their ballets resembled those of Petipa, although their dances were freer in conception and frequently incorporated ideas based on the rich sources of folk dance. These were gradually disclosed as each republic opened its own Theatre of Dance and Ballet, founded its own school and, by researching into its traditions, founded professional folk-dance groups for stage work. The growth of these groups and the founding of schools and ballet companies have developed greatly since 1945. There are now thirty-three companies resident in thirty-one towns (Leningrad and Moscow each have two). Originally these were fed from the two older schools, but already some twenty others are attached either to the Theatres of Opera and Ballet, or to the Conservatoires of the leading towns.

The next problems facing the Soviet authorities were those of repertoire and the training of choregraphers. The former depended upon the availability of libretti with firmly outlined scores by some practised composer. Such a work is produced in many towns, sometimes by the same choregrapher or his assistant (e.g. Lavrovsky's *Romeo and Juliet*), but more frequently a local or visiting choregrapher will produce his own version.

This dispersal of the same ballets throughout the U.S.S.R. allows a visitor to see that the various choregraphers set about their task in much the same way because they are bound by the score. Moreover conferences have taken place between choregraphers, dancers, teachers, musicians, critics and delegates from the audience. At these the problems of ballet production are discussed and the findings reflected in the work of the choregraphers and the Moscow Institute of Theatrical Art, where the two leading Soviet balletmasters, Zakharov and Shattin, head the faculty of choregraphic art. One reason for the founding of this Institute was to give aspiring choregraphers an understanding of their problems and help supply the demand for such artists from all over the U.S.S.R.

LEONIDE LAVROVSKY (1905–)

It was not until Leonide Lavrovsky staged *Romeo and Juliet* (Kirov Theatre, Leningrad, 1940) that a break was made with the formulas of Petipa. This work has been discussed elsewhere (*see* page 168), but it is valuable to read Lavrovsky's own comments.

> This encounter with Shakespeare's great work raised questions of artistic maturity and provoked many debates. I have endeavoured to render not only the content and tone of the tragedy, but also Shakespeare's poetic richness, vigour and tender pathos. The famous monologues of Romeo and Juliet, so full of motive and passion, to me, were not the bare bones of some subject used to strengthen a *divertissement*...
>
> I have aimed, although in danger of being told it is not dance, to sustain the dramatic depths and feelings of the actors, which arise from their need to interpret character and action. Dramatic action contains pantomime, which we underestimate because we do not fully understand its implications... True pantomime is a theatrical representation in which the thoughts, feelings and passions are expressed not by the voice, but by the movements and gestures of the body... Ballet, particularly tragic ballet demands noble, plastic and heart-felt pantomime, which arises from the dance and constitutes its most significant element. Ballet is a choregraphic play in which dance must appear as the sequel to the pantomime, and pantomime as the logical sequence of the dance...
>
> The depths of passion and action expressed so intensely by the hero and heroine of Shakespeare's tragedy demand a true merging of pantomime and dance. In ballet words are absent, but the meaning of every tiny fragment of danced-mime, or mimed-dance must reveal the appropriate language of its characters.

Lavrovsky aimed to preserve the specific features of Shakespeare's play and kept its formal structure so that he captured both the harshness of the quarrels between Montague and Capulet, and the tragic story of the two lovers. He stated (*Soviet Culture*, March, 1942) that he used a form of film technique to achieve a continuous flow of action. In this he was helped by the Soviet artist, Peter Williams, whose settings were devised somewhat as the stage in Shakespeare's day. That is, he used curtains and transparencies by which sections of the stage could be isolated or opened up as scene succeeded scene. Thus the lovers' passionate meetings were seen to be broken by violent action, which in its turn gave way to touches of humour, or solemn prayer.

Prokofiev's score supported this continuous flow of action. Its various leitmotives underlined each episode with appropriate rhythmic energy and melody, whose sentiment, solemnity or violence, deepened the moods as they changed. But what brought Shakespeare's tragedy fully to life were the outstanding interpretations of their roles, played by the Kirov dancers led by People's Artist, Galina Ulanova. Her performance as Juliet, more than that of any other Soviet dancer, serves to illustrate the difference between the Soviet choregraphers' approach to reality and the contemporary theme from that of their Western colleagues.

The great Soviet *ballerina* has placed it on record that—

> A dancer should not forget his role the moment he leaves the class or rehearsal. He should think about it all the time, without pause, for only then will he achieve a true-to-life portrait.

Thus the Soviet choregrapher, unlike his Western colleague, does not necessarily seek to create a contemporary style of dance, or choose a contemporary subject in order to present realism on the stage. Rather he chooses a theme of theatrical value, usually with contemporary or social implications and—no matter how he couches his dance—expects his dancers to bring reality to this theme by their ability to live their roles and make their audience believe in the truth and reality of their performance.

The Western choregrapher, on the other hand, in his search to be contemporary, often seeks only to find new ways of using movement, and may achieve realism within the framework of his ballet, no matter what his theme, if his dancers are artists and have learnt to live their roles. If they are unable to do this, then their modern realism in movement can only be accepted as a novelty to whet the appetites of a jaded audience.

Stanislavsky once said to a group of students—

> The "Joy of Creation" exists, but it comes to the true artist only after tremendous effort in his chosen and dearly loved field, when he attains the lofty aims he has set himself.

FURTHER READING

LAWSON, JOAN, *European Folk Dance* (London, Pitman, 1953).
LAWSON, JOAN, *Mime* (London, Pitman, 1957).
LAWSON, JOAN, *Classical Ballet, its Style and Technique* (London, A. and C. Black, 1960).
LAWSON, JOAN, *The Dancing Times*, articles and criticisms in.

Bibliography

Abraham, Gerald, *Tchaikovsky* (London, Duckworth, 1944).
Adam, Adolphe, *Score of "Giselle"* (Leningrad Archives).
Addison and Steele, *The Spectator*, No. 334 (Mon., 24th March, 1712).
Algarotti, Count, *Saggio sopra l'opera in Musica* (Naples, 1750).
Algarotti, Count, *An Essay on the Opera* (originally written in Italian) dedicated to William Pitt (London, 1737).
Angiolini, Gasparo, *Dissertation sur les ballets pantomimes des Anciens, publiée pour servir de programme au ballet pantomime tragique de "Sémiramis"* (Vienna, 1765).
Angiolini, Gasparo, *Lettere di Gasparo Angiolini* (1772).
Arbeau, Thoinot, *Orchésographie* (Langres, 1589).
Aristotle, *Metaphysics* (Walker Scott Pub. Co., 1847).
Aubry, P., *Trouvères et Troubadours* (Paris, 1909).
Augé-Chiquet, Mathieu, *La Vie, Idées et l'Oeuvre de Jean-Antoine de Baif* (Paris, 1809).
Bakroushine, Y. A., *A. A. Gorsky* (Moscow, 1946).
Baltazarino, (Beaujoyeulx, Balthasar de), *Balet comique de la Royne* (Paris, 1582).
Baron, A. A., *Lettres et Entretiens sur la Danse* (Paris, 1800).
Beaumont, C. W., *Three French Dancers of the Seventeenth Century* (London, 1934).
Beaumont, C. W., *Complete Book of Ballets* (London, Putnam, 1939).
Beaumont, C. W., *Supplement to the Complete Book of Ballets* (London, Putnam, 1942).
Beaumont, C. W. (with Sitwell, Sachaverell), *Romantic Ballet* (Faber & Faber, 1937).
Beaumont, C. W., *The Diaghilev Ballet in London* (London, Putnam, 1944).
Benois, Alexandre, *Reminiscences of the Russian Ballet* (London, Putnam, 1941).
Benserade, *Les Oeuvres de Monsieur de Benserade* (Paris, 1698).
Bisson, L., *A Short History of French Literature* (Penguin Books, 1943).
Blasis, Carlo, *The Code of Terpsichore* (London, 1830).
Blasis, Carlo, *Traité éléméntaire et Pratique de la Danse* (Milan, 1820).
Blaze, Castile, *La Danse et les Ballets* (Paris, 1832).
Bogdanov-Beresovsky, *Ulanova* (trans. Garry and Lawson) (London, MacGibbon and Kee, 1952).
Borisoglevsky, Y., *Materials for a History of Russian Ballet*, 2 vols. (in Russian) (Leningrad, 1938).
Bournonville, August, *Mon Theatreliv* (Copenhagen, 1858).
Bournonville, August, *Études chorégraphiques dediées à mes élèves et mes collègues* (Copenhagen, 1861).
Bowra, Sir Maurice, *Heroic Poetry* (Macmillan, 1957).
Buckle, Richard, Ed., *Dancing for Diaghilev, the Memoirs of Lydia Sokolova* (John Murray, 1960).
Burckhardt, Jacob, *Civilization of the Renaissance in Italy* (London, Phaidon).
Cahusac, Louis de, *La Danse ancienne et moderne ou Traité de la Danse* (Paris, 1754).
Capon, Geston, *Les Vestris* (Paris, 1908).
Caroso, Fabritio, *Il Ballarino* (1581).
Castiglione, *The Courtier* (London, Everyman, Dent).

Chambers, Sir E. K., *Medieval Stage*, 2 vols. (1902).
Chambers, Sir E. K., *Elizabethan Stage*, 4 vols. (1922).
Chambers, Sir E. K., *Shakespeare*, 2 vols. (Clarendon Press, 1930).
Cibber, Colley, *An Apology for the Life of Colley Cibber, written by himself* (London, 1739).
Clarke, Mary, *The Sadler's Wells Ballet* (London, A. and C. Black).
Compan, *Dictionnaire de Danse* (Paris, 1787).
Cunningham, Peter, *Inigo Jones, a Life* (for the Shakespeare Society, 1848).
Dacier, Emil, *Marie Sallé, une Danseuse de l'Opéra sous Louis XV* (Paris, 1907).
Daily Courant, The, From 1702 to 1730: No. 4794 2nd March; 18th Oct., 1716; 21st Feb., 1717; 16th March, 1717.
Dauberval, (Jean Bercher) The libretti for *Le Deserteur* (Paris, 1801), *La Fille mal gardée* (Paris, 1804), *Le Page inconstant* (Paris, 1805).
De Baif, Jean-Antoine, *Les Mimes enseignements et Proverbes*, with preface and notes by Prosper Blanchemain (Paris, 1880).
De Baif, Jean-Antoine, *Etrênes de Poezie Fransoçze en vers Mesurés* (Paris, 1574).
De Brosses, Charles, "Criticisms of Italian Opera" and other writings in the *Encyclopedia* (Paris, 1754).
Didelot, Charles, Libretti for *Zéphyr et Flore, Psyché et L'Amour, The Hungarian Hut, The Prisoner in the Caucasus.*
Didelot, Charles, Archives in the Lunacharsky State Theatre Museum and Library, Leningrad, and the Leningrad Choregraphic School named Vaganova.
Diderot, Denis, Collected Works in *Encyclopedia* (Paris, 1754).
Diderot, Denis, *Entrétiens sur le fils Naturel* (Paris, 1757).
Disher, Willson, *Clowns and Pantomimes* (London, Constable, 1925).
Douairière, Mme. La Baronne, *La Pure Vérite. Lettres et Memoires sur Le Duc e la Duché de Virtemberg* (Ausborg, 1765).
Du Bos, L'Abbé, *Critical Reflections on Poetry Painting and Music*, 3 vols. (Paris, 1748).
Duchârtres, Paul, *The Italian Comedy* (trans. Randolph T. Weaver) (London, Harrap, 1929).
Ducros, L., *French Society in the Eighteenth Century* (London, 1926).
Du Manoir, Guillaume, *Le Mariage de la Musique avec la Danse* (Paris, 1664).
Einstein, Alfred, *Gluck* (trans. Eric Blom) (London, Dent and Sons, 1936).
Entertainments, Three. Performed at the Theatre Royal, Drury Lane (1728).
Evans, Edwin, *Tchaikovsky* (London, 1935).
Evans, Edwin, Stravinsky, *The Firebird* and *Petrushka*, in *The Musical Pilgrim* (O.U.P., 1925).
Feuillet, Raoul Auger, *Chorégraphie* (Paris, 1699).
Feuillet, Raoul Auger, *L'Art à écrire la Danse* (Paris, 1700).
Fokine, Mikhail, *Manifesto to "Daphnis and Chloe"* (1904).
Fokine, Mikhail, Conversations with Edwin Evans, 1923–4.
Fokine, Mikhail, Archives in Lunacharsky State Theatre Museum and Library, and Leningrad Choregraphic School named Vaganova.
Fraser, Sir James, o.m., *The Golden Bough* (abridged edition) (London, Macmillan & Co., 1941).
Garrick, David, *A Catalogue of the Library, Splendid Book of Prints, Poetical and Historical Tracts of David Garrick Esq., removed from his villa at Hampton and the House in Adelphi Terrace with the Modern Works added thereto by Mrs. Garrick* (1833).
Garrick, David, Correspondence, in the Victoria and Albert Museum.
Gaunt, William, *Modern Music* (London, Novello & Co., 1937).
Gautier, Théophile, *Les Beautés de l'Opéra* (Paris, 1845).
Gautier, Théophile, *Portraits contemporains* (Paris, 1874).

GLEBOV, IGOR (ASSAFIEV), Articles on Tchaikovsky and other problems of ballet music appearing in *Soviet Musical Times and Theatre* (1935).
GLOUZHKOVSKY, ARAM, *Memoirs of a Ballet-master* (in Russian) (Moscow, 1940).
GOLDSMITH, MARGARET, *Maria Teresa of Austria* (London, 1938).
GRIGORIEV, S. L., *The Diaghilev Ballet* (London, Constable, 1953).
HARRISON, JANE, *Ancient Rite and Ritual* (London, 1931).
HASKELL, ARNOLD H., *Diaghilev* (London, Gollancz, 1935).
HOFFMANN, E. T., *Der Nussnacker und der Mauskönig.*
HOFFMANN, E. T., *The Tales of a Nutcracker Prince* (London, Chapman & Hall, 1846).
HOURMOUZIS, S., Lecture at Congress organized by International Council for Theatre Research (1955).
HUEFFER, FRANCIS, *The Troubadours, History of Provençal Life and Literature* (London, Chatto & Windus, 1878).
IVANOV, LEV, Archives in the Leningrad State Museum and Library named Lunacharsky, the Leningrad Choregraphic School named Vaganova, and the Bakroushine State Theatre Museum, Moscow.
JONSON, BEN, *The Description of the Masque Celebrating the happy Marriage of John, Lord Ramsay, Viscount Hadington with the Lady Elizabeth Ratcliffe* (1608).
JULLIEN, ADOLPHE, *Les grandes Nuits de Sceaux* (Paris, 1916).
KARSAVINA, TAMARA, *Theatre Street* (London, Heinemann, 1930).
KEMPE, WILL, *Nine Daie's Wonder* (ed. G. B. Harrison) (London, The Bodley Head, 1923).
KRAAGH-JACOBSEN, SVEND, *The Royal Danish Ballet* (London, A. and C. Black, 1955).
KRASSOVSKAYA, VERA, *Russian Ballet* (in Russian) (Leningrad, 1958).
LAVER, JAMES, *Taste and Fashion* (London, Harrap, 1946).
LAWSON, JOAN, *European Folk Dance* (London, Pitman, 1953).
LAWSON, JOAN, *Mime* (London, Pitman, 1957).
LAWSON, JOAN, *Classical Ballet, Its Style and Technique* (London, A. and C. Black, 1960).
LIEVEN, PRINCE PETER, *The Birth of Ballets Russes* (London, Allen & Unwin, 1936).
LIFAR, SERGE, *Diaghilev* (London, Putnam, 1940).
LIFAR, SERGE, *Ballet, Traditional to Modern* (London, Putnam, 1938).
MAURICE, ALBERT, *Theatres de la Foire* (Paris, 1900).
MELLERS, WILFRID, *Music and Society* (London, Denis Dobson, 1946).
MÉNESTRIER, FATHER CLAUDE FRANÇOIS, *Des Ballets anciens et modernes* (Paris, 1682).
Mercure de France (April, 1634).
METASTASIO, *Tutte le Opere di Pietro Metastasio* (Florence, 1832).
MEYER, ERNST, *English Chamber Music* (London, Lawrence & Wishart, 1940).
MICHEL, ARTUR, The Ballet d'Action before Noverre, *Dance Index*, Vol. VI, No. 3 (1947).
MOLIÈRE, *The Comedies*, with a preface by W. H. Sorley Johnston (London, 1895).
MURRAY, SIR GILBERT, O.M., *Euripides and his Age* (O.U.P. 1946).
MURRAY, SIR GILBERT, O.M., *Five Stages of Greek Religion* (Watts & Co., 1935).
NEGRI, CESAR, *Nuove Iventi di Balli* (1604).
NICHOLL, ALLARDYCE, *The Development of the Theatre* (London, Harrap, 1949).
NICHOLL, ALLARDYCE, *Masks, Mimes and Miracles* (Harrap, 1931).
NICHOLL, ALLARDYCE, *British Drama* (Harrap, 1949).
NOVERRE, C. E., *The Life and Works of the Chevalier Noverre* (London, 1832).
NOVERRE, JEAN-GEORGES, *Letters on the Dance* (trans. C. W. Beaumont) (London, 1930).
NOVERRE, JEAN-GEORGES, *Lettres sur les Arts imitateurs en general et sur la Danse en particulier* (Paris, 1807).
NOYES, ALFRED, *Voltaire* (London, Sheed & Ward, 1936).
OLIVIER, JEAN-JACQUES and NORBERT, WILLY, *La Barbarina Campanini* (Paris, 1910).

Oxford History of Music, Vol. II, O.U.P.

PARFAICT, *Les Frères, Memoirs pour servir à l'histoire des Spectacles de la Foire* (Paris, 1743).

PERRAULT, CHARLES, *Contes des Fées London* (Macmillan, 1884).

PERROT, JULES, Archives in the Lunacharsky State Theatre Museum and Library and the Leningrad Choregraphic School named Vaganova.

PERROT, JULES, Libretti for *Giselle, La Esmeralda, Lysistrata, Ondine, Catarina* and others.

PETIPA, MARIUS, Libretto *The Sleeping Beauty*, Bakroushine State Theatre Museum, Moscow.

PETIPA, MARIUS, Libretto, *Casse Noisette*, Bakroushine State Theatre Museum, Moscow.

PETIPA, MARIUS, Archives in the Bakroushine State Theatre Museum, Moscow; Lunacharsky State Theatre Museum and Library and Leningrad Choregraphic School named Vaganova.

PLATO, *The Republic.*

PLESCHEYEV, A. A., *Our Ballet* (in Russian) (St. Petersburg, 1899).

POYNTER, F. N. L., Article in the *Times Literary Supplement* No. 3,007.

PRUNIÈRES, HENRI, *Le Ballet du Cour en France avant Benserade et Lully* (Paris, 1914).

PRUNIÈRES, HENRI, *L'Opéra italien en France avant Lully* (Paris, 1913).

RAMEAU, P., *Le Maître à danser* (Paris, 1725).

REYHER, PAUL, *Les Masques Anglais* (Paris, 1909).

RICCOBONI, LUIGI, *An Historical and Critical Account of the Theatre in Europe* (London, 1751).

RICCOBONI, LUIGI, *A General History of the Stage from its Origin* (dedicated to David Garrick) (London, 1754).

RITORNI, CARLO-REGGIANI, *Salvatore Vigano* (Milan, 1838).

ROEDERER, P. L., *Memoire pour servir à la histoire de la Société polie en France* (Paris, 1892).

ROUSSEAU, F. LE, *A Chacoon for a Harlequin* (dedicated to M. Dupré) (London, 1730).

SACHS, CURT, *Rise of Music in the Ancient World* (London, Dent, 1944).

SACHS, CURT, *World History of Dance* (London, Allen & Unwin, 1937).

SACKVILLE, THOMAS, LORD, and THOMAS NORTON, *Gorboduc* (1561).

SAINT-LÉON, ARTHUR, Archives in the Lunacharsky State Museum and Library, Leningrad and the Bakroushine State Theatre Museum, Moscow.

SAINT-LÉON, ARTHUR, Libretti for *The Little Hump-backed Horse, Coppélia, Alma, Le Violon du Diable* and others.

SAINT-LÉON, ARTHUR, *Stenochorégraphie* (Paris, 1852).

SAINT-SIMON, *Memoirs*, 2 vols. (trans. by Bayle St. John) (New York, 1901).

SHAVERDIAN, A. E., *Tchaikovsky and the Theatre* (in Russian) (Moscow, 1940).

SLONIMSKY, YURI OSSIPOVITCH, *Masters of the Ballet* (Moscow, 1937).

SLONIMSKY, YURI OSSIPOVITCH, *Giselle* (Leningrad, 1930).

SLONIMSKY, YURI OSSIPOVITCH, *Didelot* (Moscow, 1958).

SLONIMSKY, YURI OSSIPOVITCH, *La Fille mal gardée* (Moscow, 1960).

SLONIMSKY, YURI OSSIPOVITCH, *The Bolshoi Theatre Ballet* (Moscow, 1956).

SLONIMSKY, YURI OSSIPOVITCH, *The Dying Swan* (Leningrad, 1961).

SOLLERTINSKY, S., *The History of the Soviet Theatre* (in Russian) (Moscow, 1935).

STENDHAL, (HENRI BEYLE), *Rome, Naples and Florence.*

STENDHAL, *Correspondence*, Vols. 1 and 2.

SYMONDS, HENRY, *Six Sets of Lessons for the Harpsichord* (dedicated to the Countess of Sunderland) (London, 1723).

TAGLIONI, FILLIPO, Libretti for *La Gitana, La Sylphide, La Bayadère* and others in a private collection.

TCHAIKOVSKY, MODESTE (Ed.), *Letters of P. I. Tchaikovsky* (in Russian) (Moscow, 1900–2).

THOMPSON, GEORGE, *Studies in the Ancient Aegean*, 2 vols. (London, Lawrence & Wishart, 1949).

THURMOND, JAMES, *Masque of Deities* (London, 1722).

TOMLINSON, KELLOM, *Six Dances*, including "The Submission" arranged for M. and Mlle. Sallé, the Two French Children in 1717 (London, 1720).

TREVELYAN, G. M., *English Social History* (London, Longmans, Green & Co., 1940).

VAILLAT, LEANDRE, *Histoire de la Danse* (Paris, 1942).

VAUGHAN WILLIAMS, RALPH, *National Music* (O.U.P., 1934).

VIGANO, SALVATORE, Libretti for *Othello, Gli Strelletsi, I Titani*, in a private collection.

WAGNER, RICHARD, *Correspondence of Wagner and Liszt* (trans. F. Hueffer) (New York, 1897).

WAGNER, RICHARD, *Prose Works* (trans., W. A. E. Ris) (New York, 1892–9).

WEAVER, JOHN, *Essay Towards a History of Dancing* (London, 1712).

WEAVER, JOHN, *A History of the Mimes and Pantomimes* (London, 1728).

WEAVER, JOHN, *The Loves of Mars and Venus* (1717).

WEAVER, JOHN, *Orchésographie*. Translation of Feuillet's book (1706).

WEAVER, JOHN, *Small Treatise of Time and Cadence in Dancing* (1706).

WEAVER, JOHN, *Anatomical and Mechanical Lectures* (1721).

WELSFORD, ENID, *The Court Masque* (O.U.P., 1926).

YATES, FRANCES A., *The French Academies of the Sixteenth Century* (London, Jarrolds for the Warburg Institute, London University, 1948).

ZAKHAROV, ROTISLAV, *The Art of the Ballet Master* (in Russian) (Moscow, 1954).

ZHITOMIRSKY, O., *The Ballets of Tchaikovsky* (Moscow, 1957).

Index of Ballets

Index of Names